Finding
Molly Johnson

MCGILL-QUEEN'S STUDIES IN THE HISTORY OF RELIGION
Volumes in this series have been supported by the Jackman Foundation of Toronto.

SERIES ONE G.A. RAWLYK, EDITOR

1 Small Differences
Irish Catholics and Irish Protestants, 1815–1922
An International Perspective
Donald Harman Akenson

2 Two Worlds
The Protestant Culture of Nineteenth-Century Ontario
William Westfall

3 An Evangelical Mind
Nathanael Burwash and the Methodist Tradition in Canada, 1839–1918
Marguerite Van Die

4 The Dévotes
Women and Church in Seventeenth-Century France
Elizabeth Rapley

5 The Evangelical Century
College and Creed in English Canada from the Great Revival to the Great Depression
Michael Gauvreau

6 The German Peasants' War and Anabaptist Community of Goods
James M. Stayer

7 A World Mission
Canadian Protestantism and the Quest for a New International Order, 1918–1939
Robert Wright

8 Serving the Present Age
Revivalism, Progressivism, and the Methodist Tradition in Canada
Phyllis D. Airhart

9 A Sensitive Independence
Canadian Methodist Women Missionaries in Canada and the Orient, 1881–1925
Rosemary R. Gagan

10 God's Peoples
Covenant and Land in South Africa, Israel, and Ulster
Donald Harman Akenson

11 Creed and Culture
The Place of English-Speaking Catholics in Canadian Society, 1750–1930
Edited by Terrence Murphy and Gerald Stortz

12 Piety and Nationalism
Lay Voluntary Associations and the Creation of an Irish-Catholic Community in Toronto, 1850–1895
Brian P. Clarke

13 Amazing Grace
Studies in Evangelicalism in Australia, Britain, Canada, and the United States
Edited by George Rawlyk and Mark A. Noll

14 Children of Peace
W. John McIntyre

15 A Solitary Pillar
Montreal's Anglican Church and the Quiet Revolution
Joan Marshall

16 Padres in No Man's Land
Canadian Chaplains and the Great War
Duff Crerar

17 Christian Ethics and Political Economy in North America
A Critical Analysis
P. Travis Kroeker

18 Pilgrims in Lotus Land
Conservative Protestantism in British Columbia, 1917–1981
Robert K. Burkinshaw

19 Through Sunshine and Shadow
The Woman's Christian Temperance Union, Evangelicalism, and Reform in Ontario, 1874–1930
Sharon Cook

20 Church, College, and Clergy
A History of Theological Education at Knox College, Toronto, 1844–1994
Brian J. Fraser

21 The Lord's Dominion
The History of Canadian Methodism
Neil Semple

22 A Full-Orbed Christianity
The Protestant Churches and Social Welfare in Canada, 1900–1940
Nancy Christie and Michael Gauvreau

23 Evangelism and Apostasy
   The Evolution and Impact of Evangelicals
   in Modern Mexico
   Kurt Bowen

24 The Chignecto Covenanters
   A Regional History of Reformed
   Presbyterianism in New Brunswick
   and Nova Scotia, 1827–1905
   Eldon Hay

25 Methodists and Women's Education in
   Ontario, 1836–1925
   Johanne Selles

26 Puritanism and Historical Controversy
   William Lamont

SERIES TWO   IN MEMORY OF GEORGE RAWLYK
DONALD HARMAN AKENSON, EDITOR

1 Marguerite Bourgeoys and Montreal,
  1640–1665
  Patricia Simpson

2 Aspects of the Canadian Evangelical
  Experience
  Edited by G.A. Rawlyk

3 Infinity, Faith, and Time
  Christian Humanism and Renaissance
  Literature
  John Spencer Hill

4 The Contribution of Presbyterianism to the
  Maritime Provinces of Canada
  *Edited by Charles H.H. Scobie and
  G.A. Rawlyk*

5 Labour, Love, and Prayer
  Female Piety in Ulster Religious Literature,
  1850–1914
  Andrea Ebel Brozyna

6 The Waning of the Green
  Catholics, the Irish, and Identity in Toronto,
  1887–1922
  Mark G. McGowan

7 Religion and Nationality in Western Ukraine
  The Greek Catholic Church and the
  Ruthenian National Movement in Galicia,
  1867–1900
  John-Paul Himka

8 Good Citizens
  British Missionaries and Imperial States,
  1870–1918
  James G. Greenlee and Charles M. Johnston

9 The Theology of the Oral Torah
  Revealing the Justice of God
  Jacob Neusner

10 Gentle Eminence
   A Life of Cardinal Flahiff
   P. Wallace Platt

11 Culture, Religion, and Demographic
   Behaviour
   Catholics and Lutherans in Alsace, 1750–1870
   Kevin McQuillan

12 Between Damnation and Starvation
   Priests and Merchants in Newfoundland
   Politics, 1745–1855
   John P. Greene

13 Martin Luther, German Saviour
   German Evangelical Theological Factions
   and the Interpretation of Luther, 1917–1933
   James M. Stayer

14 Modernity and the Dilemma of North
   American Anglican Identities, 1880–1950
   William H. Katerberg

15 The Methodist Church on the Prairies,
   1896–1914
   George Emery

16 Christian Attitudes towards the State of Israel
   Paul Charles Merkley

17 A Social History of the Cloister
   Daily Life in the Teaching Monasteries
   of the Old Regime
   Elizabeth Rapley

18 Households of Faith
   Family, Gender, and Community in Canada,
   1760–1969
   Edited by Nancy Christie

19 Blood Ground
   Colonialism, Missions, and the Contest for
   Christianity in the Cape Colony and
   Britain, 1799–1853
   Elizabeth Elbourne

20 A History of Canadian Catholics
   Gallicanism, Romanism, and Canadianism
   Terence J. Fay

21 The View from Rome
Archbishop Stagni's 1915 Reports on the
Ontario Bilingual Schools Question
Edited and translated by John Zucchi

22 The Founding Moment
Church, Society, and the Construction
of Trinity College
William Westfall

23 The Holocaust, Israel, and Canadian
Protestant Churches
Haim Genizi

24 Governing Charities
Church and State in Toronto's Catholic
Archdiocese, 1850–1950
Paula Maurutto

25 Anglicans and the Atlantic World
High Churchmen, Evangelicals, and the
Quebec Connection
Richard W. Vaudry

26 Evangelicals and the Continental Divide
The Conservative Protestant Subculture
in Canada and the United States
Sam Reimer

27 Christians in a Secular World
The Canadian Experience
Kurt Bowen

28 Anatomy of a Seance
A History of Spirit Communication
in Central Canada
Stan McMullin

29 With Skilful Hand
The Story of King David
David T. Barnard

30 Faithful Intellect
Samuel S. Nelles and Victoria University
Neil Semple

31 W. Stanford Reid
An Evangelical Calvinist in the Academy
A. Donald MacLeod

32 A Long Eclipse
The Liberal Protestant Establishment
and the Canadian University, 1920–1970
Catherine Gidney

33 Forkhill Protestants and Forkhill Catholics,
1787–1858
Kyla Madden

34 For Canada's Sake
Public Religion, Centennial Celebrations,
and the Re-making of Canada in the 1960s
Gary R. Miedema

35 Revival in the City
The Impact of American Evangelists
in Canada, 1884–1914
Eric R. Crouse

36 The Lord for the Body
Religion, Medicine, and Protestant Faith
Healing in Canada, 1880–1930
James Opp

37 Six Hundred Years of Reform
Bishops and the French Church, 1190–1789
*J. Michael Hayden and
Malcolm R. Greenshields*

38 The Missionary Oblate Sisters
Vision and Mission
Rosa Bruno-Jofré

39 Religion, Family, and Community in
Victorian Canada
The Colbys of Carrollcroft
Marguerite Van Die

40 Michael Power
The Struggle to Build the Catholic Church
on the Canadian Frontier
Mark G. McGowan

41 The Catholic Origins of Quebec's Quiet
Revolution, 1931–1970
Michael Gauvreau

42 Marguerite Bourgeoys and the Congregation
of Notre Dame, 1665–1700
Patricia Simpson

43 To Heal a Fractured World
The Ethics of Responsibility
Jonathan Sacks

44 Revivalists
Marketing the Gospel in English Canada,
1884–1957
Kevin Kee

45 The Churches and Social Order in
Nineteenth- and Twentieth-Century Canada
*Edited by Michael Gauvreau and
Ollivier Hubert*

46 Political Ecumenism
Catholics, Jews, and Protestants in
De Gaulle's Free France, 1940–1945
Geoffrey Adams

47 From Quaker to Upper Canadian
Faith and Community among Yonge Street
Friends, 1801–1850
Robynne Rogers Healey

48 The Congrégation de Notre-Dame,
Superiors, and the Paradox of Power,
1693–1796
Colleen Gray

49 Canadian Pentecostalism
Transition and Transformation
Edited by Michael Wilkinson

50 A War with a Silver Lining
Canadian Protestant Churches and the
South African War, 1899–1902
Gordon L. Heath

51 In the Aftermath of Catastrophe
Founding Judaism, 70 to 640
Jacob Neusner

52 Imagining Holiness
Classic Hasidic Tales in Modern Times
Justin Jaron Lewis

53 Shouting, Embracing, and Dancing
with Ecstasy
The Growth of Methodism in Newfoundland,
1774–1874
Calvin Hollett

54 Into Deep Waters
Evangelical Spirituality and Maritime
Calvinist Baptist Ministers, 1790–1855
Daniel C. Goodwin

55 Vanguard of the New Age
The Toronto Theosophical Society, 1891–1945
Gillian McCann

56 A Commerce of Taste
Church Architecture in Canada, 1867–1914
Barry Magrill

57 The Big Picture
The Antigonish Movement of Eastern
Nova Scotia
Santo Dodaro and Leonard Pluta

58 My Heart's Best Wishes for You
A Biography of Archbishop John Walsh
John P. Comiskey

59 The Covenanters in Canada
Reformed Presbyterianism from 1820 to 2012
Eldon Hay

60 The Guardianship of Best Interests
Institutional Care for the Children of the
Poor in Halifax, 1850–1960
Renée N. Lafferty

61 In Defence of the Faith
Joaquim Marques de Araújo, a Comissário
in the Age of Inquisitional Decline
James E. Wadsworth

62 Contesting the Moral High Ground
Popular Moralists in Mid-Twentieth-
Century Britain
Paul T. Phillips

63 The Catholicisms of Coutances
Varieties of Religion in Early Modern France,
1350–1789
J. Michael Hayden

64 After Evangelicalism
The Sixties and the United Church of Canada
Kevin N. Flatt

65 The Return of Ancestral Gods
Modern Ukrainian Paganism as an
Alternative Vision for a Nation
Mariya Lesiv

66 Transatlantic Methodists
British Wesleyanism and the Formation of an
Evangelical Culture in Nineteenth-Century
Ontario and Quebec
Todd Webb

67 A Church with the Soul of a Nation
Making and Remaking the United Church
of Canada
Phyllis D. Airhart

68 Fighting over God
A Legal and Political History of Religious
Freedom in Canada
Janet Epp Buckingham

69 From India to Israel
Identity, Immigration, and the Struggle for
Religious Equality
Joseph Hodes

70 Becoming Holy in Early Canada
Timothy Pearson

71 The Cistercian Arts
From the 12th to the 21st Century
*Edited by Terryl N. Kinder and
Roberto Cassanelli*

72 The Canny Scot
Archbishop James Morrison of Antigonish
Peter Ludlow

73 Religion and Greater Ireland
Christianity and Irish Global Networks,
1750–1950
Edited by Colin Barr and Hilary M. Carey

74 The Invisible Irish
Finding Protestants in the Nineteenth-
Century Migrations to America
Rankin Sherling

75 Beating against the Wind
Popular Opposition to Bishop Feild and
Tractarianism in Newfoundland and
Labrador, 1844–1876
Calvin Hollett

76 The Body or the Soul?
   Religion and Culture in a Quebec Parish,
   1736–1901
   Frank A. Abbott

77 Saving Germany
   North American Protestants and Christian
   Mission to West Germany, 1945–1974
   James C. Enns

78 The Imperial Irish
   Canada's Irish Catholics Fight the Great War,
   1914–1918
   Mark G. McGowan

79 Into Silence and Servitude
   How American Girls Became Nuns,
   1945–1965
   Brian Titley

80 Boundless Dominion
   Providence, Politics, and the Early Canadian
   Presbyterian Worldview
   Denis McKim

81 Faithful Encounters
   Authorities and American Missionaries in
   the Ottoman Empire
   Emrah Şahin

82 Beyond the Noise of Solemn Assemblies
   The Protestant Ethic and the Quest for Social
   Justice in Canada
   Richard Allen

83 Not Quite Us
   Anti-Catholic Thought in English Canada
   since 1900
   Kevin P. Anderson

84 Scandal in the Parish
   Priests and Parishioners Behaving Badly
   in Eighteenth-Century France
   Karen E. Carter

85 Ordinary Saints
   Women, Work, and Faith in Newfoundland
   Bonnie Morgan

86 Patriot and Priest
   Jean-Baptiste Volfius and the Constitutional
   Church in the Côte-d'Or
   Annette Chapman-Adisho

87 A.B. Simpson and the Making of Modern
   Evangelicalism
   Daryn Henry

88 The Uncomfortable Pew
   Christianity and the New Left in Toronto
   Bruce Douville

89 Berruyer's Bible
   Public Opinion and the Politics of
   Enlightenment Catholicism in France
   Daniel J. Watkins

90 Communities of the Soul
   A Short History of Religion in Puerto Rico
   José E. Igartua

91 Callings and Consequences
   The Making of Catholic Vocational Culture
   in Early Modern France
   Christopher J. Lane

92 Religion, Ethnonationalism, and Antisemit-
   ism in the Era of the Two World Wars
   Edited by Kevin P. Spicer and
   Rebecca Carter-Chand

93 Water from Dragon's Well
   The History of a Korean-Canadian Church
   Relationship
   David Kim-Cragg

94 Protestant Liberty
   Religion and the Making of Canadian
   Liberalism, 1828–78
   James M. Forbes

95 To Make a Village Soviet
   Jehovah's Witnesses and the Transformation
   of a Postwar Ukrainian Borderland
   Emily B. Baran

96 Disciples of Antigonish
   Catholics in Nova Scotia, 1880–1960
   Peter Ludlow

97 A Black American Missionary in Canada
   The Life and Letters of Lewis Champion
   Chambers
   Edited by Hilary Bates Neary

98 A People's Reformation
   Building the English Church in the
   Elizabethan Parish
   Lucy Moffat Kaufman

99 Towards a Godless Dominion
   Unbelief in Interwar Canada
   Elliot Hanowski

100 Finding Molly Johnson
    Irish Famine Orphans in Canada
    Mark G. McGowan

FINDING MOLLY JOHNSON

*

Irish Famine Orphans in Canada

Mark G. McGowan

McGill-Queen's University Press
Montreal & Kingston • London • Chicago

© McGill-Queen's University Press 2024

ISBN 978-0-2280-2299-2 (cloth)
ISBN 978-0-2280-2300-5 (paper)
ISBN 978-0-2280-2301-2 (ePDF)
ISBN 978-0-2280-2302-9 (ePUB)

Legal deposit third quarter 2024
Bibliothèque nationale du Québec

Printed in Canada on acid-free paper that is 100% ancient forest free (100% post-consumer recycled), processed chlorine free

This book has been published with the help of a grant from the Canadian Federation for the Humanities and Social Sciences, through the Awards to Scholarly Publications Program, using funds provided by the Social Sciences and Humanities Research Council of Canada.

Funded by the Government of Canada | Financé par le gouvernement du Canada | Canada | Canada Council for the Arts | Conseil des arts du Canada

We acknowledge the support of the Canada Council for the Arts.
Nous remercions le Conseil des arts du Canada de son soutien.

McGill-Queen's University Press in Montreal is on land which long served as a site of meeting and exchange amongst Indigenous Peoples, including the Haudenosaunee and Anishinabeg nations. In Kingston it is situated on the territory of the Haudenosaunee and Anishinaabek. We acknowledge and thank the diverse Indigenous Peoples whose footsteps have marked these territories on which peoples of the world now gather.

Library and Archives Canada Cataloguing in Publication

Title: Finding Molly Johnson : Irish famine orphans in Canada / Mark G. McGowan.
Other titles: Irish famine orphans in Canada
Names: McGowan, Mark George, 1959- author.
Series: McGill-Queen's studies in the history of religion. Series two ; 100.
Description: Series statement: McGill-Queen's studies in the history of religion. Series two ; 100 | Includes bibliographical references and index.
Identifiers: Canadiana (print) 20240324870 | Canadiana (ebook) 20240324919 | ISBN 9780228022992 (cloth) | ISBN 9780228023005 (paper) | ISBN 9780228023029 (ePUB) | ISBN 9780228023012 (ePDF)
Subjects: LCSH: Orphans—Canada—History—19th century. | LCSH: Church work with orphans—Canada—Catholic Church—History—19th century. | LCSH: Church work with orphans—Canada—Protestant churches—History—19th century. | LCSH: Irish—Canada—History—19th century. | LCSH: Immigrants—Canada—History—19th century. | LCSH: Ireland—History—Famine, 1845-1852.
Classification: LCC HV1006 .M34 2024 | DDC 305.23086/945097109034—dc23

This book was designed and typeset by studio oneonone in Minion 11/14

In Memory of Marianna O'Gallagher, OC
(1929–2010)
Historian, Teacher, & Friend

Contents

Tables xiii

Acknowledgments xv

Introduction: "You Will be Canadian Now" 3

1 A Much-Contested Calamity: Framing a Discussion of the Great Irish Famine and Migration 16

2 When Orphans Are Made: The Case of the Assisted Migrants and Orphans of Strokestown, County Roscommon 43

3 "The Fostering Protection of the Church" 64

4 Catholic Orphans in Protestant Towns 99

5 Assistance and Assimilation: Irish Orphans in New Brunswick 125

6 Brave New World 146

Conclusion: Finding Molly Johnson 170

Notes 177

Bibliography 213

Index 231

Tables

1.1 Major Irish ports and migration to British North America, 1847 / 39
1.2 Major British ports and Irish migration to British North America, 1847 / 40
1.3 Migration from the UK to British North America, 1843–48 / 40
2.1 Strokestown household heads by townland, civil parish, and family size / 51
2.2 Deaths of household heads by ship recorded for the Mahon Estate, 1847 / 59
2.3 Status of Mahon households in British North America, 1847 / 60
3.1 Counties of origin of Irish famine "orphans" at Quebec, 1847–48 / 71
3.2 Placement locations of the orphans of 1847–48 / 75
3.3 Placement of orphan children as located on the census of 1851–52 / 75
3.4 Ethnic origins of the placement families / 76
3.5 Irish orphans placed at Rimouski, 1847–48 / 78–9
3.6 Irish Catholic orphans in Montreal, 1847–48 / 97
4.1 Orphan placement in Bytown, 1847 / 102
4.2 Catholic children at the Hotel Dieu and their dispersal / 111
4.3 House of Industry, Kingston by religion, December 1847–June 1848 / 113
4.4 Widows' and Orphans' Asylum, Toronto, 1847–48, child placement by Catholic clergy and lay leaders / 119
4.5 Widows' and Orphans' Asylum, Toronto, 1847–48, child placement locations by occupation / 119
4.6 Widows' and Orphans' Asylum, Toronto, 1847–48, child placement locations by county / 122
5.1 Irish counties of origin of the Saint John orphans / 134

Acknowledgments

This book was written in troubled times. Although my research stretched back to 2013, the actual writing was begun and completed during the COVID-19 pandemic. Such a world event offered a contemporary parallel to the frontline health care workers who battled the typhus epidemic of 1847. Russia's illegal invasion of Ukraine not only reminded the world that imperialism was not dead, but this new war in eastern Europe's breadbasket also provided a catalyst for world food insecurity, once again recalling the tragedy of Ireland in the 1840s. On the domestic front, the re-discovery of unmarked graves of children who had been unwilling students at Indigenous Residential Schools operated by the Catholic Church, at Kamloops, British Columbia, and Cowasis, Saskatchewan, was reminiscent of the vulnerability of children when church and state place their own agendas ahead of child welfare. My mind flashed to the role of churches and the forgotten children of 1847. Although the circumstances of Irish children's deaths and assimilation differed significantly from Indigenous children later in the century, the events of the summer of 2021 were a heart-wrenching reminder of the fragility of the lives of children in history.

It is not difficult for a historian of the Great Irish Famine to be struck by the convergence of so many crises and their devastating effects on ordinary people. Events in Ireland between 1845 and 1852 formed a perfect storm of colonial landholding structures, food insecurity, poor weather, the spread of infectious disease, and ham-fisted ideologues tied to laissez-faire economics that created modern Ireland's greatest catastrophe. Close to one million people died during the famine period, and 1.5 million departed Ireland seeking refuge in British North America, Great Britain, the United States, and Australia. Thousands of children were left orphaned, and their stories have generally been forgotten. The similarities to our own times made this book both challenging to research and heart-rending to write. My role as a social historian prompted me to uncover the stories of the voiceless and chronicle their traumatic journey from their Irish homes to the cities and frontiers of North America. In the end, the story of the famine orphans offers us a portrait of how Canadians managed one of the worst refugee crises in their history to that time, how children were used as cheap labour, and how churches helped to fill the gap in public service when there were few government-sponsored safety networks in place. The orphan story also exposes how civic officials and medical professionals were at a loss to control the spread of infectious diseases carried by Irish adults and children. While writing, it was difficult not to ignore comparisons between the more than sixty persons in Canada who gave their lives the front lines of the crisis of 1847–48 and those first responders of our own time.

A work of this type is a communal one, with many hands engaged in the telling of this story. I am indebted to many people over these past few years as the "Molly Johnson project" developed. My sincerest thanks are to my colleagues engaged in diaspora research, particularly those at Strokestown's National Famine Museum and its related projects at the Irish Heritage Trust. When I was about to leave famine studies altogether in 2013, Caroilin Callery presented me with a challenge to put names and identities to 1,490 migrants from the Strokestown estate. While sometimes cursing the "needle-in-the-haystack" research undertaken because of her request, the discovery of so many orphans, prompted this much larger study of famine orphans. Jason King has been a constant support and sounding board on the project, and his own work on specific case studies of orphans has been invaluable. Christine Kinealy, director of the Great Hunger Institute at Quinnipiac University, has been a valued research partner and become a treasured friend. Ciaran Reilly, of Maynooth University has been generous to me with his own research findings and advice on matters relating to Irish estates. I am deeply grateful to John O'Driscoll and Martin Fagan of Strokestown Park who have given me free reign of the archives of the Mahon family and the estate property.

A small group of historians studying Ireland and the diaspora in Canada, gave me the idea to write the book. Huddled in our corner in the Duke of York pub in Toronto, David Wilson, William Jenkins, Elizabeth Smyth, Laura Smith, Nick Baker, and Shane Lynn made it possible for me to "launch trial balloons" (as the late John Moir might have said) and then offered me con-

ACKNOWLEDGMENTS

structive feedback that sometimes brought the balloons (often crashing) back to earth. Their collegiality and assistance over the course of this project has been remarkable and kind. I am especially indebted to my colleague David Wilson for his interest and support of my work. My successor as principal of St Michael's College, Professor Domenico Pietropaolo (2011–16), made a student research culture a priority at the college. Inspired by his initiative I created credit-granting research seminars with hand-picked students who helped with the search for the nearly 1,700 orphans included in this project. I am convinced that senior undergraduate students of history must engage in primary historical research before they graduate; I am very grateful to the five teams of students, from 2015 to 2019, who learned the heartaches and joys of doing social historical research in routinely generated records. My sincerest thanks to Julia Maher, Kiera O'Sullivan, Elizabeth McDermott, Pamela Smofsky, Jessica Bush, Chiara Fallone, Conor Finan, Meghan Drascic-Gaudio, Michaela Vukas, Britany Powell, Olivia Brasch, Rachel McLeod, Sofia Romaschenko, Emma McKean, Jaime McLaughlin, Bridget Hager, and Gabriela Escribano. Each team was given the opportunity to present their findings at international conferences in the United States, Ireland, and Canada. I am truly gratified that many of these students have now undertaken graduate work in a variety of disciplines. I also want to extend thanks to Louis Reed-Wood, one of my doctoral students, who helped me track orphans through the New Brunswick censuses of 1851 and 1861.

I am also indebted to the many archivists and local historians who assisted me in gathering the fragments. My thanks to Michael McBane in Ottawa who provided me with documents pertaining to the Grey Sisters' hospital and orphanage in Bytown. I am particularly grateful to many archivists over the years, some now retired, who were very generous in their assistance. I want to especially thank the staff of the following: Archives of the Roman Catholic Archdiocese of Toronto; Archives of the Sisters Hospitaller of St Joseph (Kingston); Sisters of Providence (Montreal); Archives of the Archdiocese of Montreal; Archives of the Sisters of Charity (Grey Nuns) (Montreal and Ottawa); Sisters of the Good Shepherd (Montreal); University of St Michael's College Archives; Queen's University Archives; Diocese of Saint John Archives; Archives of the Archdiocese of Quebec; the Archdiocese of Dublin Archives; National Library of Ireland; Russell Library of Maynooth University; and Library and Archives Canada. The pioneering work of Peter Murphy, Marianna O'Gallagher, and Marie-Claude Belley (Parks Canada), provided essential foundations for this book. I had the pleasure to present on a panel with Marie-Claude in Quebec City, in 2019, and she was most generous with research materials. I hope this book has risen to the challenge she offered in her MA thesis that there should be a study bringing all the orphans' stories together. I have been blessed with gracious and insightful collaborators. My colleague and friend at St Mary's University, Halifax, Michael Vance, read the entire manuscript and made many helpful suggestions and comments. Any errors and omissions in this book are entirely of my doing.

In the late stages of the book, I am grateful for the friendship and encouragement of Ireland's ambassador to Canada and historian Dr Eamonn McKee. As has been the case so often in the past, Kyla Madden and her team at McGill-Queen's University Press have been very supportive of this project. I would like to extend a special thanks to copyeditor Shelagh Plunkett, whose eagle eye shaped the manuscript into a much more readable book.

Finally, my work would never be completed without the support of my wife Eileen and our five adult children – Erin, Patrick, Brendan, Kathleen, and Frankie – and their partners. They made the journey joyful, tested me when I got too serious, and loved me unconditionally despite my litany of faults. My maternal grandfather Albert Geisler (1905–1991) invested in me the job of storyteller; I think of him every day and miss him greatly. In some ways, I owe my very vocation as a historian to him. This book is dedicated to Marianna O'Gallagher, OC, whose great love in life was telling the stories of the Irish settlers and sojourners to Canada, particularly in Quebec. Her life's work was left incomplete when she died suddenly in 2010; I hope this work on the orphans honours her memory and labours. When writing about children I always have my grandchildren in my thoughts. I hope that Róisín, Albert, and Marigold Lee, and Fiona O'Riley, never have to face the traumas experienced by their Irish ancestors. Their pleas should never have to be akin to those made by Molly Johnson in 1847.

Finding
Molly Johnson

Introduction
"You Will be Canadian Now"

"Molly Johnson," a priest's voice echoes over a cavernous room with a high ceiling, decorated with religious art. His summons to the girl prompts the entrance to the hall of a queue of motley and ill-clad children, who are flanked by a gauntlet of well-dressed adults. To the background music of a somber violin, they halt their dismal procession in front of an elevated throne on which sits a white-haired Catholic cleric whose pectoral cross betrays his episcopal rank. The orphaned children are told by the summoning priest that they are to be adopted by the venerable French Canadian families surrounding them and that they will surrender their Irish surnames and assume those of their new families; he adds, with some enthusiasm, that they will be Canadians now. Molly, speaking for all the children, protests in broken French that with their dying breaths their parents had told them they must keep their Irish names to preserve their heritage. The French Canadian families agree, and the bishop intervenes asking three of the children who they are: "Quel est ton nom?"; Molly Johnson, Patrick O'Neill, and Kathleen Ryan answer. The heavy violin music switches to a lively Irish jig, and all are happy, with the assumption of a storybook ending. This sixty-second vignette will be familiar to many Canadians as one of *Heritage Minutes*, which have become regular features on Canadian television. Produced by *Historica* and financed initially by the Bronfman Foundation,[1] these short films are an effort to inform Canadians about interesting and key moments in their history. Among the sixty segments this was the Irish orphans minute. The story of Molly Johnson and her orphan friends would become indelible in the minds of viewers as the Irish Famine moment in Canadian history.

In 1847 and 1848, more than 1,700 Irish children found themselves in various states of abandonment in British North America, having lost one or both parents either at sea during the horrendous voyage from Ireland or in the various quarantine stations and fever hospitals in the ports and towns in the Canadian interior. Hundreds of children were herded into hospitals, orphanages, and asylums in Saint John, Quebec, Montreal, Bytown (Ottawa), Kingston, and Toronto. While there were some similarities in the experiences of the children across all of the ports of entry, there is no single narrative that describes the orphan experience, given the varied Irish counties of origin of these children, the nature of the voyages that brought them to British North America, the communities that engaged them when they landed, and the intentions of those who stepped forward to "take care" of them.

It should be acknowledged that a single minute of film can hardly render justice to this massive refugee crisis faced by the British North American colonies in the 1840s. It would take more than a feature film to render justice to the nuances and varied stories of the Irish orphan experience. What does become clear is that the reception and treatment of these orphans opens several themes germane to Irish migration to Canada, the role of both the churches and the government in immigrant aid, and the way future generations have curated the Irish Famine experience in Canada to support national myths for the sake of Canadian unity. The famine orphans' episode also challenges some of the longstanding assumptions about sectarian relations in Canada and the other British North American colonies. The arrival of hundreds of famine refugees did exacerbate Protestant–Catholic tensions in some ports, but the reception of these newcomers was also marked by ecumenical co-operation, which has often gone unsung in the standard histories of the period. The study of these famine orphans also challenges assumptions of Canadian benevolence, especially when the historical record reveals that these children were not adopted, some were not completely parentless, and most were used as cheap labour on farms and in businesses. Far from experiencing a happy ending accompanied by Irish jigs and reels, the story of the famine orphans is complicated and contested.

This book seeks to find out what happened to these children and, in particular, what role the churches and state played in this early Canadian incidence of refugee resettlement. A detailed examination of the Quebec cohort of 619 children,[2] for example, as featured in the *Heritage Minute*, has produced some startling results.[3] While the Catholic Church played a significant role in the placements of what were overwhelmingly a Catholic cohort of

Irish orphans,[4] the placement itself did not go according to the script presented by Historica's "Molly Johnson." First, at least one third of the orphans were placed within Irish families in Quebec, who had migrated to British North America before the Irish Famine. Secondly, these were not orphans in the sense that "orphan" has been defined in our own culture – some did experience the death of both parents, but others were placed in the orphanage by one or both parents who just could not support their families after their horrendous transatlantic voyage in the so-called "coffin ships." Thirdly, these children were not formally adopted, since the *droit civile* of Canada East (now Quebec) had no such provision and would not have an adoption law until the 1920s.[5] Moreover, the census of 1851–52 identifies 90 per cent of these children as non-family members within the homes in which they had been placed. In fact, most of these children ended up as indentured servants on Quebec farms: boys worked in the fields, girls in the family home. Unlike the Barnardo children, later in the century, Irish Famine children did not emigrate with the intention of being apprentices or cheap labour. Nevertheless, their unintended "indenture" in Canada was not surprising for mid-nineteenth century colonial society, where children were treated like little adults and considered valuable to the settlement frontier and its economy.[6] Many ended up fleeing their new homes at the first opportunity. It was not quite the fairy tale ending as suggested on television.[7]

The questions raised by the experiences at Quebec, while similar to other ports of entry are not universally applicable in every detail. As had been the case in Quebec City, the presence of the Catholic Church in immigrant assistance was prominent in both Montreal and Bytown, where religious orders of sisters and priests undertook the lion's share of the medical care and hostelling of children. By contrast in Saint John, New Brunswick, the presence of the Catholic Church was weak, and Catholic children were indiscriminately sent out to Protestant homes and farmsteads with the expectation that they become productive citizens of the province. Toronto and Kingston were the principal dispersion centres for Canada West (now Ontario), from which healthy immigrants, both adults and children, were moved quickly out of the towns with the prospect of sojourning or settling in the western part of the province or in the United States. In Toronto, orphans were formally contracted out to families, with the terms of their employment or apprenticeship clearly spelled out by guardians of the Widows' and Orphans' Asylum. In the so-called "Belfast of Canada," Toronto's Catholic and Protestant leaders worked together to assure an appropriate placement for the orphans in their care. As one sifts through the historical fragments left behind by the children, their caregivers, and their employers a collage of stories emerges that help illustrate several important themes that characterize the Irish Famine orphan experience.

The principal discovery, after having examined the profiles of hundreds, is that these children were regarded by their hosts as little more than adults-in-the-making. Children were expected to pull their weight in the family context. As Tannis Peikoff and Stephen Brickey observe, "Prior to the nineteenth century, the concept of childhood as a stage in the life cycle did not exist ... [C]hildren were not considered to be especially vulnerable or in need of special attention."[8] Children in rural areas and industrial towns were expected to work to sustain the family income. For those orphans, who found themselves severed from the family, there were concerns from civic officials and reformers that idleness and isolation would lead to crime. It was not until the early nineteenth century that such attitudes began to shift, where in Upper Canada apprenticeship with adults was thought to be the preferred manner to keep orphans and other children productive, industrious, and out of trouble.[9] Similarly, mid-nineteenth century elites regarded education as a means of providing sound foundations for the children, so it should come as no surprise that orphan asylums in both Saint John and Toronto were staffed with a teacher who managed daily instruction for the children. In the Catholic convent settings, schools were usually adjacent to where the children were housed. Thus, institutions for homeless children served dual functions: they were both centres to educate the "orphans" and serve as a placement agency for work in the community. As one contemporary observer commented: "Adoption, Sir, is when folks gets [sic] a girl to work without wages."[10] While the placement of Irish orphans in 1847 and 1848, varied in terms of levels of apprenticeship, contracted wage work, or work in exchange for board, the expectation was still the same – these children were not to be idle but to become productive citizens.[11]

Another theme that emerges quite clearly from the outset is that the famine provided the opportunity for the Roman Catholic and Protestant churches to step forward as the primary providers of social service in early Canadian society. The reception of famine immigrants was a moment in which the Catholic Church engaged all its energies from fundraising to front line care. The work of the Catholic laywomen of Quebec, the Grey Nuns of Montreal and Bytown, the Sisters of Providence and the Sisters of the Good Shepherd in Montreal, and the Sisters Hospitaller of St Joseph of Kingston, all repre-

INTRODUCTION 7

sented actions described later as "heroic" by the Church. Sisters themselves were stricken with fever and several died, as did clergy in Quebec, Montreal, on the quarantine station at Grosse Ile, and in Toronto. The forty-two-year-old Catholic bishop of Toronto, Michael Power, tended to the fever sheds in his city when all his priests were ill. He supervised the triaging of children to the orphans' asylum, but he also contracted typhus and died, becoming the most prominent Catholic cleric to succumb to "famine fever."[12] Currently the Archdiocese of Toronto is promoting his case for sainthood, as a "martyr of charity." Thus, the famine moment and the orphan reception can be considered one of the Catholic Church's triumphs as it staked out its place in colonial Canadian society.

The efforts by several Christian churches to accommodate and place Irish orphans in homes and businesses also marked a time of understated cooperation between colonial Protestants and Catholics. The refugee crisis and the proliferation of Irish orphans drew the traditionally hostile churches into common cause both for charitable and sectarian reasons. Just as Catholic agencies provided a strong charitable network for the orphans, so did the Anglican Church. Secular Protestant leaders, particularly in noted sectarian hotbeds such as Kingston and Toronto, worked together with Catholics to bring aid to the Irish children, who were predominantly but not exclusively Roman Catholic. The benevolent motivations by the churches also disguised fears among church leaders on both sides that the "other" might use this as an opportunity to proselytize the youngsters. It was known by many Catholic leaders that in Ireland, Protestant evangelizers were active in the slums of Dublin and in many Poor Law unions, where children without identifiable religious affiliation, or without parents, were routinely turned over to the Church of Ireland (Anglican) for their education.[13] Another development in the orphan episode involved one church or another exploiting the weakness of the minority denomination, thus allowing such fears of proselytizing and apostasy to come true. Such was the case in Saint John, New Brunswick, where Protestant churches exerted a clear religious hegemony over the Catholic refugees, largely because of the underdeveloped Catholic institutional presence in that port city.

The orphan relief effort and the religious benevolence it characterized could also be used as a blunt weapon by Catholic Church leaders over their faithful. Bishop Ignace Bourget of Montreal, who also suffered from typhus but survived, remembered the famine orphan moment selectively and could conveniently draw this card when dealing with Irish Catholics who challenged his authority. In the 1860s, when the Montreal Irish, including Thomas D'Arcy McGee and parish pastor Patrick O'Dowd, challenged Bourget's effort to redraw the boundaries of St Patrick's national parish in the city, he conveniently reminded them of how French Canadians had cared for famine victims, particularly Irish orphans, when the Irish were in such need twenty years before. Infuriated by the bishop's selective memory, McGee and others publicly pronounced their own agency in making new lives and livelihoods in Montreal.[14] Nevertheless, the memory of the famine orphans, selective or not, could be used as a powerful example of French Canadian kindness to the "English-speaking" population and a reminder of the bonds between the principal settler/colonizing peoples of Canada.[15]

The theme of mythmaking based on the famine orphans worked very well outside of the ecclesiastical context. In his book *The Irish in America* (1880), author John Francis Maguire retold the story of the Church and its people adopting the Irish orphans and paints a very vivid scene of Bishop Signay and the commissioning of the adoption process: "Half-naked, squalid, covered with vermin generated by hunger, fever, and the foulness of the ship's hold, perhaps with germs of the plague lurking in their vitiated blood, these helpless innocents of every age – from the infant taken from the bosom of its dead mother to the child who could barely tell the name of its parents – were gathered under the fostering protection of the Church."[16] Maguire's scene could have served as a story board for the *Heritage Minute*, as the French Canadian benevolence is enhanced at a time in the mid-1990s, when national unity in Canada was under severe strain and a second referendum on sovereignty was pending in Quebec in 1995. Here the Irish are an Anglophone bridge, even in so far as the names "Johnson" and "Ryan" were concerned. It was no small coincidence that three premiers of Quebec were Johnsons, and a leading journalist and federalist politician was named Ryan (Claude Ryan). Such links from the orphans to the present has been carefully curated to show how the seeds planted by kindness in 1847–48 blossomed over the course of Quebec's history, as the descendants of these orphan children contributed greatly to the province's political culture and beyond. Both Bourget and Maguire, for different reasons, had singled out the orphan moment as something that could be used repeatedly to enhance the unity of Canada's peoples. Even the French-language inscription on the memorial Celtic Cross at Grosse Ile, erected in 1909, speaks of the valiant efforts of French Canadians to assist

INTRODUCTION

the starving Irish, though the inscription in the Irish language is decidedly anti-English and Irish nationalist in its content and tone.[17]

The story of the famine orphans also forms part of a much larger contribution to the writing of Canadian history under the guise of "nation building." The processing of immigrants at various ports of call, the building of sheds, enhancements of hospitals, provision of internal transportation, and the supplying of emigration agents with the tools to provide Irish migrants with daily necessities came at a heavy financial cost to the Canadian and New Brunswick governments. While the Colonial Office and its chief minister, Earl Grey, dickered over practically every request for reimbursement from the colonial emigration service, the famine migration provided colonial politicians with an opportunity. Governor General Lord Elgin argued strenuously for a full reimbursement of the government's costs in 1847, which eventually was conceded by Westminster. The conditions accepted by Elgin, however, would see the colonies assuming control over their own immigration service, with the concomitant responsibility for raising their own revenues to provide for immigrants. For those whiggish historians, mostly in the past, who were searching for yet another example of Canadian autonomy, they would surely find this acquired colonial independence over immigration as furthering the process of "building the Canadian nation." The famine refugees, both adults and children, were unaware of their agency in this process.

What follows is an analysis of the chronology of how Irish children, generally living in rural circumstances in the country of their birth, find themselves orphaned in Canada after having survived a harrowing journey across the North Atlantic in the 1840s. The first chapter assesses the Irish famine, its impact on rural Ireland, and the way it was interpreted by both contemporaries and commentators over time. Some journalists and historians have described the famine as a calamity caused by the British government's inaction during the initial stages of the potato blight or, worse, a deliberate act of genocide committed by British officials on the Irish. Revisionists have downplayed the nationalist rhetoric and anti-British positions, demonstrating the inherent flaws in the rural Irish economy and society, the dependence of so many persons on the potato monoculture, and the obvious inadequacy of the Irish Poor Law to handle the crisis after 1845. The famine, therefore, is viewed through a variety of lenses, and it is important to sift out the various positions of commentators, their biases, and the complicated web of circumstances that transformed the potato blight into one of the greatest humanitarian disasters in Irish history. The trauma suffered by Irish migrants during the famine years is a most suitable context within which one can place these displaced Irish children.

The second chapter puts one group of famine migrants under scrutiny in order to understand how Irish children became orphans. The case study presented here is the assisted emigration scheme of Major Denis Mahon, landlord of the Strokestown Estate in County Roscommon, in the spring of 1847. Mahon made it possible for 271 families, constituting 1,490 persons, to leave his estate with the goal of settling them in Upper Canada. He compensated these tenants for their existing chattels and tenancy agreements, underwrote and provisioned them for their journey: first 160 kilometres from Strokestown to Dublin, then by steamship from Dublin to Liverpool, and finally by sailing ship from Liverpool to Quebec. In the four ships that had been chartered by his land agent and chief business officer, there was a horrendous loss of life. Of all the orphans landing at Quebec in the 1847 sailing season, the highest percentage among all of Ireland's thirty-two counties originated in County Roscommon. They are also among the few orphans that can be traced from famine conditions in their Irish townlands to their eventual placement with French and Irish Canadian families. Their journey is echoed in many other stories of children from different counties who ventured across the Atlantic but whose paper trail is much thinner. The story of the Roscommon orphans gives one a close-up of the struggle of Irish children amidst the chaos created by hunger, eviction, and trans-Atlantic travel. It is a story of orphans from the ground up.

Until recently there has been little written about the experience of the Irish migrant on both sides of the Atlantic. Robert Scally's excellent microstudy of resistance and eviction on the townland of Ballykilcline, very near Mahon's estate in Roscommon, documents the Irish story well but really leaves the migrants' story hanging just after their landing in the United States.[18] Similarly, Jim Rees and, more recently, Kevin Lee have chronicled the assisted migration of Lord Fitzwilliam's tenants from his Coollattin estate in County Wicklow. While Rees' study leaves the trail of the migrants in St Andrew's, New Brunswick[19] without much sense of what happens next, Lee's work is the culmination of years of labour connecting the records from the Fitzwilliam estate to the genealogies of Canadians and Americans who are descendants of the original migrants. His "Coollattin–Canada Connection" project is among one of the most ambitious and successful historical endeavours to uncover what happened to famine migrants over several generations.[20] Gerrard Moran's work moves the story of migrants along by examining the conditions on a variety of estates, particularly in counties Galway, Sligo, and Mayo, and makes an attempt to plot the lives of some of the refugees as they make a new life in North America, particularly the young women transported to Canada and Australia under Lord Grey's emigration scheme.[21] Mary Lee Dunn picks up the strands left by Scally and tracks many of the Ballykilcline migrants to Rutland, Vermont.[22] In a similar fashion, Tyler Anbinder's masterful account of Lord Lansdowne's assisted migration from his Kenmare estate to the Five Points ghetto of New York City, demonstrates not only migrant settlement but the migrants' ability to save money and take advantage of a degree of upward social mobility. Anbinder had the advantage of excellent primary sources, including the records of the savings bank where many of the Irish Famine migrants built tidy accounts.[23] Finally, Cian McMahon's study of Irish migration, titled *The Coffin Ship*, uncovers emigrant life before, during, and after their transportation either across the Atlantic to North America or down the Atlantic and across the Indian Ocean to Australia.[24] In all of these works, however helpful in unpacking various aspects of the emigrant experience during the famine, none offers special focus on the children who were separated from their families and faced a new life, in a new land, with little in hand.

At times the attempt to give voices to the "voiceless" in the past can be as frustrating an action as trying to make proverbial "bricks without straw." Unlike Australia, Canadian historians have no orphan databases to facilitate their research.[25] In the absence of a significant manuscript repository to provide evidence for what happened to these children, the research process in Canada relied on a selection of routinely generated records from across all the British North American colonies. In Quebec, the principal list of orphans was supplied by the Charitable Society of the Catholic Ladies of Quebec, later transcribed by my late colleague Marianna O'Gallagher. Referred to in this book as the "O'Gallagher List," this comprehensive ledger, committed primarily by the "Dames," includes the names of each child, date received, parents names, county of origin, age, ship from which they disembarked, and, whenever possible, the name of the so-called adopter and the place of relocation. The entire list was reprinted, for easy use, in O'Gallagher's *Grosse Ile: Gateway to Canada, 1832–1937*, ergo the origin of our reference to the name of the list.[26] A third important foundation has been a little-known Master's thesis written by Marie-Claude Belley at Université Laval in 2003. Belley carefully examined the 619 orphans on the O'Gallagher list but included additional names derived from ecclesial and civil sources. Her data set was 702, but the names of the addition eighty-three children were not appended to the thesis, so the current research is grounded solely in data pulled from the O'Gallagher list.[27]

The foundational records upon which the Montreal lists of children were based came from three primary sources: a list provided by Mother Elizabeth McMullen of the Grey Nuns who were the front line responders at Point St Charles; the registers of the Sisters of Providence who established the orphanage of St Jerome Emiliani (the Catholic patron saint of orphans), and the *Canada Gazette*, the official newspaper of the Government of Canada, which included lists of Protestant children placed in the care of Bishop George Mountain, who at the time was responsible for both Anglican dioceses in Quebec City and Montreal. From these foundational texts, a data set of 414 names was produced. Three problems quickly presented themselves. First, the transcription of the St Jerome's lists (one for boys and one for girls) was highly problematic because of the spelling of surnames, likely the result of misunderstandings created when French Canadian sisters recorded the names from Irish and English-speaking children, and poor penmanship on the original document. Secondly, some children were transferred to the Sisters of the Good Shepherd, whose records now are less accessible due to the congregation's move from their original residence; much the same could be said of the records of the Protestant children who were taken on by the Montreal Protestant Orphans Home, which were not made available to the author.

The lists generated in Bytown and Kingston also came from religious sources. In Bytown, the Grey Nuns, under Mother Élisabeth Bruyère, recorded the names of orphaned children in the register of the General Hospital. With each there was indicated the home of a local family where small groups of children were lodged until such time as they could be properly placed by the local Church. The Sisters Hospitaller of St Joseph in Kingston also created a ledger of their orphans, including the method of discharge and destination of each child as they left the Sisters' care. Unfortunately, the trail of these children often runs cold in Kingston because many were placed there and the manuscript census records for 1851–52 do not exist for Kingston.

The lists generated for Saint John, New Brunswick, and for Toronto were far more complete but presented their own challenges to the researcher. The Saint John lists were transcribed by Peter Murphy for his Master of Arts thesis earned under the auspices of the Atlantic Canada Studies at St Mary's University in Halifax.[28] Murphy's valuable transcriptions included the names of children, parents, ship of origin, age, and placement family, all of which were derived from the Orphans Asylum in Saint John. The problem with tracking these children was the fact that the census of New Brunswick, in 1851, did not record the religion of children. While knowing that most of the recipients of the orphans were Protestant farmers and businessmen in the province, it cannot be ascertained if the children who were found in the census of 1851 retained their Catholic faith. The next census, taken in 1861, did include religion but most of these young Irish wards were now fourteen years distant from their placement and most could not be found. In Toronto, the records of the Widows' and Orphans' Asylum for 1847 were detailed in offering the child's name, placement family or business, and the contractual obligations of the placement. Nevertheless, the absence of manuscript census data for the city of Toronto and many townships to the north of the city, in 1851–52, make the process of identifying any of these children beyond the asylum sojourn, a near impossible task. When this work was begun, with all the lists combined, there were 1,644 names of Irish children who were recorded as "orphaned" during the sailing seasons of 1847–48.

The next stage was to try to track the first point of contact of these children with civil records, particularly the manuscript census of Canada East for 1851–52. It was the second government-initiated head count in the British North American colonies of New Brunswick, Nova Scotia, Canada East, and Canada West. The census was not without its problems. The maritime colonies conducted their censuses in 1851, while the United Province of Canada delayed its until January 1852. The human count was also accompanied by an agricultural census which enumerated the land cleared, crops under cultivation, degree of animal husbandry, and housing among other things. While the presence of the agricultural census is a great aid in determining the level of economic activity of settlers and their relative wealth and status, not all the agricultural census sections have been preserved, making data retrieval and comparison difficult. Moreover, whole sections of the two provinces were enumerated and the records have been lost, including areas of the city of Montreal and some rural sections of the surrounding region.

To make matters even worse, the census copy, now digitized and machine readable, is an exercise in frustration. As eminent Canadian historical demographer David Gagan explained, "Phonetic spelling which reduces surnames to gibberish, terrible penmanship, and sloth which most frequently manifested itself in a too heavy dependence on the 'Ditto' all conspired in the hands of some enumerators, to render the entries for entire households and whole districts at best unreliable, at worse undecipherable."[29] As an extra difficulty, the Canadian census did not report the date of immigration on the census form until 1901, forcing any researcher of the 1851 census to exercise considerable creativity in determining the actual date of migration. Thus, the search of the census had to be supplemented by Ancestry.ca and FamilySearch.com, both of which contain errors of transcription and record interpretation. Ecclesiastical records, newspapers, government documents, and a few manuscript sources helped to fill in some of the gaps.

The results confirmed the original findings of the research team engaged with uncovering the whereabouts of the Irish orphans. First, the research for this book underscores that historians ought to be careful in how they define "orphan." Three different types of orphans could be identified – those missing both parents; those who had one parent who could not afford to keep them; and children with two parents who would collect them in the spring of 1848, when they had scratched together enough money to care for them. Secondly, it is clear that clergy, both Anglican and Catholic, became major players in the placement of children in homes where the head of household was of the same faith as the orphan, thus confirming that the Churches prioritized the faith of the children being nourished and protected in their new home. The officials in Saint John were the exception. Thirdly, Irish children were not legally adopted by patrons because at the time there was no mechanism in British North America for legal adoption; the transfer of property to a non-genetic family member could only be made through the services of a notary. Fourthly, in the case of Quebec City and Montreal, Irish, Scottish, and English families were patrons of these children as well as French Canadians. Finally, in most cases the census reveals that these children were not considered family members, and it is clear that they were put to work or sent to school by their placement families. This reflected both the placement family's need for cheap labour but also the social expectation that for orphan children, idle hands resulted in disorder, crime, and sin.

Finally, the orphan relief efforts, as described in this book, form part of a new and burgeoning public history of the famine in both Ireland and North America. The stories of several orphans from the Strokestown Estate in Roscommon have formed part of the public narrative at the National Famine Museum in Ireland, the National Famine Way, and the Great Famine Voices oral history project, sponsored by the Irish Heritage Trust.[30] The orphans' stories open up new and creative links between communities of scholars in

INTRODUCTION 15

both Ireland and Canada, strengthening partnerships between national parks, historians, genealogists, tourism offices, and national museums. The seeds that were planted by the "Molly Johnson" vignette underscore the fact that the Irish Famine story is also a Canadian story and one that has captured, in an increased way, the public imagination. To know this story, however, one must sift through the conflicting narratives that tangle within the history of the Irish Famine itself. It is now to this context that we must turn.

1

A Much-Contested Calamity
Framing a Discussion of the Great Irish Famine and Migration

Gerald Keegan was a schoolteacher from County Sligo. In the early spring of 1847, he and his young bride, Eileen, decided to leave famine-ravaged Ireland and begin a new life with relatives in Canada. As a literate man, Keegan kept a journal of his journey, chronicling the horrors he discovered on board the ship bound to Quebec from Dublin. He was graphic in his details of the crowding on board ship, the stench and filth below decks in steerage where many of his fellow travellers were entombed for the better part of the six-week passage. Keegan was also horrified by the number of deaths at sea that resulted from poor food, poorer sanitation, and the dreaded "ships fever." Several times Keegan found himself in conflict with the ship's first mate and captain as he vehemently protested the treatment of his fellow migrants on what would universally be referred to in the months to come as a "coffin ship." When he and Eileen arrived at the Quebec quarantine station of Grosse Ile, he volunteered to assist the sick and dying off the ship to convalesce in the island's medical facilities. Unknown to him, his wife and baggage were unloaded from the ship by the unscrupulous first mate, and he and Eileen were left stranded on the island. In time, Eileen contracted typhus and died, as did Keegan himself, mostly because of his selfless volunteer work in the fever sheds.

Keegan's diary is a gripping testimony to the Irish Famine and the plight of tens of thousands. In the 1980s, as the sesquicentennial of the famine period approached, the diary was published as *The Voyage of the Naparima* and became a best seller in Ireland.[1] Through its pages readers were struck by a gripping narrative of hunger and death caused by greed, heartless landlords, and the dastardly policies of the British government. The diary helped confirm the anti-British opinions pronounced a century before by Irish radical John Mitchel when he penned, "the Almighty had brought the blight, but the English created the famine."[2]

There was one thing standing in the way of confirming Mitchel's certitudes on the Famine: Keegan's diary was a fake.[3] In fact, it was written fifty years after the famine, in 1895, by an Anglo-Canadian newspaper editor, Robert Sellar, who serialized his famine story, titled "The Summer of Sorrow," in his weekly paper *The Huntingdon Gleaner*. Sellar's original manuscripts are held by Library and Archives Canada and clearly show the work of a literary craftsmen, including his deletions and edits to the make his text that much more appealing to his readers. While some commentators still claim that Sellar based his serial on real events, there is no evidence that he was plagiarizing an actual diary from the famine period.[4] When the diary was first reprinted in 1988, in a double volume set *The Irish in Canada: The Untold Story*, editors assumed that the diary was real and that there had been a conspiracy afoot to keep it hidden in an effort to deflect attention away from British responsibility for the catastrophe that beset Ireland and saw the loss of over two million of its people in less than a decade.[5]

There are other famine diaries of dubious origin, but none so notorious as Keegan's. It is still available in bookstores with the proviso that it is based on real events.[6] More importantly, it has become symbolic of the struggle between historians, politicians, and pundits over the "facts" of the famine and the way in which collective memory and empirically based scholarly study collide over Ireland's worst disaster in its modern history. The story of Molly Johnson and the famine orphans is just one Canadian chapter in this much larger contested narrative of the events during the "great hunger" and who ultimately bears responsibility for the Irish Famine. Despite the thrust and parry of nationalist, revisionist, and neo-revisionist historians over the details of the famine, the Mitchellite version of events retains its strength among many in Ireland and the Irish in the American[7] and Canadian diasporas, particularly as the famine is increasingly commemorated by public monuments.[8]

It is within this context of the contested narratives of the Great Irish Famine that the study of the famine orphans in Canada must be placed. Sifting through the versions of what happened during the famine and its migrations can becoming enormously frustrating, with one contending with wildly different scholarly and populist interpretations.[9] Ironically, the historical record in Ireland did not focus on the famine period with any seriousness until the 1940s, when then-president Éamon de Valera commissioned several notable scholars, principally from University College Dublin, to produce an official history of the Great Famine. Published in 1956, nearly a decade after its anticipated date of publication, Dudley Edwards and T. Desmond Williams' edition titled *The Great Irish Famine* assigns no blame for the famine, exorcises some of the famine myths of previous writers like Mitchel, and offers some pithy insights into the politics of the relief efforts but in the end demonstrates the weakness of having been written without much sense of social historical method.[10] Six years later, however, Cecil Woodham-Smith's *The Great Hunger* (1962) became the standard text on the famine, as she filled its pages with heroes and villains and tapped into some of the worst and most emotionally gripping episodes of the famine.[11] American Irish nationalists and others lapped up Smith's work, particularly her critique of Charles Edward Trevelyan, secretary of the treasury, and the text became the touchstone for a nationalist perspective on the famine. In recent years a new generation of scholars, including Cormac Ó Gráda, Mary Daly, and Joel Mokyr, have challenged Smith's work and Mitchel's rhetorical flourishes, providing revisions that have enflamed Irish nationalists on both sides of the Atlantic.[12] The research and writing of historians such as Peter Gray, Christine Kinealy, and James Donnelly in the 1990s, as the famine approached its 150th anniversary, provided a balance between revisionist corrections of economic and political circumstances and an acknowledgment that the famine was real and marked a period of untold human suffering in all of Ireland including areas of the north.

Despite the more recent nuanced and evidence-based appraisals of the people and events of the Great Famine, it comes as no surprise that stories of the famine touch emotional chords and produce passionate interpretations of this national tragedy. But as is the case with the Keegan journal, let the buyer beware. The publication of Tim Pat Coogan's *The Famine Plot* in 2012 renewed controversy when he claimed, "John Mitchel's stark analysis that God sent the blight but the English created the Famine rings true ... Whig policy was directed at getting the peasants off the land and if it took mass death to achieve that directive, so be it."[13] Dismissive of contemporary scholarship, it was as if, in Coogan's appraisal, no meaningful research in the area had been done since Mitchel. Responding to Coogan's charges of genocide against Britain,[14] Liam Kennedy, a professor emeritus at Queen's University Belfast, published *Unhappy the Land: The Most Oppressed People Ever, the Irish?*[15] Kennedy's counterargument cut to the quick, demolished the genocide theory, and exposed the divide that has long existed between professional historians and their popularizing counterparts on the claims of English acts of genocide against the Irish. Kennedy's book, however, did little to thwart sales of Coogan's tome.[16] Thus, despite the hundreds of litres of ink spilled on the effort to understand what actually happened during the famine, the debate continues, and one must take great care to reconstruct events that led to the appearance of so many orphan children in British North America in "Black '47" and beyond.

The question at present is essentially uncovering what set of circumstances prompted the families of Molly Johnson and other orphans to leave Ireland in the late 1840s. Nothing is as clear cut as it first appears.[17] When addressing the events that affected Irish families, one discovers that there were few people of means and power, on both sides of the Irish Sea, who "stood with the angels" when it came to relieving the hunger, sickness, and death that stalked Ireland after the failure of the potato crop. Merchants, both Catholic and Protestant, priests and ministers, Irish nationalists and pundits, landlords, land agents, and farmers with larger and more productive farms all collectively shared culpability for the persistence of Irish suffering from 1845 to 1851. In the end, the ideology of political economy based on "*laissez-faire*" and simple self-interest doomed the Irish peasant classes, who either suffered and died in their homeland or sought new life abroad. Not all families fled Ireland for the same reason, but assuredly all families had lost hope in sustaining their lives within Irish social structures that had virtually collapsed following the repeated potato blights and crop failures after 1845.

It was the generations-old landholding system and the colonial economic structures in Ireland that set the stage for what happened during the potato crop failures of 1845 to 1850 and account for the frustrated attempts at alleviating mass starvation. From the time of the British plantations in Ireland in the sixteenth century and throughout various historical manipulations of land tenure imposed by the British Crown, Ireland had emerged with a landed class that held property on the one side and much of the population that rented and farmed as tenants, on the other. Complicating matters was the fact that the landlords were primarily Protestant (as strengthened by the Penal Laws imposed in the late seventeenth century), English-speaking, and often absent from their demesnes. Their tenants were primarily, but not exclusively, native Irish, Roman Catholic, and officially (until 1829) effectively barred from public office and the liberal professions.[18] In the wake of the Napoleonic wars agricultural prices declined although agricultural exports grew, yet those at the bottom of the agricultural pyramid failed to advance in their economic status. Moreover, the cottage linen trade in the northern counties of Ireland went into steep decline as larger urban industrial textile mills replaced them.[19] Of the landlords themselves, who numbered close to ten thousand, it is estimated that one in twelve were insolvent in 1845.[20] Faced with these new convulsions in the economy, many Irish, both Protestant and Catholic, regarded emigration to Britain, the United States, and British North America as their only recourse.

For those farmers who remained, rural life faced new population pressures as their families grew, along with the commensurate pressure to feed them. The potato became a wonder food, rich in vitamins and carbohydrates; it is said that the average Irish male consumed around twelve pounds per day, prepared in various ways.[21] Moreover, contemporary commentators of the state of the Irish people noted that the Irish peasant was identified as one of the most robust and healthiest in Europe.[22] A ready food supply facilitated population growth, but as tenant families grew, so did the familial obligation to provide older sons with their own land to farm. Tenancies shrunk because of these subdivisions, but the "lumper" variety of potato was an ideal crop, yielding large harvests from "lazy beds" planted on even the most marginal and tiniest patches of land.[23] By 1840, Irish tenants – small farmers, cottiers, and conacre labourers –particularly in the west of Ireland, were trapped in a potato monoculture.

Phytophthora infestans, a fungus that attacked potato stalks and then gradually turned the subterranean tubers into a stinking, putrid mess, struck the Great Lakes and St Lawrence Valley of North America in the early 1840s.[24] In most regions, both Canadian and American, farmers were able to adapt to the loss of the potato because the agricultural economy of the region was diversified. In Eastern Nova Scotia, however, poor land and frontier type settlements had produced a farmer reliance on the potato akin to Ireland. When disaster struck that colony in 1845 and 1846, the local government in Halifax sent immediate financial aid and new seed to develop and diversify the local farm economy.[25] Ironically *phytophthora infestans* was likely carried to Ireland by merchant ships from the Americas and born on the winds and rain from continental Europe where potato blight had been reported in the Low Countries. In the autumn of 1845, what on one day appeared to be beds of healthy potato plants soon turned black, and as much as one third of the late autumn crop of potatoes was destroyed, although the losses varied from county to county, with heaviest losses in the east of Ireland.[26] There was no sense of panic among farmers themselves: first, the entire crop had not failed; second, the blight was not universal; and finally, within living memory, crops had failed before in 1817 and 1821, on both of which occasions Irish tenant farmers muddled through and anticipated a return of the potato harvest the following year.[27]

While there had been concern for the quantity and quality of seed potatoes for the crop intended for 1846, most Irish farmers thought that the worst dangers had passed. In the autumn of 1845, the administration of Prime Minister Sir Robert Peel had made arrangements to import American maize, to be sold at a penny per pound, in order to relieve any distress to those farmers who had lost the previous year's crops. The sale of the maize, however, did not begin until March 1846,[28] due to the inability of American grain to be shipped expeditiously and perhaps a lack of urgency, given the limited scope of the blight the previous autumn. Peel's government also dramatically altered British trade policy in June that year when it abolished the Corn Laws, which had protected UK farmers by restricting the importation of cheap foodstuffs. Inherently a free trader, Peel had seen the potential Irish food crisis as sufficient reason to facilitate a more liberal trade in agricultural products.[29] The potato crop in the summer and autumn of that year appeared to flourish, but just in advance of the harvest the blight returned, destroying much of the potato crops in all of Ireland's thirty-two counties. The new crisis had to be faced by a new administration. Peel's repeal of the Corn Laws had alienated protectionist members of his own party and his government eventually fell (although on a "Coercion Bill"). Subsequently, Lord John Russell and his Whig (Liberal) Party assumed the government, bringing with them a zealous adherence to *laissez-faire* capitalism and a reluctance to engage the state in actions that might inhibit the natural economic forces at play in the marketplace. Charles Edward Trevelyan, the secretary of the treasury, held on tightly to the dictums of *laissez-faire*, fearing that the redirection of Irish food exports would disrupt the Irish economy irreparably and that government handouts to the Irish poor would create an unnatural dependence on government assistance, which would also hamper values of hard work, productivity, and thrift.[30]

Charles Trevelyan and his allies were unwilling to deviate from a very strict application of allowing the free market to respond to natural economic forces. They placed considerable faith in the ability of the economy to right itself and little faith in the Irish people, whom they thought would become too dependent on government aid and lose incentive to fend for themselves. Such a bureaucratic response to the famine was dictated by doctrinaire capitalist theory and a repugnance to Irish Catholic culture, although it should be noted that Protestant Irish, even in the northern counties, also suffered from the devastation of their potato crops and the hunger and disease that came thereafter.[31] Therefore, while one might characterize British relief policy in Ireland as bearing an anti-Catholic bias, it is not a sufficient explanation of government policy when Protestant Belfast, Lurgan, Armagh, and large sections of northern County Down were stricken by the blight and subsequent food crisis as well. In so far as British North America was concerned, many families fled these northern counties during the famine, using Derry (Londonderry), Newry (from Warrenpoint), and Belfast as points of departure for Saint John, New Brunswick, and Quebec. Margaret Conlan was living proof of such decisions. Her Protestant family left Belfast during the migration of 1847, and all died except Margaret, only six years old, who was left alone at the dock of Quebec, hoping that an uncle would come and fetch her.[32]

The results of this *laissez-faire* policy were an unmitigated disaster. The poor law unions, which had been hastily established in 1838 and were completely unsuited to the Irish social structure, were overwhelmed by destitute cottiers (small tenant farmers), conacre farmers,[33] and labourers.[34] In addition, many of those local gentry who were obliged to support the poor through the Poor Law rate found that their finances were stretched thinly. Tenants who defaulted on rent sent a chain reaction through the local economy, ultimately inhibiting some landlords from being able to meet their own obligations.[35] The government-sponsored soup kitchens and the private relief offered by the mainline churches and the Quakers provided needed immediate relief but no long-term strategy to solve the food crisis in Ireland. The government also put in place local public works projects, designed to put money in pauper hands to buy food and not to disrupt local markets. While the economic theory behind putting cash in the hands of the poor to help reignite the economy might appear to be a sound approach in the eyes of some economic theorists today,[36] it was short-sighted to think that starving and ill people could successfully carry out the heavy labour required to build stone walls or roads to nowhere. The harsh winter of 1846–47, one of the worst in Irish memory, just hastened the death and destitution of the Irish people. In recognition that the public works programs did not work and were subject to local corruption, Trevelyan began to scale back and ultimately cancelled the state-sponsored initiatives and, in an effort to thwart undue dependence on the state by its citizens, ended the subsidized soup kitchens.[37] Ironically, the soup program had been modestly successful in feeding thousands who might have otherwise perished in Black '47. The crisis continued that year even though there was a modest harvest of potatoes by year's end. This ray of hope was dashed by two successive years of crop failure in 1848 and 1849. By the early 1850s, one million Irish people had died and 1.5 million Irish had emigrated, out of an 1841 population of 8.1 million.[38]

John Mitchel, who at the time was a member of the politically radical "Young Ireland" movement, laid the blame for this catastrophe squarely upon England's politicians. In his recounting of how ships laden with Ireland's agricultural bounty set sail for foreign markets while Ireland starved, he condemned the policies of the British government. To this day, Mitchel's reasoning has fuelled charges of genocide against Russell, Trevelyan, and the Whigs who supported their *laissez-faire* policies. Such blanket criticism of British policy, however, overlooks some important facts. It is inaccurate to say the government did nothing – their expenditure on Ireland during the famine was £9.5 million or the equivalent of £712 million in today's currency (roughly $1.5 billion CAD).[39] Clearly, the real question ought to have been did the government spend the money effectively and as generously as it might have had the famine taken place on the island of Great Britain. Moreover, one might ask, had the famine ravaged England and destroyed its agricultural economy, would there have been far greater financial intervention from Westminster?[40] Long-standing prejudice against the Irish, both in cultural and religious terms, and "Irish fatigue" among politicians and British voters who despaired at ongoing troubles in Ireland, may account for a less than robust response to the Irish food crisis. There is no doubt that the Peel government effected significant relief projects to alleviate what was thought to be a passing trouble in Ireland. Although Peel might be chastised for political opportunism in enacting free trade in agricultural products by means of the abolition of the Corn Laws,[41] the fact remains that allowing for the importation of cheaper foodstuffs should have been a key measure in alleviating Irish hunger.

While the policies of the Whig Government regarding Ireland may have been misguided, doctrinaire, and ultimately ineffective, such initiatives were often frustrated by the apparent inaction of the Anglo-Irish landlord class. Parliament's broadening of the Poor Law to include outdoor relief and the imposition of the principle that "Irish property would pay for Irish poverty" were ill-conceived and eventually abject failures. What Westminster perceived was a fattened landholding class in Ireland not pulling its weight, whereas in reality many landlords and their agents struggled to cover their own debts when rent revenues from impoverished tenant farmers were drying up.[42] It has already been noted that public works programs, while theoretically a reasonable approach to inject capital into a failing economy, if introduced early, also failed. Introduced too late, and without forethought or much planning, subject to local corruption, and relying on starved and ill labourers, the scheme failed. Even when successful programs such as the soup kitchens were enacted, the government, ill-advisedly having declared "the worst to be over," terminated them.[43] There was always the lingering fear that government-sponsored assistance would breed overdependence on the state and instill a culture of laziness in Ireland.

By their often half-hearted and self-interested actions, landlords also added to the misery of their tenants during the famine period. The inability of tenants to pay rents became a convenient excuse for mass evictions from some estates, thereby providing the opportunity for landlords to consolidate the small tenancies and to create pasturage for the more lucrative agricultural practice of animal husbandry. Landlords claimed that they were impoverished by defaulting tenants (a practice that had gone on for decades) or having inherited lands from those who left their properties deeply in debt. The famine crisis provided an opportunity for many landowners to rid themselves of tenants who were perpetually in arrears and to initiate long-sought land reform that would dismantle the small farms that had multiplied on their estates over the previous half century and open the land for new economic opportunities.[44] Some landlords were notorious in their attitudes toward the peasantry and their opportunism. George Bingham, Lord Lucan of Castlebar, County Mayo, Ballinrobe, evicted 2,000 tenants (he was in arrears in paying his poor rate) and his tenants were cast out onto the roads, landless, unemployed, and without hope.[45] Nearby, in the Doolough Valley, in 1849 hundreds of tenants trekked the twenty kilometres from Louisbourgh in the north of the valley to Delphi in the south, where they were rebuffed by the landlord's agents when they begged for food. A gale and snowstorm blew in off the north Atlantic as they trudged back to their homes.[46] Most of them died, and to this day the valley is nearly devoid of human habitation. In another act of callousness, in 1847 William Gregory, a member of Parliament and landlord in Galway, proposed his famous "Gregory Clause," which amended the Poor Law to allow for outdoor relief but only for those tenants holding a quarter acre of land or less; tenants with holdings greater than a quarter of an acre would have to abandon their lands to be eligible for relief.[47] While on the surface the policy appeared to be a generous extension of relief at the workhouses within poor law unions, in reality, however, it was a means whereby landlords could rid themselves of their responsibilities to their disadvantaged tenants and reclaim their tenancies.

Other landlords were seemingly contradictory in their approaches to their tenants. Elizabeth Smith, wife of a prominent landlord at Baltiboys (also Baltyboys), County Wicklow, wrote, "We determined to get rid of the little tenants and to increase the large farms – and we did it – not at once – just watched for opportunities and managed this delicate business without annoying anyone – even causing a murmur [sic] ... Envy, malice, evil-speaking, hatred, lying and all uncharitableness ... how I wish we had not one tenant in Baltyboys." If one based their judgment of this landlord simply on her diaries one would miss the disconnection between her words and her actions. Smith was known to travel from cabin to cabin and got to know her tenants personally. She was sympathetic to those who worked hard and highly critical of those she deemed indolent. When she was faced with a crisis on her husband's estate in the early years of the famine, she was noted for her generosity to most tenants in supplying them with food and shelter. Based on her experiences of rural poverty on her estate and neighbouring ones, she publicly criticized the policies of the Russell government.[48] Major Denis Mahon, who will feature in the next chapter, displayed similar conflicted behaviour with regards to his tenants at Strokestown in County Roscommon.[49]

There were also landlords who provided more complicating challenges to the stereotype of the evil landlord. John Plunket Joly of Clonast, Kings County, appeared almost completely oblivious to the starvation and disease taking place all around him. His diaries dating from the period make little or no mention of the human suffering in his midst. Joly, who wrote about his many travels through Ireland and sketched what he saw along the way, demonstrated a preoccupation with music, peasant dances and customs, and his many hobbies. Joly appeared to live somewhere in a fantasy world of his own creation.[50]

Despite the general negative images of landlords, both in the historical record and the popular mind, several orphans in Quebec and Saint John could be traced back to estates managed differently. Some landlords rose to the fore in the time of crisis and assisted their tenants in extraordinary ways. Stephen De Vere, a nephew of Lord Mountjoy and a landlord in County Limerick, travelled with his assisted tenants to Quebec and then complained formally to the British government about conditions on board the emigrants ships, thereafter immortalized as "coffin ships"; De Vere's testimony in front a Parliamentary Board of Inquiry became a catalyst in the revision of the Navigation Acts to ensure better food and health care for passengers on transatlantic voyages.[51] Lady Catherine, the Marchioness of Sligo, whose son George was a landlord in Mayo, took personal interest in the relief of suffering within her family's estate, becoming one of the most noted philanthropists during the famine.[52] At the end of the crisis she was personally responsible for the erection, near her estate, of the first known monument to those who lost their lives during the calamity. Similarly, there was John Hamilton, who at the age of twenty-one in 1821 inherited 20,000 acres in south Donegal near Donegal town. He was loved by his tenants and for good reason; he nearly bankrupted his estate to aid tenants in need both before and during the famine.[53] In Wicklow, Earl Fitzwilliam, knowing that there was little for his tenants left in Ireland, paid for the transport of hundreds of Irish to begin new lives in Canada and New Brunswick. Although many of the migrants struggled and faced discrimination from the communities that they entered, the migration plan offered hope to those that had virtually lost any sense of a future in Wicklow.[54] Nevertheless, the landholding system had failed the small farmers, cottier farmers with only a few acres, and the oft-landless labourers and conacre farmers. Those who had means were among the families who hoped to begin again in Canada.

The question remains, landlord or not, could these families have remained in Ireland had there been sufficient food to feed them? It has been argued, that had these foodstuffs been retained in Ireland to feed the destitute, the Great Hunger could have been diverted there. The historical record is clear that food was exported from Ireland during the famine – grains, livestock, distilled products, etc. It was evident to Trevelyan and those who held principles of free trade and *laissez-faire* capitalism that any disruption in Irish trade would have had a most serious long term-effect on the Irish economy. The fear of long-term dependence on the government and persistent Irish poverty as a result stood as principal arguments against ceasing agricultural exports during the time of the potato crop failure. Careful scrutiny of the economic history of the period indicates that the amount of food exported would never have fed the hungry of Ireland if diverted to domestic use.[55] The food crisis was compounded by Roman Catholic and Protestant merchants who refused to divert their exports of agricultural goods from foreign markets to feed the local population. Many merchants also used the market forces argument to keep food prices high[56] and appeared to be equally convinced that the market forces ought not to be disrupted. Self-interest governed the behaviour of the mercantile community, who desired neither to disrupt the flow of trade nor their own profits and livelihood to unduly assist the starving masses around them. While a reduction of exports in the first year of the crisis may have mitigated some of the worst effects of hunger and disease in 1845–46, the British *laissez-faire* policies appeared to have had considerable support among the merchants of Ireland.

The merchants and exporters, however, formed only one link in the chain of trade that connected foreign markets with domestic producers. Each link in this food supply chain contributed to the misery of poor Irish families because each failed to engage the food crisis with a sense of great urgency and a level of compassion for their neighbours. Within the land holding system there were tenant farmers with large holdings (middlemen) who had diversified farming on their land and did not depend solely on the potato for sustenance. It was these mid-level farmers who had subdivided some of their large tenancies, subletting them to cottiers and seasonally to labourers. In a time of crisis, these middlemen demonstrated little willingness to divert their surpluses to relieve the distress around them. It should also be pointed out that this division between the small and middle-sized tenancies did not correspond to a sectarian divide. Middle-sized holdings were in the possession of both Roman Catholic and Protestant farmers, neither of whom appeared willing to make sacrifices for their sub-tenants and both of which continued to export food stuffs to foreign markets.[57] Moreover, during the crisis, larger farmers refused to pay cash wages to their agricultural labourers, who were then forced to return their meager rented plots and then leave the land, perhaps to face starvation as an army of the rural landless poor.[58] One of the great tragedies within famine Ireland was the fact that many of the individuals closest to the scenes of starvation and who may very well have helped to make some difference locally failed to do so. One does not have to look all the way to the Parliament in Westminster to discover that there were more than just economic theorists, capitalists, Malthusians, and merchants who thought that in the greater scheme of things, profits outweigh persons.

It also comes as a bit of a surprise that when families resorted to appeal to their Christian communities, the response was often less than what had been expected by the petitioners. Churches, whose Christian teachings underscored the necessity to serve the poor, weak, marginalized, and the proverbial "widow and orphan," were called upon ceaselessly to assist those in need: some rose to the challenge while others did not. The Roman Catholic Church, which represented most Irish persons in the provinces of Connacht, Leinster, and Munster, and a large minority in Ulster, did provide assistance during the famine, through food/soup kitchens, outdoor relief, the distribution of relief money from abroad, and the provision of charitable aid in a variety of ways. In Limerick, Bishop John Ryan established soup kitchens and a "Soup Society" to alleviate hunger in the city, eliciting great praise from *The Limerick Reporter*, which claimed that such works were evidence that "he who gives to the poor, lends to God."[59] In Dublin, Archbishop Daniel Murray became a central source of charitable donations made by persons, institutions, and churches around the world. From Dublin, Murray would respond to requests for assistance from across Ireland, therein creating a network of Church-based relief that fanned out to all counties but particularly those worst afflicted in the west of Ireland. The priests in his archdiocese became a major source of information on the spread of disease and the depletion of the food supply.[60] Likewise, Father Laurence Renehan, president of Patrick's College, Maynooth, kept in contact with a network of priests and alumni, from who he gleaned first-hand accounts of the famine, and sent aid from the college to Kerry, Longford, and Tipperary.[61] Moreover, priests were recorded as having kept calm in riot-prone areas, working feverishly to relieve suffering and maintain order.[62]

Acts of charity and self-sacrifice offer only part of the story of religious institutions' engagement in the famine. While some politicians, landlords, and philanthropists regarded emigration as an opportunity for starving landless tenants to start anew and perhaps have a better life in America, Archbishop John McHale of Tuam discouraged emigration, as did Archbishop Paul Cullen, who with many clergy regarded "exodus" as an attempt both to denude Ireland of its Catholic majority and to play to the advantage of scheming landlords.[63] In fairness, McHale had been an outspoken critic of the government's *laissez-faire* policies and had also been instrumental in the distribution of aid to the starving masses in Connaught.[64] As had been the case of Denis Mahon (see chapter 2), one may read several motives behind assisted immigration schemes and, perhaps, those who resisted emigration projects might have been more forthcoming in assisting those who were to remain in Ireland, landless, poor, and malnourished. It should be pointed out that, despite the temper of the times, the Roman Catholic Church also continued to engage in capital projects during the famine, thereby limiting the relief they could offer, while still demanding collections for local and papal charities. Some have judged the Church's collective effort as more reactive than proactive, with the hierarchy unable to speak as one powerful voice for change under the conditions brought by the famine; "instead the majority [hierarchy] busied itself with burying the dead and curbing social unrest."[65]

Much more might be said of organized Protestantism and its engagement with the famine. The legally established Church of Ireland (Anglican) did charitable work locally but did not discontinue tithing in Ireland, nor did they sacrifice the lavish parochial lifestyle in the ministerial manse.[66] Moreover, rumours spread with varying degrees of evidence that, in some locations in Ireland, Protestants were dolling out soup on the condition that Catholic recipients denounce their faith and become Protestant. The term "souperism" still persists to denote apostasy that is motivated by the want to better one's earthly conditions.[67] While there has been much made of souperism in popular literature on the famine, it was clear that documented cases are fewer than expected and the Quaker charities in no way engaged in the practice.[68] Nevertheless, the images of such proselytism, particularly from testimony from contemporaries in West Cork, Kerry, and Mayo, suggest that the famine became an opportunity for churches to accelerate their mission programs when they felt the Catholic population was vulnerable. Even Church of Ireland Archbishop of Dublin Richard Whatley admitted "attempts were made ... in some instances to induce persons to carry on a system of covert proselytism by holding out relief of bodily wants and suffering as a kind of bribe for conversion."[69]

Curiously, the small Anglican weekly publication in Quebec City, *The Berean*, eagerly reported the evangelical works of Protestant missionaries at Achill Island and Dingle, praising their efforts and assuring readers that their donations to such causes were the Lord's work.[70] Children, notably those without parents present, were particularly vulnerable. Unable to identify their religious affiliation, missionaries immediately incorporated them into the Church of Ireland. This proselytizing practice became general policy throughout Ireland when the attorney general mandated that "where the religion of an orphan or deserted child was unknown, the child could be brought up in the religion of the state, the Church of Ireland."[71] Understandably some Catholics families, with whatever they could scratch up for fare, fled Ireland to save both their bodies and their souls.

The self-interest of the churches may also be reflected in the general religious attitudes that may have determined some policy and public perception of the Irish during the famine. In the mid-nineteenth century, there was an acknowledged religious bias, particularly among Anglican Evangelicals like Charles Trevelyan, who saw the hand of providence in the potato blight; perhaps, it was thought, God was meting out divine punishment to Irish Catholics who had slavishly obeyed the dictates of a foreign potentate in Rome and persisted in superstitious and outrageous religious beliefs and practices.[72]

These prejudices held sway among large numbers in the English propertied classes and in some members of the Whig caucus and civil service. Such providentialism, when combined with the low opinion of the Irish as a people, provided a fertile social and political context in which ideas of massive relief to Ireland might be dismissed or rendered in mere half measures.

One irony of this providentialism was the fact that those who were starving were not exclusively Catholic. The famine knew no sect. It is a long-standing myth in Northern Ireland that the famine was essentially a southern and Catholic problem.[73] As has been acknowledged earlier in this chapter, Protestants suffered in the Belfast area, in Lurgan, and in Counties Antrim, Armagh, and Down. Working-class areas of Belfast were overwhelmed by starving refugees from the countryside, in addition to those who starved in the mill towns and linen-producing villages around the Laggan. In 1847, 38,000 migrants, mostly famine refugees, entered the Upper Canadian inland port of Toronto, which then had only about 20,000 citizens. It is estimated that one in five of these migrants were Irish Protestants. Today, St James Anglican cemetery in the city has the only known memorial in the world dedicated exclusively to Protestant victims of the Irish Famine.[74] Thus, the irony of providentialism becomes clear and certainly challenges notions that the famine can be seen clearly within a sectarian context of Protestant overlords who oppressed and Catholic peasants who suffered, died, or emigrated. Moreover, despite its ironies, providentialism may have lain at the heart of indifference for some Evangelicals during the famine, but Catholics themselves may have felt that they had earned the displeasure of the deity in some way and the famine was a punishment for their tepid religious practice. It has been suggested that this sense of guilt and need for God's forgiveness launched Irish Catholics willingly into Archbishop Paul Cullen's militant and triumphant devotional revolution in the 1850s.[75]

The food crisis and religious complications from which Irish families fled, where also compounded by deep divisions among Irish politicians. Daniel O'Connell's great movement for the repeal of the Act of Union between Ireland and Britain, in 1801, was bitterly divided by the mid-1840s. While O'Connell had marked notable success in forcing Catholic emancipation in 1829, and his monster meetings were drawing tens of thousands of Irish to the cause of repeal,[76] his movement was coming apart at the seams. A growing movement within repeal, known as "Young Ireland," grumbled that O'Connell's means of constitutional reform were too cautious and ineffective. This edgier nationalist movement eschewed the "old leader's" non-violent and constitutional approach to Irish autonomy from Britain, with a brand of Irish radicalism that regarded physical force as one of the tools to secure Ireland's freedom. When, in 1843, O'Connell was threatened by the law and called off a mass meeting at Clontarf, outside of Dublin, it was clear to Young Irelanders that the cause of repeal now had to mount new and aggressive means by force of arms to secure Ireland's independence from Great Britain.[77] O'Connell's reform newspaper the *Freeman's Journal* faced stronger rhetorical competition from *The Nation*, the more radical voice of the Young Ireland movement.

Amid the row between O'Connellites and Young Irelanders, the famine unfolded. O'Connell, who himself was a landlord, was infirm, old, and a weaker voice in Westminster. He spoke about Irish relief, admitting at first that Ireland had more than enough food to satisfy its needs,[78] but had been a supporter, politically, of the Whig faction in Parliament and became associated, and therefore tainted, with the policies perpetuated by Russell and Trevelyan. While his pleas for relief in both 1845 to Peel and 1846 to Russell fell on deaf ears, he continued to supply relief in the form of maize and oatmeal to his own tenants in County Kerry.[79] In 1847, while travelling to Italy for a rest, O'Connell died. His final years had been a pale imitation of the energy and passion that had earned him the title "The Great Liberator."

As for the Young Irelanders, their approach to the famine was to discourage charitable aid to Ireland, fearing that the Irish people would be demoralized and reduced to pauperism. "Young Irelanders," writes historian David Wilson, "were closer than they realized to Charles Trevelyan."[80] In fact, many Young Irelanders thought that the famine might open the opportunity for the most important issue of the day – the independence of Ireland. Future Canadian politician, Thomas D'Arcy McGee, then a member of Young Ireland, told potential American donors promising economic relief that such a move was bound to interfere with the free trade that ought to be made open to Ireland as a result of the repeal of the Corn Laws. With almost a Trevelyanesque reasoning, McGee did not want any interference in the correcting of the Irish economy and the subsequent strengthening of Ireland which, in the short term, might bring about the repeal of the Union: "American political aid was welcome, American economic assistance would be counterproductive."[81] It is ironic that John Mitchel, whose writings have been so often cited because of their implication that the British created an artificial famine, was rank and file among the Young Ireland leadership which tried to block relief for ideological reasons.

In some ways, the devastation of the Irish people that came because of the repeated crop failures was not entirely something that leaders could remedy easily. There is little doubt that conditions for the Irish families failed to improve because of poor government policy; an ineffective Poor Law system; struggling and, in some cases, self-serving landlords; ideologically driven politicians of all stripes; some double-souled churchmen; and less than charitable merchants and larger landholders. There were also reasons for the prolonged suffering in Ireland that were outside the capabilities of civil servants and local officials to remedy. Trustees of the workhouses and local physicians were helpless in their efforts to treat effectively the diseases that emerged, sometimes in pandemic proportions, as a result of hunger and starvation. Rudimentary epidemiology and microbiological skills of physicians were no match for cholera, typhus, and typhoid, which carried off many of those rendered destitute by hunger. In the case of typhus, for instance, also known as "ship fever" or by its scientific name *Rickettsia prowazecki*, there was no known cure and it was highly communicable. Today this bacterial infection can be fought easily with antibiotics.[82] Archbishop Daniel Murray, in gathering information in October 1847, reckoned that of the 74,065 deaths reported to him from nearly 300 districts across all four Irish provinces, 51,884 or 70 per cent were from disease and the remaining 30 per cent were from outright starvation.[83] While governments could have been more effective in the administration of food and shelter and less eager to put so many of the ill in crowded quarters, physicians were still certainly limited in their abilities to fight the bacterial infections that ravaged the weakened bodies of the malnourished.[84]

Accounting for the actions of parliamentarians, churchmen, merchants, landlords, and political agitators tells only one part of the famine story as it unfolded in Ireland. On the ground, the lives lived and the lives taken in ordinary families is truly the untold story of the famine. These were illiterate and semi-literate people, unlike the fictional Gerald Keegan, who did not have the skill, opportunity, or materials to record their story. The hunger and disease and a sense of hopelessness among the Irish cottiers and labourers led to considerable social unrest. Often the make-work projects sponsored by the government were the foci of the unrest. Labourers found the wages too low to provide for their family. In August 1846, 3,000 to 4,000 people gathered in Westport, Mayo, to protest their wages; later, in October, on the Knock road, County Clare, a "check clerk" and an overseer were brutally assaulted by a gang. In December, on the Pullough Road, County Limerick, Private George Windsor of the Royal Sappers and Miners was attacked by "two armed men in women's clothes" in retaliation for fraud and corruption by officials on the road works.[85] In the fall and winter of 1846–47, disruptions in the public works were a daily occurrence across Ireland. In January 1847, an inspecting officer in the North Riding of County Tipperary confessed that suspensions of local road works would normally "remedy the evil" of idleness and protest, but "with the existing destitution, I conceive it to be a step which could not safely be adopted."[86] The problem in Ireland in 1846–47, however, was that such projects came far too late and people were unable to earn enough because they were physically weak due to malnutrition.[87] In Killaloe, County Clare, however, the wages of poor labourers on the relief works simply could not sustain both their food purchases and rents.[88]

Hunger and violence went hand-in-hand, particularly in the devastated areas of Munster and Connaught in the south and west of Ireland. In the early winter of 1847, as food supplies were depleted and as the price of available food soared,[89] the number of starving families exploded and their desperation took a violent turn. In January, in Adare, County Limerick, public works labourers protested when the daily wage was reduced from ten pence to nine. The Viscount Adare called in troops who engaged in "striking and thrusting the people" with their bayonets. A serious riot was avoided when the local parish priest, Father Leahy, intervened and placed himself as a human shield between the soldiers and the mob.[90] Shortly thereafter, in nearby Askeaton, a couple described as "an industrious and inoffensive" were mutilated to death by a hatchet-wielding burglar who stole their valuables.[91] In another act of desperation, seeking whatever money could come, a couple living near Youghall, County Cork, were arrested after they attempted to sell the corpse of their dead child.[92] In May 1847, "drunken mobs" attacked food wagons on the turnpikes of Munster, and an unruly group of patrons smashed all the windows of St John's Church Soup Kitchen in Limerick City.[93] Irish peasants lived lives of desperation that called for desperate measures uncontemplated in "normal" times. Hungry people ate anything that appeared palatable. A story was told of a family at Ballina, County Tipperary, who had to put down their donkey. Nothing, it was reported, was as miserable as seeing "a poor man salting down his ass for the consumption of his family."[94] The workhouse appeared as the only alternative to such extreme conditions of want.

What is also clear from the routinely generated records from the period and local newspapers was that children were at the heart of this story. In the 1840s, children comprised about one third of Ireland's total population, and children under the age of ten, in combination with adults over the age of sixty, accounted for three fifths of recorded deaths during the famine.[95] Moreover, half of the rations at the government-sponsored soup kitchens in Ireland were given to children under the age of nine.[96] Across Ireland, journalists and officials often focused on the plight of families and children during the worst of Black '47. American philanthropist, Asenath Nicolson was shocked by what she found when visiting a National School in Ballycroy, County Mayo:

> the national school gave not a favourable impression of the state of the children; nearly a hundred pale-faced and bare-footed little ones were crowded into a cold room, squatting upon their feet, cowering closely together, waiting for ten ounces of bread, which was all their support, but now and then a straggling turnip-top[97]

Similarly, at Crookhaven, in west County Cork, local physician James McCormick reported his discovery of dead babies at their mothers' breasts and "children who were fine and plump a few months since, now nothing but sinew and bone, with their eyes larger than their sockets."[98]

The plight of children during the famine was most evident in the workhouses that were a fixture in local poor law unions. The Poor Law had been imposed on Ireland in 1838 as a means of assisting the "deserving poor," but as we have already witnessed, these unions were completely overwhelmed by families seeking respite from the famine. When families surrendered themselves to relief at the workhouse, they were separated by sex with children segregated along the same lines as their parents with little regard given to their age or family circumstances. In some larger workhouses, children under the age of nine were sent to nursery wards.[99] In general, children were essentially regarded as little adults and were treated accordingly. Christine Kinealy, one of the leading experts on the Poor Law during the famine, has written, "Children in the 19th century were regarded as the responsibility of their parents, but who was responsible if those parents were ill, or destitute or disappeared, or were dead? When families and communities had been destroyed, who was to fill the vacuum. Neither the public works nor the Poor Law provided sufficient relief to keep people healthy. More shockingly, they were failing to save lives."[100]

Once having separated children from their parents, it was easier for workhouse supervisors to engage in a form of social engineering. The children subject to the plans of the guardians were of four specific types: those who had parents also residing in the workhouse, those children who had been orphaned, those children who had been declared as illegitimate, and many children who were abandoned or deposited at the workhouse by their parents.[101] In the case of the latter, boys and girls waited for remittances from their estranged parents to help them leave the workhouse and perhaps join them in their new places of employment, including Britain and America. Some of these children found their hope unrequited as they languished in the workhouse for a decade or more. Regardless of the reason for their presence, many poor law unions opened schools in the workhouses with the intention of training children not to continue the indolence and vices of their parents. Guardians believed that education was the best way to prevent crime, develop skills in children, and thereby train a new generation of Irish to be useful and productive citizens. To this end, workhouses often released their children for indentured work locally in an effort to offer them sound supervised work experience and spare them the life of fecklessness that they might have otherwise lived.[102] It was this type of thinking, engineering the poor gormless child into a productive one, that lay behind even larger government-funded schemes that would witness poor law unions release hundreds of young women and adolescent girls to travel to Australia and Canada to become domestic servants and, in the case of the Antipodes, potential wives for the colony's largely male population.[103] For families, the poor law union had always been a last resort; for their children it was the beginning of a life of indenture, or worse.

In the 1840s, Irish families faced the decision of staying in Ireland, with all the dire consequences of disease and starvation, or scraping together the means to escape and start a new life elsewhere. The poorest individuals and families had no recourse but to remain in Ireland because they did not have the means to leave. Other families with modest means elected to travel by foot or cart to Dublin and embark on cattle boats and steamers to Liverpool, where they would fan out all over Britain seeking nourishment and a steady income. Others, depending on the cost of passage flocked to Irish ports – Sligo, Derry, Dublin, Cork, Limerick, or Newry – to venture across the Atlantic to the Americas. The Irish also sought out Liverpool as a port of departure and for its cheap fares. But as will be seen in the next chapter, the securing of a passage did not necessarily mean safe and healthy travel to a new life. One's selection of a destination – Quebec, Saint John, New York, Boston, or New Orleans often determined the price of a ticket and, perhaps, the conditions on board ship. Tickets to the United States were the most expensive. Ports in the USA levied stiff head taxes on any ships landing diseased passengers or paupers and there were recorded cases of ships from British and Irish ports being refused entry because of diseased passengers.[104] This did not mean that American ports were closed to Irish refugees; it just meant that it was harder to enter the United States. Contrary to popular belief, more than 119,000 passengers from Irish and UK ports entered American ports during Black '47.[105]

Canada was often seen as a second choice but a necessary evil. Acknowledging that America had been his first choice, a recent Irish emigrant to Boston reported that "It is not well for those who are thinking of leaving their beloved homes in Ireland (wretched though they may be) to think of Canada as a home ... the employment which grows from enterprise and the enterprise which grows from freedom are not to be found in Canada. It is a second edition of Ireland, with more room."[106] Similarly discouraging, in May 1847 *The Limerick Reporter* summed up the dreadful choice facing so many of the dispossessed Irish: "In the present day there is a refinement on the edict of the Protector [Cromwell's famous ultimatum 'to hell or Connaught'], and the word is 'Death or Canada.'" The columnist went on to express grave misgivings about the mass migration of the Irish people: "Nay, some very few honest men, but mistaken men, have espoused this wild and impracticable project. The grand inducement held out is, that death awaits the people in their own country, and they ought, therefore, to leave it as quickly as possible, without knowing whether as speedy a death does not await them in the wilds of Canada."[107] Canada, it was claimed, was a difficult country, both in terrain and in climate. The Irish in their "new Ireland" would "roam like a flock of sheep without a shepherd, indebted to a new landlord: the Land Company." Nevertheless, in 1847, approximately 90,000 emigrants, mostly Irish, set sail for Quebec, nearly 17,000 ventured to New Brunswick, and about 2,000 intended Nova Scotia as their new home.[108] For Canada, it would be the largest mass migration of Irish people to its shores in history.

In terms of the voyage in 1847, the popular motif of the "coffin ship" was well suited to some of the vessels arriving in British North American ports, particular Quebec and Saint John. Some ship's captains interpreted the Navigation Acts very loosely and failed to provide adequate food and water for passengers crowded below decks on ships that were intended to carry chattels, timber, and grain – not humans. Ships were overcrowded because captains were in collusion with unscrupulous shipping agents who oversold tickets and promises. Crammed below decks on a six- to eight-week voyage, weak, underfed, and vulnerable to the spread of infectious disease, it is little wonder that a high volume of deaths at sea or in quarantine earned the vessels the infamous moniker. While it may be moot that landlords and government officials were aware of such conditions, the captains and agents of such vessels were culpable for prolonging the agony of the Irish families over this period. Certainly, officials had to take note when a person of prominence made a complaint. As previously mentioned, Stephen De Vere, an Irish landowner in County Limerick and convert to Catholicism, made the startling passage to judge for himself the conditions on board the "fever ships." In a letter to Lord Earl Grey at the Colonial Office and in testimony repeated later to a Select Committee of the British Parliament, De Vere reported:

> Before the emigrant has been a week at sea he is an altered man. How can it be otherwise? Hundreds of poor people. Men, women and children of all ages, from the driveling idiot to the babe just born, huddled together without light, without air, wallowing in filth and breathing a fetid atmosphere, sick in body, dispirited in heart, the fevered patients lying between the sound, in sleeping places so narrow as almost to deny them the power of indulging, by a change of position, the natural restlessness of the disease.[109]

Ironically, De Vere's testimony reflected similar comments made in the fabricated diary of Gerald Keegan, and in the problematic journal of Robert Whyte.[110]

Nevertheless, one must not be too hasty in generalizing about all ships, particularly those making the voyage from the United Kingdom to North America after 1847. In fact, during the sailing season of 1847, there were ports of departure that were more responsible than others for the implementation of the provisions of the Navigation Acts. In 1847, the port of Limerick sent fifty ships to British North America, the largest number of any Irish port.[111] The port served some of the most ravaged areas of the famine including devastated poor law unions in Counties Clare, Limerick, north Kerry, and Tipperary. The captain of the port, Richard Lynch, was evidently scrupulous in the way in which ships were maintained and provisioned. Perhaps his perspicacity was responsible for the fact that ships departing Limerick lost on average only four passengers at sea, whereas Cork lost twenty-seven on average, Liverpool twenty-six, and Dublin nine. Specific examples of safe passages include *The Dunbrody*, sailing from New Ross, County Wexford, which lost very few passengers on its many transatlantic voyages and the Quebec-built *Jeanie Johnston* which could boast that it lost none. The strict conditions on board the *Jeanie Johnston* were emphasized clearly in posted regulations by the ship's master James Attridge, which warned passengers that no fighting, drinking, open flame, swearing, gambling, or spitting would be permitted below decks.[112] As in all things contested about the Irish Famine, care must be taken regarding sweeping statements even about the coffin ships.

The year 1847 marked the high watermark for famine migration to British North America, as is indicated in table 1.3. Before addressing the orphans that were created during this migration, it is best to be clear about the principal characteristics of the Irish departing for British North America. First, the Irish families among the nearly 90,000 who ventured to Quebec came primarily from the counties of Munster and Connaught, in the south and southwest of Ireland, although there were some who hailed from Leinster and Ulster.[113] The region of origin is important in this case because of the fact that in Connaught and Munster the Irish language was often the first language or only language of prospective migrants at this time.[114] These were also primarily Roman Catholic regions of the country. In Saint John, New Brunswick, however, because of the pre-existing shipping ties between New Brunswick and the Irish ports of Cork and Derry (Londonderry), the families and individuals arriving on the Fundy Shore were primarily from Ulster's northern counties and the Cork region in Munster. In so far as Derry was concerned, this would have been a principal port of departure for many families who were members of the Presbyterian Church or the Church of Ireland.

As table 1.2 indicates, the large numbers of Irish leaving the port of Liverpool account for an undocumented listing of Irish hailing from all counties in Ireland. This smattering of migrants from all counties differs significantly from earlier pre-famine migrations which witnessed specific regions of Ireland being transplanted to the British North American colonies. Newfoundland's Irish, for example hailed from the southeast of Ireland: Waterford, Wexford, Kilkenny, Tipperary, and east Cork.[115] Prince Edward Island's Irish had strong representation from County Monaghan, primarily a Catholic region of Ulster.[116] New Brunswick's Irish migrants, in addition to the aforementioned regions during the famine, also witnessed Irish migrants from Newfoundland, or "two boaters," resettling on the mainland after a sojourn in eastern Newfoundland.[117] The central Canadian colonies were typical catch basins for a mix of migrants from across Ireland, with Quebec (Lower Canada) welcoming mostly Irish Catholics, while Ontario (Upper Canada) populated by a majority of Protestant Irish from the midland counties and from Ulster. The famine migrants would mark a shift in the dispersal of Irish from almost all Irish counties.

Table 1.1
Major Irish ports and migration to British North America, 1847

Port	Ships departing	Total cabin	Average persons steerage	Assisted persons pership	Percentage assisted total	Sick persons average per vessel	Dead at sea average per vessel
Limerick	50	9,174	183.5	1,287	21.06	4.0	4.2
Cork	33	10,322	312.8	680	11.13	50.3	26.9
Dublin	27	6,568	243.3	2,079	34.03	18.8	8.9
Sligo	26	5,732	220.5	802	13.12	14.9	14.2
Belfast	21	6,913	329.2	5	0.07	10.1	6.7
New Ross	15	4,395	293	251	5.71	16.1	7.8
Waterford	14	3,050	217.9	64	2.10	4.6	2.6
Derry	11	3,526	320.6	156	4.41	18.4	5.6

Source: British Parliamentary Papers, vol. 17, Buchanan Report; Andre Charbonneau and Andre Sevigny, *1847 Grosse Île: A Record of Daily Events* (Ottawa: Canadian Heritage, Parks Canada, 1997), 21.

Table 1.2
Major British ports and Irish migration to British North America, 1847

Port	Ships	Total cabin steerage	Average per ship	Assisted persons	Percentage assisted persons	Sick average	Dead at sea
Liverpool	72	27,039	375.5	512	1.9	43.4	25.8
Glasgow	30	2,019	67.3	0	0.0	2.7	2.0
London	19	1,985	104.5	0	0.0	0.3	3.3

Source: British Parliamentary Papers, vol. 17, Buchanan Report; Andre Charbonneau and Andre Sevigny, *1847 Grosse Île: A Record of Daily Events* (Ottawa: Canadian Heritage, Parks Canada, 1997), 21.

Table 1.3
Migration from the UK to British North America, 1843–48

Colony	1843	1844	1845	1846	1847	1848	Total	Percentage
Nova Scotia	1,203	747	615	698	2,000	702	5,965	2.3
PEI	529	257	242	286	536	59	1,909	0.7
New Brunswick	987	2,489	6,412	9,690	16,589	4,346	40,513	15.4
Newfoundland	448	684	618	523	993	343	3,609	1.4
Canada	20,350	18,747	23,884	32,242	89,738	25,582	210,543	80.2
Total	23,517	22,924	31,771	43,439	109,856	31,032	262,539	100.0

Source: LAC, Colonial Office Papers, Reports of the Colonial Land and Emigration Commissioners, 1845–50, CO 384/78–83.

A second, major distinction to acknowledge, as both tables 1.1 and 1.2 reveal, is that most Irish emigrants at this time came in steerage, among the cheapest ways to travel on the trans-Atlantic voyage. As one can assess in the coming chapter, from the investigations done by Major Denis Mahon's agents in Liverpool, both self-funded individual families and those families who were part of a landlord-sponsored scheme, were by necessity of their social position paying some of the most inexpensive rates available to them. Fares for the journey varied from port-to-port and depended on the quality of travel. A person departing Liverpool for Quebec would spend £5 10 shillings for passage "with full allowance of provisions" or £3 if he was willing to carry his own provisions in addition to the legal allowance of water and meat to be provided from the ship's stores. The fares from Ireland to Quebec were cheaper; the scale in Cork ranged from £5 for full allowance to £3 5 shillings for legal allowance and in Dublin from £4 10 shillings for full allowance to a mere £3 for legal allowance. Children between the ages of one and fourteen travelled at half price, while infants were given passage for free.[118] Of course, these rates could vary given the availability of ships, the season, and the port of embarkation. Included in the fare was the tax per capita paid to the port of entry, in Quebec it was far less than taxes levied in ports in the United States.[119]

Finally, it should be noted that only a small proportion of those Irish families arriving at the port of Quebec had been assisted by their landlords. In 1847, the worst year of the famine to that point, 441 ships landed in Quebec carrying as many as 90,000 of the nearly 110,000 emigrants, mostly Irish, who would venture to British North America in search of refuge.[120] Because of the way children under fourteen years were counted as only half of a statute adult, as reflected in their ticket price, the numbers of passenger on board ship could have been much higher. Nevertheless, despite popular myths to the contrary, only 6,000 of the migrants who set out for the Port of Quebec were recorded as having been subsidized by their landlords.[121] While the documents provided by the Quebec newspapers have notable gaps in their reporting, the figure of acknowledged assisted immigrants is below 10 per cent of the total. The overwhelming majority of the Irish emigrants to Canada had scraped up enough money themselves or had received remittances from friends and family in "America,"[122] to pay for their passage and provisions while on board ship. Even though their number only constitutes a small proportion of the total who arrived in Canada, the story of assisted immigrants is often better documented than the sagas of those families travelling on their own. Landlords, shipping agents, and government officials left a paper trail in many of these migration schemes, offering us insights into who made the journey, their reasons for doing so, and the extent of the family network engaged in the scheme. When assessing how orphans are created, to put it crudely, emigration schemes like that of Major Denis Mahon's in County Roscommon, offer insights not available from most of the migrants who made the decision to leave Ireland on their own.

It is somewhat ironic that even during the height of the misery witnessed in Ireland during Black '47, some pundits were already aware of how contested the story of the famine would become. Reprinted in *The King's County Chronicle*, from Parsonstown (now in County Offaly), an opinion piece from the *Times* of London appears almost prophetic:

> Historians and politicians will someday sift and weigh the conflicting narrations and documents of this lamentable year, and pronounce, with or without affectation, how much is due to the inclemency of heaven, and how much to the cruelty, heartlessness, or improvidence of man. The boasted institutions and the spirit of the empire are on trial.[123]

Each phase of the famine appears contested depending on one's perspective of Irish history and that of the Irish diaspora. The British government, political ideologues, landlords, merchants, farmers, and churches all must shoulder some of the responsibility for enabling the horrific sequence of events from 1845 to 1852. No doubt, while not all the ships and their agents in port were the unscrupulous operators of coffin ships, many persons must bear responsibility for the huge death toll that resulted in ill-fitted vessels, unsanitary conditions, and the easy spread of disease on board the ships themselves. There is plenty of blame to be shared. At the ground level, one in every five Irish migrants to British North America in 1847 was dead by the time the new year was "rung in." What remained of some Irish families were some 1,700 children and young adults left stranded on foreign shores, in a different and sometimes hostile climate, and in some places unable to speak the local language. It is now time to turn to how, during Ireland's tragedy, these orphans were made.

2

When Orphans Are Made
The Case of the Assisted Migrants and Orphans of Strokestown, County Roscommon

John O'Connor lay on the embankment of the Niagara River for much of the night. He was cut, sore, and he did not know if he had broken any bones. But the eight-year-old Irish lad tried not to move. He was terrified that Thomas Brennan might reappear and finish the murderous work that he had begun. In May 1848, after a night of drinking and rough housing, Brennan strangled Mary O'Connor and beat Patrick O'Connor to death with his own hammer. He then threw their bodies down the steep embankment leading to the Niagara River, where their corpses would decay for weeks before being discovered. Perhaps thinking that the fall would be enough to kill him, Brennan then hurled young John O'Connor over the cliff but miscalculated the child's resilience. Tangled in branches and brush, John never reached the bottom and by dawn had sufficient energy left, to crawl and stagger to the cabin of Mrs Hopkins who lived near Queenston. There he took shelter and was comforted by a fellow traveller from his home country, but he never said a word, terrorized by the thought that either Brennan or his teenaged daughter might return to the area to finish the deed.[1] The Brennans, Hopkins, Daltons, and O'Connors all came from the townlands owned by Major Denis Mahon, the landlord at Strokestown, County Roscommon. In 1847, he had assisted 271 families off his estate and subsidized their passage from Ireland, to Liverpool, and finally Quebec. Some resettled as far in the interior as Niagara, but close to a third of the 1,490 migrants who left Strokestown that spring died at sea or at the quarantine station of Grosse Ile. Among the survivors were more than forty orphans, who were, in time joined by yet another, John O'Connor, rendered parentless in a horrific way.

The story of the assisted migrants from the Mahon estate, known more popularly in Ireland today as "the 1,490," presents an interesting case study of how orphans came to be during the Great Famine. When they set out from Strokestown, County Roscommon, in May 1847, the 1,490 included no orphans by any standard definition. It was a migration of extended families, young couples, and single men and women who were facing near starvation in some thirty-two townlands within the 11,000-acre estate of Major Denis Mahon. The landlord's intention was to remove them from their lands, and lighten his long-term financial burdens, by offering them a stipend for cancelling their leases and a "generous" subsidy to rebuild their lives in Upper Canada. They would walk the 160-kilometre (100 miles) distance along the Royal Canal to Dublin, secure passage by steamer to Liverpool, and finally be dispatched on four chartered ships of dubious quality, bound for Quebec. Their trek offers, in microcosm, a vivid picture of how one of the greatest challenges for Canadian hosts, during the famine, was the care of hundreds of orphans who survived the journey. Typhus, dysentery, sea sickness, accidents, and even murder took a huge toll on adults and children alike within the 1,490; the stories of the surviving orphans, however, help open a window on the famine migration itself and the reception of these refugees by provincial authorities in British North America. Through the Strokestown 1,490 one comes to appreciate the complete cycle of events that prompted Irish migration during the worst years of the famine and how it came to pass that many families were destroyed, and the fate of the surviving children rested in the hands of strangers in a strange land.

The migration of the 1,490 from Strokestown offers the historian a rare opportunity to study a large group of migrants, hailing from the same townlands, travelling on the same ships, with the intention of sojourning or settling in British North America. In the last twenty years there have been a handful of similar stories of transatlantic migration focusing on New Brunswick, Vermont, and New York City,[2] but none have ever attempted successfully to track such a large group of migrants through Quebec, plot their dispersal throughout North America, or follow several generations of family members beyond the time of migration.[3] The landlord, Major Denis Mahon has received mixed treatment in the historiography of the famine and in local collective historical memory. To some scholars and contemporary residents of the area, Mahon was simply another landlord who wanted to maximize his own profits on a failing estate and who shipped out hundreds of families to rid himself of even greater debt by trying to subsidize relief efforts for them at home. Others regard the major as a victim of circumstance, inheriting an estate that had been poorly managed and was deeply in debt. His title to the property coincided with the potato blight and repeated crop failures that triggered misery for the cottiers and labourers on his estate and throughout Ireland. His offer to subsidize the passage of 271 families to Canada was, at best, an effort to give some of his tenants a chance at a new life.

History is rarely so simple. The case of Mahon's tenants has become somewhat of a *cause célèbre* in the Irish famine historiography, perhaps because in the wake of learning that many of his tenants perished on route to Quebec, Mahon was assassinated, the first landlord to die at the hands of tenants during the *Gorta Mor*.[4] Unfortunately journalists and historians have heaped too much attention on the murder, with its salacious "who dunnit" qualities, and not enough on examining the evidence regarding what actually happened to the people Denis Mahon assisted off his estate.[5] For some writers, the murder was an expression of general unrest on the estate, created by the mass migration and further evictions approved by Mahon and executed by his agent, John Ross Mahon.[6] Padraig Vesey has been more pointed in the allocation responsibility: "Mahon's assassination was a protest not against landlordism as such but against his land agent's management process."[7]

Other writers take a less harsh view of Mahon, seeing him as being overwhelmed by circumstances beyond his control: the inheritance of a highly indebted estate on the eve of the famine,[8] the circumstances of the famine itself, and the ongoing rent strikes in adjacent townlands to Strokestown.[9] In managing these affairs Mahon failed, thereby enraging many tenants and creating the incentive for two tenants, supported by the local Molly Maguires[10], to kill him as an example to other members of his class.[11] Mahon is also vilified by those writers taking the side of local parish priest Father Michael McDermott, who allegedly denounced the landlord from the pulpit, claiming that "so many died while he lives."[12] The scene in Strokestown was allegedly akin to Henry II's calling out of Thomas Becket – "will no one rid me of this troublesome priest" – except in this case it was the clergy lamenting the alleged malevolence of the landlord. Mahon's reputation is a subject of continuing speculation – some see him as victimizer, others as victim, and still others are ambivalent. In contemporary memory in Roscommon[13] it is the assisted migrants of 1847 – the 1,490 – that have been identified as victims: shipped off to Canada, to die on board coffin ships, or in the lazarettos of Grosse Ile, the quarantine station in the St Lawrence River often referred to as Quebec's charnel house. From this group, our first sampling of Irish orphans is drawn.

When the manuscript evidence is re-examined and new evidence comes to light from unlikely sources, one is forced to pause, reflect, and reassess. Perhaps the murder of Mahon has obscured by the way that some historians have looked at life on his estate, prior to November 1847. Is it wise to analyse the events preceding the dastardly deed as a natural trajectory to that fateful event on the evening of 2 November 1847? Mahon's own correspondence in the Strokestown Park Archives and in the National Library of Ireland, suggests the events on the Strokestown Estate from 1845 to 1847 can be read differently, without acting as a subliminal reference point to Mahon's murder and the tendency to bias that all events on his estate inevitably led to that end. Perhaps it is important to step back and examine the events for their own merit and what they might relate to us, without recourse to the filters provided by the murder, which can tempt the mind to read events backwards forming a natural trajectory to the killing. In addition, an obscure Anglican weekly paper in Quebec City, *The Berean*, may force a complete scholarly re-thinking of the migration itself and the agency possessed by the 271 families that took up Mahon's offer to leave in the spring of 1847. What follows is a reflection on new questions raised by these sources and the way scholars and local collective memory have considered the dramatic events on Mahon's estate in 1847. It is also an accounting of how just 271 families accounted for forty orphans, stigmatizing County Roscommon as the county with the highest number of orphans who landed at Quebec in 1847.

The English and Scottish plantations in Ireland, beginning in the time of the Tudor dynasty, created two classes in the landholding system: Anglo-Irish landlords, of who at least one third were absentee, holding more than 9,000 properties where the majority of the Irish population were reduced to tenancy.[14] In the nineteenth century Ireland was divided into four provinces, which in turn were subdivided into thirty-two distinctive counties. For administrative purposes each county was subdivided into baronies, the number of which varied from county to county according to its size. In turn, each barony was divided into civil parishes, which themselves were divided into small townlands, which varied in size from a few hundred acres to several thousand. The Mahon family, originally from County Clare, moved to County Roscommon where the newly restored King Charles II awarded them their estate during the post-Cromwellian Restoration of the 1660s and 1670s.[15] Nicholas Mahon received 2,000 acres in the Ballynamully area, known now as Strokestown, an anglicized name harkening to the historical swings of weapons during the battles between the O'Connors and Mitchells near the stream that still runs through the town. In 1696, the Mahons commenced the building of a large estate house on the old clan O'Connor seat and eventually, by the middle of the eighteenth century, completed a large manor home in the Palladian style.[16] By 1845, when Denis Mahon inherited the estate following the death of his cousin "mad" Maurice, the third and last Baron Hartland, the Mahon estate exceeded 11,000 acres and included 11,958 people living on sixty-eight townlands, in roughly six civil parishes.[17]

By the 1840s the estate was in dire financial condition. Denis Mahon faced a whopping debt of more than £30,000, accumulated over several decades through his predecessors' land purchases, estate improvements, endowments to widows and children, and some eccentric investments on the estate.[18] Worse still, many tenants had been truant in the paying of their annual rents. Some tenants simply could not afford the rates given the limited yields on plots often less than five acres.[19] Others, following the lead of tenants in the nearby Crown-controlled townland of Ballykilcline, Kilglass Parish, simply went on strike, refusing to pay rent for their marginal holdings. Tenant resentment of policies of lease-shortening and eviction, as invoked by landlords' agents and middlemen, and grinding rural poverty in many townlands, spawned episodes of violence in the area.[20] Nocturnal raids of retribution against those who violated "rural codes of behaviour" or against those who served the landlord became more frequent in Roscommon.[21] The secret society "the Molly Maguires" was often thought to be at the heart of this exercise of vigilante justice. Mahon faced an increasingly violent situation on his estate, and by the autumn 1845 the drama worsened when there was a partial failure of the potato crop upon which most of his tenants depended.

Mahon's estate was subdivided between large tenant farmers or middlemen, such as the Brownes, Hagues, and Conrys, with holdings of as much as 400 acres each and small-scale farmers who held several dozen acres.[22] Most of Mahon's nearly 12,000 tenants held tenancies of anywhere between two and five acres.[23] Many townlands, such as Kilmackenny in the parish of Lissonuffy, from which murderer Thomas Brennan and victim Patrick O'Connor hailed, were of marginal agricultural value, with poor soils and plenty of bog land. Lissonuffy was also adjacent to the highest point in the area, Slieve Bawn mountain, which offered rocky slopes and little promise for cultivation. As a result, the Brennans and their neighbours cultivated potatoes, which provided a high annual yield and plenty of nutrition for the family's subsistence. Cottier farmers like the Brennans however, were not at the bottom of the agro-social scale. That position was reserved for conacre farmers – essentially labourers who engaged short one-year leases to secure a cabin and a small potato patch to feed their families. These conacre labourers were by no means supine; when lands appeared available for their use on larger tenancies in Strokestown but were denied them, they often squatted and battled with larger farmers to secure their meagre means to sustain their families.[24] When the potato blight struck repeatedly in 1845 and 1846, it was these conacre labourers and cottiers like Brennan, with modest but marginal holdings, who fell victim to hunger and disease.

Major Denis Mahon was not idle during the early phases of the potato blight. Although frequently absent from his estate, attending to his business and family interests in London, Mahon wrote a steady stream of letters to his agent, the local relief committee, and to his larger farmer-tenants, to remediate some of the short-term effects of the crisis. Many of his tenants were in arrears on their rent, and some had years of accumulated debt. Mahon knew that they would have little means to pay when the food supply in the county collapsed. He reduced rents for many of the smaller tenants— those he considered the deserving poor (although he never used the term). He noted, however, that he would not relieve those tenants he suspected had the means to pay but simply refused, imitating the rent strikers in the neighbouring townland of Ballykilcline, which was owned directly by the Crown. When American maize was made available through Prime Minister Sir Robert Peel's relief operations, Mahon set up dispersal centres which on some days witnessed the distribution of maize to destitute tenants for free and on alternate days at the modest cost of a "penny a pound" for tenants with means.[25] It should be noted that very few of the 271 families initially included in the emigration scheme ever availed themselves of the free American corn, perhaps indicating that they were not among the most destitute of Mahon's tenants. Finally, Mahon also worked with the local relief committee, promoted the establishment of a soup kitchen,[26] and served on the local Board of Guardians for the Roscommon and Strokestown Poor Law unions.

In 1846, in an effort to reorganize and strengthen the estate's finances, Denis Mahon hired the services of John Ross Mahon, a distant cousin and a partner in the Dublin firm of Guinness & Mahon. John Ross would come to the estate armed with a businesslike attitude towards all aspects of life at Strokestown, demonstrating a management style that left little room for emotional attachment to the people for whom he was responsible.[27] Major Denis Mahon continued his policy of suspending the rents of many tenants who he knew were unable to pay, which seemed consistent with his earlier efforts to provide a loan fund for tenants in need,[28] but now even these were unable to repay the earlier loans at the agreed rate. As the situation at Strokestown worsened, Major Mahon decided that the distribution of seed might assist tenant farmers directly – in a sense having farm labourers and cottiers help themselves.[29] At the other end of the spectrum, the major insisted that the tenants, some of whom were among his largest landholders, be forced to pay him what he was owed. He directed his agent to collect these rents and evict these "rent conspirators" if they refused to pay. Not surprisingly, John Ross Mahon met with considerable resistance when trying to carry out these orders.

John Ross Mahon, however, had other ideas and decided to embark upon another tactic to keep the estate afloat. Considering the maintenance of tenants on their lands, in addition to paying the poor rate for growing numbers of tenants relying on the relief provided in the Poor Law union, John Ross proposed a less expensive solution. Migration, claimed the agent, would be cheaper than maintaining the tenants in Strokestown or in the relief works; migration would also provide the major with an opportunity to consolidate vacated lands for grazing or for other more profitable purposes. The agent and his landlord disagreed to the point where John Ross threatened to resign.[30] In early 1847, Major Mahon relented and suggested that the assisted tenants be sent to the closest port, Sligo Town, where their passage to America could be subsidized, akin to what the major considered the successful precedents set by Lord Palmerston on his Sligo estates.[31] Once again, John Ross Mahon had other plans. Through his firm, his agents could book passage through Liverpool on ships bound for Quebec, for which fares were substantially cheaper than those ships bound for ports in the United States. The major relented and tenants were invited to participate in the migration scheme.[32] In exchange for passage and supplies from Dublin to Liverpool and then to British North America, subscribers would abandon their cabins, terminate their leases, and be compensated for crops, chattels, and animals relinquished. They were not permitted to return to their former holdings once the deal had been consummated. In any event they would have known their cabins would be tumbled by John Ross's men upon their departure. While the figure has been disputed, about 271 families representing thirty-two townlands, agreed to sign on to the plan.[33]

The tenants who seemed to opt for the emigration scheme were not the poorest of the poor. Evidence from the estate papers demonstrates that few of these families had previously applied for the "maize" gratuity, and many had come from townlands where some rents had been paid. The records from the estate archives suggest that these prospective emigrants may have been the least impoverished of Mahon's tenants. In fact, in their correspondence, during the application process, in April 1847, the major lamented to John Ross Mahon:

> I have been considering over the numerous applications we have had for assistance on the score of Emigration, and it strikes me that many of those applying are of the better sort of tenant and if possible should be kept home, but at all events if determined to go they should do so at their own expense. I think the first class for us to send is those of the poorest and the worst description.[34]

The letter should not be interpreted with too much malice of intent. Mahon was suspicious that tenants may have been holding back rent and, if such was the case, they should pay their own passage. From a business standpoint, and with the original intentions of the emigration scheme in mind, if Mahon lost his most productive tenants, he would be no farther ahead because he would be liable to the poor tax for the poor who wished to stay. In one sense, John Ross Mahon's plan would have been completely undercut, but the fact remains that in the official documents of the "assisted" many of the "better" tenants left. Finally, one interesting detail that might be overlooked is that there were "numerous" applications – many tenants simply wanted to leave the estate. Initially, what one is left with from a close reading of the estate papers is that Mahon was less the tyrannical and heartless stereotype of the famine landlord, as might first appear, and that the tenants who opted for the migration scheme may have been far better off than their peers who stayed behind. Thomas Brennan, his wife Bridget, and their two children, for example, surrendered their three-acre holding and joined the scheme with forty-six families from their townland, the largest number sent from any corner of the Mahon estate.[35]

Of the 271 families that decided to take up Major Mahon's offer, it is estimated that there were perhaps as many as 900 children and teenagers included among the assisted families.[36] The assisted group of 1,490 people[37] that constituted these 271 migrating families did not leave *en masse* but departed Strokestown in two waves, travelling along the banks of the Royal Canal and then proceeding by steamship from Dublin to Liverpool about a week apart.[38] The canal linked the city of Dublin with the rural hinterlands as far as the Shannon River, where it met near the villages of Tarmonbarry on the Roscommon bank

Table 2.1
Strokestown household heads by townland, civil parish, and family size (N=271)

Townland	Civil parish	Households	Total migrants
Aughadangan	Lissonuffy	10	56
Ballyhubert	Lissonuffy	4	19
Castle of Leitrim	Kilbride	3	11
Cloonhain	Cloonfinlough	14	66
Cregga Feehily Quarter	Kiltrustan	6	37
Cregga House Division	Kiltrustan	6	31
Cregga Plunkett Quarter	Kiltrustan	6	31
Culleen Park	Lissonuffy	10	54
Culliagh	Bumlin	19	96
Curdrummin	Bumlin	2	15
Curhouna		16	109
Curnashina	Kilbride	9	58
Curries	Kiltrustan	3	33
Dooherty		8	57
Farnbeg	Bumlin	1	5
Goortoose Holmes	Bumlin	8	45
Goortoose McGuire	Bumlin	10	55
Goortoose Murray	Bumlin	8	39
Graffogue	Bumlin	4	22
Kilgraffy	Kilglass	14	71
Killinlosset	Kilgefin	5	27
Killinordamore		5	20
Killmackenny	Lissonuffy	47	249
Lacken	Cloonfinlough	1	7
Laughboy	Aughrim	3	11
Lower Culliagh	Bumlin	8	38
Mullivetron		9	46
North Yard	Bumlin	3	6
Pasture		1	6
Scramogue	Bumlin	5	24
Tooreen	Lissonuffy	13	72
Tully	Kilglass	10	49
No Shows		29	
Total		271	1490

Source: Strokestown Park Archives (SPA), STR/74, Lists of Assisted Tenants by Townland, 1847.

and Cloondara, in County Longford. Each side of the canal had steep banks that separated the waterway from adjacent pasture, farmland, or bog. It was upon these narrow banks that the families, including their hundreds of children, were herded by the estate employees led by chief bailiff, John Robinson.[39] The aim was for Robinson to literally move these tenants as quickly as possible, without delay or casualty, along the canal to the port of Dublin, where they would embark steam ferries to Liverpool. The narrow banks would have to be shared between this mass of humanity and horses pulling the barges along the canal. Ironically, these boats would be filled with seed, headed to the interior, or food stuffs intended for export. Children and their parents would have found it difficult to move on the narrow banks, avoiding the barge horses, feces, muck, and the lure of respite in a neighbouring field. They would also be struggling to move carts filled with their earthly possessions and the food provided to them by Mahon for their journey.

What is known about their journey, which is very little because of the few surviving records, is that the first wave of assisted adults and their children arrived at the quay in Dublin, on 24 May 1847, without injury and in a timely fashion to make their connections to the trans-Atlantic vessels waiting for them in Liverpool. In June 1847, *The Berean*, a small Anglican weekly newspaper published in Quebec, printed a short article from a Dublin newspaper, *Saunder's News-letter*, reporting the arrival, on 24 May 1847, of Major Denis Mahon's assisted migrants at Dublin. It confirmed a previously known newspaper report[40] that Mahon's assisted migrants left for Liverpool, provisioned by the landlord, on 27 May 1847. *The Berean* article, however, included a number of other surprising details about the state of these famine refugees:

> This afternoon an unusual long train of emigrants, evidently from the same townland, and presenting marks of comfort not recognizable in the bulk of people fleeing from the famine, passed along our quays to the emigrant offices, near the Customs House. There were fifteen cars, well laden with baggage, and a party of about 130 persons followed them. One of the leaders stated that they had come from the lands of Kilglass, part of the estate of Major Denis Mahon, the successor of the late Lord Hartland in the county of Roscommon, and that their destination was Upper Canada. He admitted that they had formed a community of about 2000 persons, the tenants of Major Mahon, and that allowed him rent. He had obtained <u>venires</u> against them, and when nothing remained to be done but to send the sheriff to take possession of their holdings, the

gallant Major sent for several of them, and proposed to forgive them all of their rents, pay their passage to America, and supply them with provisions to the end of their voyage, and on condition of their levelling of their cabins and giving up quit possession. The proposition was deemed advantageous, hardly any opposition was offered, the majority of the cabins levelled, and nearly 2000 poor persons, who should have been supported by the ratepayers, are now on their way to America.[41]

The Berean's account is one of the few newspaper sources for the Strokestown migration. What the report confirmed, however, was that these adults and children travelled in groups based on their townland, had plenty of baggage in fifteen carts to support them,[42] had been provisioned amply by Major Mahon, and had an appearance much better than other famine refugees arriving in Dublin. This report also indicated that Mahon's families were not setting out blindly but that their destination was a new life in Upper Canada, one of Britain's expanding overseas colonial possessions.[43]

If reading daily life on the Strokestown estate in 1846–47 through the lenses of the murder of Major Denis Mahon is methodologically problematic, so is reading the nature of the migration scheme through the lenses of the trans-Atlantic passage itself. Denis Mahon was in England at the time the first group of migrants departed and was busy making sure that he had borrowed sufficient money for the scheme, that this money was spent properly, and that John Ross Mahon and his bailiffs ensured that the boarding and departure of the assisted migrants was executed smoothly.[44] The major actually stayed in Liverpool as the first wave of tenants departed.[45] There is nothing in the archival records to suggest that Denis Mahon deliberately cut corners or that he was only half-hearted in his support of the tenants. The fact that, without sufficient capital or savings, he forced himself to approach lenders and bankers to underwrite the entire scheme, thereby placing the Strokestown estate in deeper debt, attests to his determination to see that the migration scheme worked. What he may not have known was that the shipping agents of J & W Robinson, retained by John Ross Mahon, through his own firm's business ties, had a rather poor reputation in Liverpool.[46] The Robinson's attractive price point may have veiled the fact that the ships they retained were negligent in taking proper health regulations seriously and the provisions on board ship were substandard. Had John Ross Mahon known the shady business that was the Robinson agency, he was never formally held to account for what happened on the voyages. In fact, in the wake of the emigration tragedy and mass evictions on the estate thereafter, in 1851, he was celebrated at the Strokestown Fair as having been a kind and just land agent.[47] Nevertheless, since he was ultimately in charge of the scheme, Major Denis Mahon would be held responsible for what happened to the 1,490 assisted tenants.

In Liverpool, John Ross Mahon, his business colleagues, and the estate bailiffs would make the final preparations for the journey. Major Denis Mahon paid for the tickets for each of his tenants, with adults at full fare and children under the age of fourteen listed as half of a statute adult. In the absence of sailing lists for most ships heading to Quebec before 1865, it is nearly impossible to reconstruct how many men, women, and children were on each ship. The fare, food, bill, and baggage bills leave few clues as to how to determine how many children were on board these ships. The early correspondence between Major Mahon, John Ross Mahon, and Mr Samuel Gale indicated that the cheapest destination was Quebec, with a minimum fare of £3. 3s.0d per statute adult.[48] Although trying to economize on the scheme, Major Mahon did not pay this rate. As late as 24 May 1847, when the first wave of emigrants set out from the estate, the major reported that he had paid for up to 390 (statute adult) places on the *Virginius*, in addition to £200 in stores and provisions.[49] Three days later he wrote to the agent telling him he had raised £550 to pay for the "first batch" and he was pleased that his agent John Ross Mahon was also to be in Liverpool to see the first group depart.[50] On 28 May, one assumes from the correspondence that John Ross was present when the *Virginius* sailed with 476 passengers and on 1 June, when the remainder of the first wave of assisted tenants departed on *Erin's Queen*. Major Mahon continued to spend time in London, frantically raising money for what he thought might be as a many as 400 statute adults in the second group.[51] His letters within the week confirm that he had raised an additional £1400. 16s.7d to subsidize the 405.5 statute adults who sailed on the *Naomi*, on 15 June 1, and the overflow of fifty-five statute adults who were dispatched on the *John Munn* a day later.[52] By mid-June Denis Mahon had accepted an additional £3,590. 16s 7d in debt to finance the two waves of the migration scheme.[53] While it is difficult to determine exact numbers of migrant children from the fragments of records preserved from the scheme, the majority of Mahon's assisted tenants embarking in Liverpool were children.[54]

Liverpool was not a hospitable place for prospective migrants.[55] The women and children from the Mahon estate must have been overwhelmed, save for their very brief sojourn in Dublin, waiting for the ferry, most had never ventured outside of their townland. Liverpool was a lively and mesmerizing port city to these poor Irish farmers. Thieves, crooks, swindlers, and flim-flam men laid in wait for easy targets. "Runners" in the employ of substandard hotels and hostels would feign friendship with the unsuspecting migrants, seize their baggage, and drag them to filthy lodgings, where the prices were high and the quality of the rooms were poor. Other Irish migrants, who had languished in port, waiting for passage on a ship, were more than willing to buy an unsuspecting migrant's ticket. Major Mahon had sent his bailiffs not only to assure himself that his adults and children would board the ships and not return to the estate but also to police the assisted tenants and to make sure that they were not conned by the scum of the Liverpool docklands. Although John Ross Mahon reported that the embarkation of the first wave was a success, there is evidence to suggest that not all of the intended estate migrants actually made the journey. The *Virginius*, for example, was said to have been exclusively for Mahon's tenants. Lists of the dead, credited to the *Virginius*, however, contain the names of passengers who bear surnames that are not on John Ross Mahon's list of tenants who agreed to the terms of the emigration scheme.[56] There was "spillage" in Liverpool. Whole families disappeared to make a new life in Britain, presumably with money pocketed from the sale of their tickets.

These runaway tenants may have counted themselves lucky because there is no doubt that the crossing of the Atlantic for the remainder of Mahon's 1,490 was not easy. The first group of migrants departed Liverpool on board the *Virginius*, with surplus passengers boarding the *Erin's Queen*. The *Virginius* left Liverpool on 28 May 1847 under the direction of Captain Thomas Austin with 476 statute adults on board. Captain Joseph Davidson's *Erin's Queen* left four days later, on 1 June, with a steerage complement of 493 statute adults, with 100 of these being listed as Mahon's people.[57] John Ross Mahon prepared for a second batch, the largest group, 350.5 out of 421 statute adults, set sail under Captain Thomas Wilson on the *Naomi* on 15 June, while the overflow of fifty-five statute adults sailed on James Watt's ship, the *John Munn*, the following day.[58]

The crossing of the Atlantic of at least three of the ships – *Virginius*, *Naomi*, and *John Munn* – confirm the worst descriptions of the "coffin ships" that made the ocean voyages during Black '47. First, the ships were not properly outfitted for passenger travel. All the vessels were essentially cargo ships that normally would unload their timber, grain, and raw materials in British ports and then make the return trip to North America with rocks or salt as their ballast. Both the *Virginius* and the *Erin's Queen*, had recently arrived at Liverpool, having left New Orleans likely filled with cotton and foodstuffs.[59] For the *Erin's Queen*, the New Orleans to Liverpool run appeared to be its regular trade route, with Quebec appearing as a brief detour.[60] During the famine migration, the steerage compartments were refitted with makeshift bunks, usually two high, to allow for human cargo to serve as ballast for the journey back to America. With hundreds of passengers crammed below deck, in poorly lit areas, and whole families consigned to a single bunk that may have measured eight feet by six feet, with about eighteen inches allowance per passenger and a six-foot clearance between lower and upper bunks, the ocean voyage was a misery.[61]

In the spring and summer sailing, the north Atlantic could be perilous. Prevailing winds and the Gulf Stream naturally moved from west to east, necessitating that ships tack against the current and the trade winds. At this rate, the voyage from Liverpool to Quebec could take from six to eight weeks. Cooking fires were only permitted on deck and only when weather permitted, which meant food was often eaten raw and cold, when passengers were able to eat at all. It is safe to say that none of Mahon's tenants had ever been to sea; they became easily seasick spending much of their time vomiting, urinating, and defecating below decks. The smell in steerage was ungodly, and the lack of sanitation made for horrendous conditions. The mandatory water supplies became contaminated, and biscuits often were infested with maggots or soiled by vermin. Rats became a common travelling companion, spreading disease and biting the young and the sick.

In such conditions disease flourished. Diarrhea, malnutrition, and dysentery were common on these ships. As indicated in chapter 1, the most common problem below decks was the outbreak of typhus or "ship's fever." The *Rickettsia prowazeki* bacteria[62] often lived in the feces of the common louse. Lice abounded in the conditions on board these ships. When a louse bit a passenger, it defecated at the site of the wound. When the wound became itchy, an unsuspecting victim scratched the affected area, which effectively rubbed the bacteria into the wound after which it invaded the victim's system. One effectively became the agent of one's own infection. A further problem was that the bacteria was very hardy. It could survive for days on clothing, bedding, bunks, and surfaces where it might infect other passengers. Once infected, the victim would not know symptoms for the better part of a week. In that time the bacteria were multiplying in one's body and attacking vital organs. In time, victims would display a high fever, headaches, abdominal pain, profound thirst, rashes, skin lesions, and a dopiness or fuzziness (hence the name Typhus: the Greek word for smoke or cloud). The condition ran its course in two weeks and most of those who contracted typhus died. In the modern period it could be treated with antibiotics, but in 1847, doctors attempted a variety of remedies – poultices, plasters, brandy, milk – without much success. For hundreds of famine migrants, including Mahon's families, typhus would end their journey to a new life in America.

This crowding on board the ships had disastrous effects. The *Virginius* did not sink as was assumed by some local people in Roscommon,[63] although it did sail off course and its complement of dead was as high as reported later by both Canadian and British newspapers.[64] Data from the death registers reveal that of the 476 passengers recorded on the ship, of which children under fourteen were counted as half a person, there were 267 (56.1 per cent) deaths. Of the known 271 household heads that represented the entire 1,490, 31 either died at sea on the *Virginius* or once the ship disembarked its sick at Grosse Ile (see table 2.2). Included among the dead was the captain of the *Virginius* and almost all his officers.[65] On the other hand, the overflow passengers from Mahon's estate on the *Erin's Queen* fared somewhat better: 100 of its 493 registered passengers were from Mahon's 1,490. Of these, only fourteen appear in the death registers at Grosse Ile, included therein are only 2 household heads from the original 271 assisted families. The death rate on the *Erin's Queen*, when all passengers are considered, was 136 or 27.6 per cent, still startling but half as many deaths as on the *Virginius*. If you had been in Mahon's overflow group, you counted yourself lucky.

The second batch of Mahon's families fared little better than their kinsmen and neighbours on the *Virginius*. Of the 196 dead on the *Naomi* 126, or 35.9 per cent of the ship's passenger list, were from the Mahon estate – a shocking statistic but, nevertheless, not the numbers that were reported back to the estate in the fall of 1847. On the *John Munn*, twenty-six, or just under half of the total complement of Mahon passengers, either died at sea or at Grosse Ile. About 41 per cent of the *John Munn's* complete roster of passengers perished. When the dead on-board these two ships are added to the dead among the first wave of migrants who left in May, about 387 migrants of the 1,490 perished or just over one in every four. Similarly, fifty-eight of the 271 household heads, or just over one in five heads of families, never realized the "new start" that had been promised them in Upper Canada (see table 2.3). While the numbers of dead do not jibe with the dead of popular memory, the death toll is still a testament to horrific conditions on board the four ships and accounts for the blame that would be laid at the feet of the landlord. It is no small coincidence that after the reports of the dead reached Ireland in the autumn of 1847, Major Mahon became a marked man.

The quarantine station at Grosse Ile presented anther grim chapter in the journey of Irish families to Canada during the Irish Famine. If one survived the horrendous voyage – the *Virginius* did not land at Grosse Ile until 11 July, after having spent fifty-one days at sea – the quarantine station was the next risk to one's life. Both the *Erin's Queen* and the *Naomi* arrived at Quebec in advance of the Mahon's lead ship.[66] Established in 1832 as a quarantine station during the cholera epidemic, Grosse Ile was the first Canadian stop for the surviving Mahon families. Located in the St Lawrence River approximately fifty kilometres northeast of Quebec City, Grosse Ile's quarantine facility was under the supervision of Dr George Mellis Douglas and his medical staff. The island had been inundated with unprecedented numbers of refugees from Ireland in 1846 and Douglas anticipated a similar if not greater flow of migrants to the station in 1847. To prepare Grosse Ile appropriately, he petitioned the Canadian government for £3,000 to outfit the island properly. The station had several sheds for the sick, a hospital, and quarters for the physicians and workers. Not sensing the urgency of Douglas, the government responded with a warrant of £300 and use of the steamship *St George* to ferry healthy emigrants from the island to Quebec City.[67] Decisions made in the ports of entry in the United States, to levy heavy fines on captains carrying infirm emigrants and a larger levy on each passenger landed, made Quebec and Saint John, New Brunswick, appear cheaper and more advantageous destinations for those financing and outfitting trans-Atlantic vessels. While the United States did not ban emigration from Ireland,[68] they certainly made it more difficult, and Canada became the alternative.

Early in the shipping season the arrival of numerous ships with hundreds of sick and dying passengers proved Douglas' prognostications correct.[69] The island was quickly overwhelmed, and ships had to anchor off the island by the dozens until an attending physician could inspect the passengers on board. In late May, the *Montreal Herald* reported that "the forebodings of evil with respect to emigrants arriving in the St Lawrence, are at this moment too sadly verified."[70] In the first few weeks of receiving the arrivals, Douglas boarded the ships himself to assess who would have to be taken to the island for treatment. When they learned of this practice, government officials insisted on the letter of the law, forcing Douglas to disembark entire shiploads of passengers, sick and healthy to the station, for inspection. When it became clear that

Table 2.2
Deaths of household heads by ship recorded for the Mahon Estate, 1847

Ship	Estimated passengers	Strokestown assisted	Estimated total deaths	Strokestown deaths, verified	Strokestown household head deaths
Virginius	476	476	267 (56.1%)	221 (46.4%)	31
Naomi	421	350.5	196 (46.6%)	126 (35.9%)	16
Erin's Queen	493	100	136 (27.6%)	14 (14.0%)	2
John Munn	452	55	187 (41.4%)	26 (47.3%)	7
At sea					
Not defined					2
Total Statute adults	1,842	981.5	786 (42.7%)	387 (39.4%)	58 of 271 (21.4%)
Total of 1,490		1,490 Includes children under age fourteen			387 (26.0%)

Source: Strokestown List prepared from the Strokestown Park Archives and entered into a database by Dr Ciaran Reilly of Maynooth University. There are 274 families who appear on the glass memorial in front of the Strokestown Park Museum, although three families ended up remaining on the estate; Canadian data is from Marianna O'Gallagher and Rose Dompierre, *Eyewitness: Grosse Isle 1847* (Ste-Foy, Quebec: Livres Carraig Books, 1995); André Charbonneau and Doris Drolet-Dubé, eds, *A Register of Deceased Persons at Sea and on Grosse Île in 1847* (Ottawa: Canadian Heritage, Parks Canada, 1997).

Douglas and his staff and their small facility could not handle the crush of emigrants, the government rescinded its order and permitted quarantine to take place on board ships, without disembarking all passengers.[71] Matters were made worse by the fact that waiting passengers were drinking water directly from the St Lawrence, causing numerous cases of dysentery.[72] By summer, new sheds were being built on Grosse Ile, tents were erected as temporary shelters, more physicians were sent by the government,[73] and the army was deployed to the island to keep order. But the result was much the same; unable to be treated, most of the typhus cases, thousands, died. In 1847 alone, 3,238 emigrants died in quarantine, and 5,424 emigrants in total (from ships and hospitals) were buried on Grosse Ile, including Thomas Brennan's wife, Bridget, and their young son.[74]

Table 2.3
Status of Mahon households in British North America, 1847
(N=271)

Status of the household head	Number	Per cent
Died at sea or in quarantine	58	21.4
Located in Canada	71	26.2
Located in the United States	29	10.7
Location/status unknown	113	41.7
Total from estate	271	100

Source: Census of Canada, 1851–52; Registers of Catholic Parishes in Canada East and Canada West (online Familysearch.com); Library and Archives Canada; RG 19 D-5, v.2532, Department of Finance, Travel Vouchers and Expenses, 1843–54; André Charbonneau and Doris Drule-Dubé, *A Register of Deceased Persons at Sea and on Grosse Ile in 1847* (Ottawa: Canadian Heritage, Parks Canada, 1997).

If the statistics provided by the Grosse Ile burial records stand as the source of record, then much can be hypothesized about the state of Mahon's people and the creation of so many Irish orphans from this single estate. At least 387 people of the 981.5 statute passengers recorded as embarking the ships chartered by Mahon died either at sea or in the quarantine station at Grosse Ile. Fifty-eight household heads are included in this number. Often their partners died with them, leaving the surviving children in the family without parents when they arrived at Quebec. The most conservative estimate possible, based on the available data suggests that perhaps as many as 300 children died on route from Mahon's estate to Quebec City. The fact that often infants were not included by name in the counts, complicates matters, as does the fact that John Ross Mahon's records indicate that 1,490 tenants agreed to participate in the migrations scheme, while only 981.5 statute adult passengers are officially recorded on board these ships. What appears clear, however, is that, although any firm number is pure speculation, there were far more children under the age of fourteen on these ships, than what the official record implies. The death toll could be far higher than the official death registers suggest.

The question remains whether Mahon was culpable for this catastrophe at sea and in the quarantine station. The booking agents certainly made the cheapest arrangements possible, cutting corners which seemed to be part of John Ross Mahon's economizing on behalf of the estate. Clearly the passengers were not inspected carefully when boarding the ships, there were not sufficient supplies of fresh water and edible food for the passengers registered, and, in the case of the *Virginius* the navigators were handicapped by weather and currents and ended up off course. If *The Berean* report is to be treated with any weight, it appears that at least in the case of the first wave of migrants from the townlands including Kilgraffy, Tully, and Kilmackenny Mahon had done his due diligence in supplying them with food and providing wagons for the cartage of their personal belongings. Invoices in Mahon's papers indicate that he was liable for not only the fares for each of the passengers but also for considerable baggage, thus confirming the observations made by the reporter investigating the first wave of the 1,490 on Dublin's Custom House Quay.

The fate of the 1,490, however, did not go unnoticed and judgement was passed on Mahon expeditiously. When word of the devastating loss of life was reported back to Roscommon, via a short article reprinted from the Toronto *Globe* focused on the *Virginius*, there was general outrage in Strokestown, particularly from the pulpit of the local Catholic parish. It may have been no coincidence that in November 1847, while returning from a meeting regarding local Poor Law union business, Denis Mahon was gunned down, becoming the first Irish landlord to be assassinated during the famine.[75] It was unfortunate that the *Globe* had recorded only part of the story; research into the records of Grosse Ile reveal that while the *Virginius* casualties were accurate as reported, overall mortality may only have been around 39 per cent, if based on the actual passengers recorded, or 26 per cent if based on the entire original number of 1,490, or just 21 per cent if based on the household heads alone, on board all four ships.

What is known, and central to our purpose at hand, is that the voyage and the quarantine experience left forty-two children from the Mahon estate without parents. In the sailing season of 1847 these orphans account for the highest number of children from any Irish county recorded in the ledgers of the Charitable Catholic Ladies of Quebec.[76] These children represented eighteen families from the Mahon estate, whose parents and extended family did not survive the journey. The largest group of siblings were the children of James Sheridan and Mary Connelly of the townland of Curhouna, in the parish of Lissonuffy. The Sheridans and their ten children were in the second batch of Mahon's assisted emigrants and the set sail on the *Naomi*. At least four of the Sheridan children died on route, including the eldest boy, John.

As they waited for the *St George* to take them to Quebec, only six Sheridan children remained: Catherine (twenty), Mary (nineteen), Ann (fifteen), Owen (fourteen), Ellen (twelve), and Patrick (ten). It may be assumed that Catherine took charge of this little group, who faced an unknown future in a foreign land where they did not speak the language of the majority in Quebec. At least they could be led by a sibling, who would be considered an adult in the new world. Not so for Patrick and Thomas Quinn, whose parents James and Margaret also died on the *Naomi*. They were also from the townland of Cuhouna, but these lads were only twelve and six years old respectively, not only having lost their parents but two siblings as well.

Notable among the surviving orphans were Daniel and Catherine Tighe. Originally from Lissonuffy Parish, they had lost their father in Roscommon and their widowed mother, Mary, took her five surviving children with her brother William Kelly. As they waited for the *St George* to come and fetch them off Grosse Ile, they left behind the graves of their three siblings, and their uncle. While Mary Tighe, their mother, was not recorded on the Grosse Ile list of the dead, it is likely she expired shortly after reaching Quebec City. Daniel was twelve and his sister was nine. Little is known of what these children could claim to bring with them as they awaited the ferry to take them. The hospital steward collected the baggage and money of the dead for redistribution among surviving family members. In the case of George and Mary Cox, aged nine and seven, their parents Martin Cox and Mary Maloney both died on the *Virginius* but left them £1 2 shillings in cash, as the two orphans continued their journey.[77]

The saga of the Mahon migrants helps to reveal the nature of the flight from famine in Ireland during Black '47. While the assisted migration scheme experienced by the 1,490 was more exceptional than the rule for emigrants during the Great Famine, the pilgrimage of these 271 families does bring to light the relationships between some landlords and their tenants in Ireland, the graphic nature of the emigrant journey, the horrendous conditions on board ship and in quarantine, and how orphans came to be during this time. The Mahon orphans form only a handful of the nearly 1,700 Irish orphans that needed the attention of colonial governments and churches in 1847–48, but in the absence of diaries and written correspondence from many of these emigrants, the Mahon scheme allows us to recreate with some detail, the devastation of so many Irish families and the plight in which young children were found. For his part, Thomas Brennan worked on Grosse Ile for several months and in early 1848 left the quarantine station with his surviving daughter.[78]

They headed to Niagara, where his friends the O'Connors had emigrated, likely before Mahon's proposed scheme. There was work available on the Welland Canal, and there were already other Connaught men there, repairing the great ditch that helped shipping bypass the legendary falls at Niagara.[79] He would set up among his own kind. But, unknown to anyone at that time, Brennan's journey to the Niagara would provide yet another case of how orphans came to be.[80]

3

"The Fostering Protection of the Church"

They were all alone, standing hand in hand at the Marine Hospital in Quebec. Not long before, Daniel and Catherine Tighe and their mother Mary had embarked the steamer *St George* that had taken them on the next leg of their journey to Quebec City.[1] Daniel, twelve, and Catherine, nine, were now the only survivors for the Kelly and Tighe families who had left the Mahon estate in Roscommon and taken passage on the *Naomi* out of Liverpool. Their father Bernard had died on Major Mahon's estate and their widowed mother, Mary Tighe, had gathered her five children and joined her brother William Kelly who had accepted the major's assisted emigration offer. Neither Will Kelly nor the Tighes had any known plans to link with family or friends in the new world; they just clung to a dream that they would begin a new life. Daniel and Catherine lost their three siblings and their uncle on route to Quebec, and now their mother Mary had passed away at the Marine Hospital.[2] Daniel and Catherine, in the company of dozens of other Irish orphans were entirely at the mercy of their new hosts, most of whom spoke only French, a language the orphans did not understand.

Having taken the steamer and landing at Quebec, Daniel and Catherine and the other children were escorted to the Quebec Marine Hospital, where they were screened for any signs of typhus or other infections, and then were taken to a home on Prince Edward Street, where the orphans were housed and quarantined by the Society of Charitable Catholic Ladies of Quebec. Within days of their arrival, a Catholic priest, Father Edouard Faucher,[3] entered the building, accompanied by one of the ladies who represented the Charitable Society. The priest checked the list handed to him by the woman in charge, and healthy children were picked out of the dozens sitting and lying in the dormitory, frightened, hungry, and completely confused because they could not understand what the priest and woman were talking about. While the presence of the priest, a community spiritual leader they would have known back in Ireland, may have offered them some solace, the moment must have been confusing and frightening to children who had already been traumatized by a transatlantic voyage of six weeks or more during which time they witnessed the sickness and death of their loved ones. The priest and his assistant directed Daniel and Catherine to a wagon, where they joined less than a dozen other children who had already been selected.[4] They left the city and began a slow journey through the forests and farmsteads outside of Quebec City. They had crossed the great river again and were making their way towards the town of Nicolet on its south shore, periodically stopping, so that children could be directed off the cart and into the presence of strangers. When the cart stopped at another farmstead in the parish of St-Croix in Lotbinière County, the priest directed Daniel to leave the cart and join the woman and man who were waiting nearby. What happens next has become the stuff of legend in contemporary Strokestown.[5]

François Coulombe and his wife Marie were the couple waiting for the priest. They were middle aged and childless and had sought a young man to help them work their farm. The arrival of Daniel fulfilled their request to Father Faucher who had journeyed from their parish to collect Irish orphan children who might be taken in by some of his parishioners. The request for this action had come directly from the archbishop himself. Upon the sight of Daniel stepping down from the cart and joining the Coulombes, the Tighe descendants recount how Catherine flew into a fit of screaming and crying, clutching her brother, who was the only person left from the family and world she had known. The Coulombe's had only asked for a boy, but now they accepted a girl as well in what has been considered a great act of charity. In time, the Coulombes retained a notary and signed title to the farm over to Daniel upon the event of their deaths. By 1871, Daniel and his wife Virginie had two children and he had Gallicized his name to Tye.[6] Daniel inherited the farm, as planned, and Catherine, who never married, worked as a housekeeper for the new parish priest, Father E.B. Coté, at St-Croix.[7] On the surface, the story of the Tighes appears to be a rags-to-riches tale of young orphan children "making good" in the new world. Moreover, their story enhances the image of French Canadian largesse as they "adopted" the seemingly helpless little Irish children and gave them a new home. Finally, the Catholic Church emerges as the primary agent of making certain that Catholic children were cared for and given to pious Catholic homes – saved for the faith. However, as happens many times after intense historical research, not all is or was as appears.

An analysis of the surviving routinely generated records from this period casts a different light on the actions of the Canadian churches and people in their engagement of the Irish famine orphans of 1847–48. In the process of examining the lives of more than 1,300 famine orphans, at Quebec City and Montreal, and a number of other Irish "foundlings", discovered along the way, there appear a variety of life trajectories for these orphans who, unlike the sedentary Tighe children, were on "the move" much like other immigrants in this era.[8] The idea that the host society and the Irish children were engaged in a type of the mass "adoption" requires considerable nuance. Firstly, adoption is not an appropriate term to be used in the context of this story; secondly, many children were essentially placed in semi-indentured service to the families in both the city and countryside; thirdly, siblings were separated from one another and sometimes at great distances; and fourthly, many orphans were keen on leaving their placements as soon as possible in order to secure independence or re-unite with extended family members elsewhere in British North America and the United States. Many of the children who remained in Canada learned French quickly and assimilated into French Canadian society. As well, it is problematic to refer to all these children as orphans, since some were placed in the Catholic Charitable Ladies shelter, and other orphanages, while one or both of their parents were still alive. In fact, the famine orphan stories, like that of Daniel Tighe of Lotbinière or even the invented tale of Molly Johnson of the *Heritage Minute*, were atypical of the orphan experience. Few orphans were embraced by their placement families and fewer appear to have inherited property because of the nature of the work they were forced to do for their new hosts.

Fundamental to understanding what happened to these children is recognizing that, in the absence of a state-funded social safety network, the day-to-day tasks of caring for these "orphans" fell to the Roman Catholic and Anglican Churches in Lower Canada or Canada East. Catholics, who comprised most of the inhabitants of this section of Canada, had a well-established infrastructure of social services, schools, and hospitals as a means of preserving the Catholic faith in a province which contained a powerful Anglophone Protestant minority and a sister province, Canada West, which was thoroughly Protestant with a tiny and precarious Catholic minority. The Roman Catholic Archbishop of Quebec, Joseph Signay, continued the tradition of protecting the Catholic faith by enhancing this Catholic social service network while continuously allying the Church with Protestant British Governors and their civil policies. As a means of preserving language, religion, and culture, the Catholic episcopacy's policy of co-operation with the colonial administration had been generally effective since the British Conquest in 1763.[9] Bishops and most of their priests and members of religious orders were clear in their intention to "render unto Caesar," even if the Crown was Protestant and English. The Canadian hierarchy in the mid-1840s, knew the Irish crisis well, and funds had been raised at the request of Signay himself to help relieve Irish hunger.[10]

The question of the day in 1847 was what to do with hundreds of Irish Catholic children left abandoned in their section of Canada. Alarmed, Signay was unequivocal when he wrote to the Irish bishops, claiming that the calamity that faced their people was now being repeated as they arrived in his diocese: "The voice of religion and humanity imposes on me the sacred and imperative duty of exposing your Lordship to the dismal fate that awaits thousands of unfortunate children of Ireland who come to seek in Canada an asylum from countless evils affecting them in their native land."[11] Under Signay in Quebec and Bishop Ignace Bourget in Montreal, the Catholic Church mounted a disciplined effort to accommodate what one newspaper termed these "hopeless little travellers."[12]

As has been witnessed, the children that were greeted by Signay had already been traumatized by the horrendous journey across the Atlantic and by the conditions awaiting them in the quarantine station of Grosse Ile. George Mellis Douglas, the chief physician on the Island, had hoped for restrictions on the landing of sick immigrants, with regulations in place akin to the ports in the United States.[13] His hopes were unrequited. Instead, the children saw a drama of illness, death, and despair unfold in front of them after they disembarked their ships. The spread of the contagion, mostly ship's fever, was something that all officials, medical or otherwise, wanted contained on the island. Up river in Quebec City one editor cautioned readers about the potential catastrophe if medical protocols on the island were not strictly enforced: "We must entertain the hope that no necessary precaution will be neglected and we think it reasonable to give the authorities credit for every willingness, on their part, to use the greatest vigilance and strictness in carrying into effect appropriate measures for preventing the spread of contagious disease."[14] While there was no bacteriological sense of how contagion spread in the 1840s, the sight of impoverished, ill-clad, and hungry strangers and their "urchins" landing on the quays of Quebec was sufficient to throw the local population into near panic. The site of unattended children landing in large numbers in Quebec's Lower Town, raised the additional question of who would care for them now that their parents were dead or nowhere to be seen.

Signay and others did not exaggerate the emergency they faced as dozens of Irish children poured into Quebec City daily. In the sailing seasons of 1847 and 1848, alone, the Catholic Charitable Ladies recorded at least 619 children's names in their ledgers.[15] Most children were listed with the names of their parents, county, and parish of origin and often the names of the families and institutions in which they would be placed if they did not succumb to their illnesses. Added to this number were at least eighty-three additional children who had been recorded by either parish priests or civic officials.[16] The original 619 names and details from the "Ladies Ledger" were transcribed by historian Marianna O'Gallagher in her study of the Grosse Ile quarantine station and this O'Gallagher List forms the source of information for the children who are examined in this study.

The children's first point of reference in this new world would have been the Emigrant Reception Office on Champlain Street,[17] a narrow street that ran below the heights and parallel to the St Lawrence River and fed into streets and alleyways where there were shops and warehouses. The chief emigration agent for Canada, A.C. Buchanan, had his offices there. Close by, the city had established a soup kitchen where the children may have received a hot meal before being moved to the nearby Marine Hospital.[18] It was at the hospital where the children would be checked for contagion, and then Catholic children were separated from Protestant children to facilitate the work of the clergy who moved the healthy children to the care of their respective Christian denominations. The Anglican Church co-ordinated the gathering of all Protestant children regardless of denomination.[19] Children who were unable to be moved remained at the Marine Hospital to be treated for typhus, dysentery, and other ailments. One of the causes for so many entering the hospital was the emigrants' eagerness to drink water directly from the St Lawrence River which "caused something like dysentery" thus necessitating immediate medical attention.[20] As the hospital filled beyond its capacity, with as many as 500 patients at a time, the provincial government released a cavalry barracks for the exclusive use of typhus patients.[21] At any given time, dozens of children were treated alongside hundreds of men and women suffering from similar maladies. In the week of 3–10 July, for instance, of the 388 admittances to the hospital, forty were children. During that week, sixty-five children were in care at the hospital, and only nine were discharged. For seven of the children in treatment that week, their journey to Canada ended at the Marine Hospital's cemetery.[22]

Volunteers led the healthy Catholic children from the hospital to the orphan asylum, run by the Charitable Catholic Ladies, on Prince Edward Street.[23] Here the children were processed, and their names and information were inscribed in the ledger. Such documentation had at least two purposes: first, to track each individual child in terms of their residency and those potential "adopters" who might seek children to be placed in their homes and second, to maintain records for the purposes of collecting the subsidy per child paid for by the Canadian government.[24] The children, once the ladies had received their per capita child subsidy, would be recorded in the *Canada Gazette*, with additional information identifying with whom they were to be placed.[25] The subsidies did not make these children wards of the state; they were in the protective care of the churches until such time as placement occurred. As will be observed in all provinces, there was little follow up as to what happened to the children once placed, and few records remain attesting to the church's due diligence once the children were handed off to patrons. The Charitable Catholic Ladies eventually surrendered the asylum, in 1849, to the care of the Souers de Charité de Montreal (Grey Nuns). At that time, the Catholic Church in Quebec City had no non-cloistered order of religious women to undertake such a task, therefore the Grey Nuns answered the archbishop's call.

One can only imagine the pandemonium at the Prince Edward Street orphan asylum. Dozens of Irish children were admitted each day. Some spoke English, some Irish, and some nothing but blather because they were infants under the age of two. For the youngest, the ladies recorded the infant's names only if there was an older sibling to identify them. The children also came from all counties of Ireland bringing with them different types of accented English and different dialects of Irish depending on their Munster, Connaught, or Ulster origins (see table 3.1). In general, the analysis of the O'Gallagher List shows several interesting patterns in terms of county origins and primary placement or, in the words used by contemporaries, location of the "adoptions." Of 360 orphans who could be identified by county, Roscommon led all others with fifty-two orphans or just more than 14 per cent of the total in this subset. Tipperary followed with thirty-three or just over 9 per cent; Clare had twenty-six orphans at 7.2 per cent of the total, while Fermanagh and Laois had twenty each or about 5.6 per cent, respectively. The first caution is the high numbers of Roscommon orphans, particularly for a county which generally was remarked as having lower levels of migration to British North America in the period than other counties. The inflated numbers are likely because of the concentration of the aforementioned assisted migrants from the estate of Major Denis Mahon and the horrendous conditions on board his chartered vessels. The *Virginius* and the *Naomi* were notorious for their high rates of deaths at sea and in quarantine and produced a disproportionate number of orphans, with the possible exception of the ships *Lady Sale* and *Aeolus*, which landed in Saint John, New Brunswick.[26] The fact that the *Virginius* was filled exclusively with Roscommon migrants and the vast majority of passengers on the *Naomi* were also from Roscommon, helps to explain why the numbers of Roscommon orphans appear inflated when compared to general migration figures for the county among the arrivals in British North America in the sailing season of 1847.

With a holding centre containing hundreds of "orphans" weekly, the local Roman Catholic Church sprang into action. Archbishop Signay used both his pulpit and circular letters to mobilize his clergy and laity to collect the children and place them with upstanding Catholic families.[27] Priests had already been drafted for duties at Grosse Ile to administer to the Irish once they disembarked from their ships. Signay had seconded priests from across the diocese for this minimum one-week placement on the quarantine station.[28] As the letters of Fathers McGauran and Taschereau have already attested, in chapter two, the scenes they witnessed at Grosse Ile left an indelible imprint on these priests. Many clergy who had previous experience on the island and had survived the typhus epidemic were among the many priests who stepped forward to gather children for placement in their local parishes. In fact, several priests would accompany the children on the steamer *St George* from Grosse Ile to the Marine Hospital at St-Roche.[29] As had been the case with the Tighe children, priests returned home, canvassed their parishioners, and then travelled back to the orphans home on Prince Edward Street to fill their parishioners' requests. To co-ordinate the entire operation efficiently, Signay assigned Father Charles-Felix Cazeau, his secretary, to manage the allocation of children to priests for distribution in local parishes.[30] Cazeau may very well have been the model for the priest crying "Molly Johnson" in the *Heritage Minute* vignette. Regardless, he would become a pivotal figure as the Church implemented its plan to place children, and he assured observers that groups of Irish siblings would not be broken up.[31]

Table 3.1
Counties of origin of Irish famine "orphans" at Quebec, 1847–48 (N=619)

County	Number	Percentage	County	Number	Percentage
Roscommon	52	8.4	Meath	7	1.1
Tipperary	33	5.3	Limerick	7	1.1
Clare	26	4.2	Louth	6	0.9
Fermanagh	20	3.2	Armagh	4	0.6
Queen's	20	3.2	Antrim	3	0.5
Leitrim	20	3.2	Donegal	3	0.5
Mayo	18	2.9	Derry	3	0.5
Kildare	17	2.7	Monaghan	3	0.5
Tyrone	16	2.6	Waterford	2	0.3
Kilkenny	16	2.6	Carlow	2	0.3
Sligo	13	2.1	Kerry	2	0.3
Galway	11	1.8	Kings	1	0.2
Wicklow	11	1.8	Longford	1	0.2
Cork	11	1.8	Non-Irish	5	0.8
Westmeath	11	1.8	Unknown	259	41.8
Cavan	10	1.6	Total	619	100.0
Wexford	7	1.1			

Source: Marianna O'Gallagher, *Grosse Ile: Gateway to Canada, 1832–1937* (Ste-Foy: Carraig Books, 1984), appendices. Note neither Dublin nor Down were represented. Non-Irish consisted of two from each of England and Scotland and one from Quebec.

The orphan lists reveal several very important correctives to the myths generated by the famous *Heritage Minute*. First, these children were not necessarily orphans in terms of the common contemporary usage of the word – both parents absent or dead. While the majority had lost their parents, there were dozens of others who had been placed in the care of the ladies by a surviving parent who was incapable of supporting the child or, in several cases, multiple children. The case of John Patrick Mahoney serves as an illustration of the depositing of "half-orphans" at the asylum. In 1848, Mahoney's wife, Honora Kelly, died, and he and his six daughters, ranging in age from thirteen to four years old, set out from Coolmean, County Clare, for a new life in Canada. Mahoney's ship, the *Governor* arrived at Grosse Ile from Cork in late May, 1848. The family was placed in quarantine and the second youngest daughter, Ellen, died there on 24 May. Mahoney took his five surviving daughters to Quebec on board the *St George* and on 2 June placed Bridget (eleven), Mary (ten),[32] Catherine (six), and Nancy (four), at the orphan asylum. He kept the eldest daughter, Elizabeth (thirteen), with him, presumably to be responsible for her father's care. Each of the four youngest sisters were placed with French Canadian farm families in the Rimouski area, both Mary and Nancy with the family of Antoine Larouche and the two other girls with the Mavinon and Pineau families.[33] With the four Mahoney girls safely ensconced in the Rimouski region, John Patrick and his eldest daughter rejoined them there. He and Elizabeth moved into the home Hubert Levesque and Genevieve Ruest, who owned a farm in the area, and it appears both Mahoneys worked for their keep.[34] In one sense the family was reunited, although the other Mahoney daughters were scattered in the region on different farmsteads, contrary to Father Cazeau's intention to place all siblings in a single household rather than splitting families. The story of the Mahoney settlement underscores that orphans were not necessarily parentless, and placement in the asylum became a strategy used by one or two parents to have their children cared for while they acquired the resources to reclaim their children and begin anew.[35]

A second correction comes with the meaning of adoption. Although the term had been used colloquially since the settlement of New France to describe children being taken in and cared for by families,[36] there were no legal grounds for the practice. In 1873, the province of New Brunswick, at which point was one of the founding provinces of the Dominion of Canada, was the first Canadian jurisdiction to create the category of legal adoption.[37] In the 1840s, the *Droit Civile* of Canada East (Quebec) did not anticipate legal adoption nor did the revised *Code of 1866* on the eve of Canadian Confederation. There were provisions made for the legal transfer of property to heirs, which in some cases might be *de facto* orphans, but no legal adoption. The only reason for doing so would have been to provide for the smooth transition of inherited property between a deceased person and his/her children. No law existed to transfer property to formally adopted children because legal adoption did not exist in the province of Quebec until the 1920s. In fact, the census of 1851–52 allowed the enumerator to indicate whether households contained family and non-family members. Most of these Irish children, when traced in the census were not considered family members in either the French Canadian or Irish

Canadian homes in which they were placed. Thus, the case of Daniel Tighe (Tye) appears exceptional as the Coulombes allowed for his inheriting of the farm, not by any right of adoption but because they retained a notary to prepare legal documents that transferred title of their property to Daniel upon their deaths.[38] While the term *de facto* adoption might be suitable for identifying the Irish orphans in their new domestic situation, the term's legal adoption would be an anachronism.[39] Perhaps when one refers to the situation of these children, it would be more accurate to say that they were "placed" and not adopted.

A third myth is also exploded by a careful examination of the O'Gallagher List. French Canadian families, although dominant among the domestic placements for Irish children, did not monopolize the Church's placement operation. Irish families constituted about one third of the families in which Irish children were received. About 357 adopters were identified in the list of 619, and of these 118 or 33.0 per cent were of Irish in origin and sixteen others, or 4.5 per cent, had English or Scottish surnames. The remaining 222 individuals (or 62.2 per cent) were identifiably French Canadian by their surname. Only one person could not be identified ethnically by the spelling of the surname (see table 3.4). This prominence of Irish families among the placements should come as no surprise knowing that the Quebec City area and some adjoining rural areas had long been to home of Irish settlement.[40] This was in keeping with the migration patterns of early nineteenth century British North America, which witnessed 450,000 Irish migrate, sojourn, and settle in the British colonies prior to the famine.[41]

It should also be noted that not all children placed in Irish households shared the same experiences even though among those who likely spoke their language and shared elements of the same culture. Thomas Kearin, from County Cavan, for example, lost both his parents on the *Ganges* and was placed in the home of Patrick McGowan, a dry goods merchant who lived on Baude Street in Quebec City. Unfortunately, the placement lasted only eight months because the twelve-year-old Kearin died in April 1848 and was buried from Quebec City's basilica.[42] Several other Quebec City-based Irish families took on orphans, including that of Patrick Boylan of St-Roche which agreed to take in Bridget Lynch, a half orphan whose mother still lived in County Westmeath but whose father had died during their voyage on the *Yorkshire*.[43] She would not remain with the family but eventually entered domestic service in the Ottawa Valley. Eleven-year-old Edward Nealon, who like the aforementioned Mahoney sisters was also from Coolmean, Clare, was housed with the family of Cornelius McCarthy. Edward remained in the city for decades and married another Celt, coincidentally named Alice Irish.[44]

Finally, the case of the McManus brothers deserves some attention because it reveals that the mythology of Christian charity bestowed by local Catholic families and Father Cazeau's pledge not to separate siblings ought not be taken at face value. John McManus, age eleven, and his brother Patrick, age eight, were from County Tyrone in Ulster and arrived on Prince Edward Street well past the end of the sailing season, in December 1847, suggesting that their parents Hugh and Catherine died either in quarantine or in the Marine Hospital. The brothers were sent to Riviere-de-Loup but were separated, with John being assigned to a Mr Spencer and Patrick to a local tavern keeper, Mr Kelly, in nearby Fraserville. In due time both brothers were discovered slinging beer in the tavern accompanied by another Irish child, Jane Harvey, who was likely employed for domestic chores.[45] It appeared John Kelly knew and appreciated cheap labour when it landed on his doorstep.[46]

Cazeau's plan for orphan deployment was focused in four significant geographic clusters in Canada East (see table 3.2). There was some demand for children particularly from Trois Rivieres,[47] but the needs of Catholic families there were subordinate to the individual efforts of priests from other parishes in filling their demands by arriving at the orphan asylum first. The largest number of orphans were placed in the Quebec City area including the city itself, the suburbs, and the county. This cluster also included Quebec City's neighbouring counties of Portneuf and Montmorency. The second largest cluster was in the frontier area of Rimouski, about 300 kilometres to the northeast of Quebec City on the south shore of the St Lawrence River. The third area of significance was the agricultural county of Lotbinière, located west of Quebec City on the south shore of the St Lawrence, across the river from the city of Trois Rivières. The fourth cluster was found adjacent to Lotbinière in the town and county of Nicolet (see table 3.3). The prominence of these regions appears dependent upon the parish priests from those areas who took the initiative to personally transport Irish children to their home parishes, not coincidently in Rimouski, Lotbinière, Nicolet, and St-Grégoire.[48] In these cluster areas outside of Quebec the overwhelming number of placements were in French Canadian Catholic homes. In the census returns of 1851–52 for these regions the orphan children did retain their Irish surnames, although many of their given names now appeared as French: Mary as Marie, John as Jean,

Table 3.2
Placement locations of the orphans of 1847–48
(N=420)

Location	Number	Percentage
Quebec City and region	107	25.5
Rimouski and area	57	13.6
Nicolet and St Grégoire	56	13.3
Lotbinière and region	25	6.0
United States of America	22	5.2
Upper Canada	19	4.5
Montreal and region	5	1.2
Other placement areas	129	30.7
Total	420	100.00

Source: Marianna O'Gallagher, *Grosse Ile: Gateway to Canada, 1832–1937* (Ste-Foy: Carraig Books, 1984), appendices. Many of the "other" placement areas involved less than three children per place.

Table 3.3
Placement of orphan children as located on the census of 1851–52
(N=77)

Location	Number	Percentage
Rimouski and area	24	31.2
Quebec and area	20	26.3
Nicolet and St Grégoire	16	21.1
Upper Canada	9	11.8
Montreal and area	5	6.6
Lotbinière	2	2.6
United States of America	1	1.3
Total	77	100.00

Source: Marianna O'Gallagher, *Grosse Ile: Gateway to Canada, 1832–1937* (Ste-Foy: Carraig Books, 1984), appendices. The one foundling was not included in the count since she did not appear on the O'Gallagher List. Census of Canada, 1851–52, Canada East.

Table 3.4
Ethnic origins of the placement families

Ethnic origin	Number	Percentage
French Canadian	222	62.2
Irish	118	33.0
Scottish and English	16	4.5
Unknown	1	0.3
Total	357	100.00

Source: Marianna O'Gallagher, *Grosse Ile: Gateway to Canada, 1832–1937* (Ste-Foy: Carraig Books, 1984), appendices.

and Henry as Henri. There were also smaller groups of children who were sent to extended family and relatives in the United States and Upper Canada (Canada West), some of whom had settled prior to the famine in the Canadian interior or the United States tidewater ports or the opening frontier in western New York and Ohio valleys.

Once the Irish children departed from the care of the Charitable Catholic Ladies, their whereabouts are difficult to locate. Several children died at the orphan asylum and their stories ended in Quebec City. Infants were often recorded as nameless by Church facilities in both Quebec and Montreal because there was no other family member present to confirm either the age or name of the child. The gaps in the census data of 1852, missing counties and urban neighbourhoods in the census, children who simply ran away from their placements, and the inaccurate transcription of Irish names by Francophone enumerators complicates the search for the orphans. As table 3.3 indicates, at least seventy-seven (12.4 per cent) of the 619 orphans on the O'Gallagher List can be traced with some accuracy due to their inclusion in the census and the added bonus of being able to search for the names of the placement hosts. There are about ninety-four other children who are possible matches (15.2 per cent), but among these are questions about their given names, ages, religion, and surnames that raise doubts about an exact match between the census and the O'Gallagher List. Thus, the conclusions of this study are based on an assessment of close to one in four of all the orphans recorded by the ladies in 1847 and 1848.

Perhaps the most important revelation regarding these orphans was the manner of their placement. The majority of the seventy-eight orphans (seventy-seven plus one foundling) were not listed as family members, with many serving as day labourers on farms, domestic servants in the cities and towns, and some just labelled as "none" for occupation. Regardless of the ethnic background of the placement family or business, Irish or French Canadian, these children were regarded as an opportunity for patrons to exploit them for their labour. They appear less as integrated members of the families in question and more valued for their work, particularly when families needed teens and pre-teens to labour, because the family's children were in infancy. While certain general patterns of orphan placement appear, individual stories help illuminate orphan experience more vividly.

One should not be surprised to find that these children were used for little more than indentured labour on French Canadian farms and Irish Canadian businesses. In the mid-nineteenth century children were still regarded as little adults, and work and education were considered the two means by which children could be properly formed. The academic literature on children for this period as rich and certainly points to the necessity of keeping orphans from idleness by giving them skills, tasks, and learning in order to make them moral and productive citizens. When one strips away any romantic notions conjured by the *Heritage Minute* regarding adoption and the preservation of culture by keeping one's Irish name, one is left with the stark reality of being a child in mid-nineteenth century British North America. In Upper Canada, for instance, Veronica Strong-Boag comments that apprenticeships "were the only legislative provision for poor or orphaned children from 1799 to 1851."[49] In the Maritime provinces children could be auctioned off to serve on farms or other local businesses. As Bettina Bradbury reports on nineteenth-century Montreal, children were expected to work to support their impoverished families.[50] Given the practical attitudes towards children and labour that prevailed in the colonies in the period, the revelation that Irish orphans were put to work in their new homes is no surprise as that was simply among the expectations placed on children in early and mid-nineteenth-century Canada.[51]

The way Irish children were treated once placed with families by the local parish priest may be illuminated by looking at Rimouski as a case study. Rimouski provides a good laboratory not only because it was the second largest placement area for orphans coming from the ladies' orphan asylum in Quebec but also because the census records for 1851–52 are complete for the region, as are the registers for the local Roman Catholic parish of St Germain. Lotbinière County, on the other hand, which was another area of heavy placement, is frustrating to study because of gaps in the census data for sections of

Table 3.5
Irish orphans placed at Rimouski, 1847–48
(N=25*)

Name	Age	Father	Mother	County	Placement	Religion	Ship	Status
Francis Brady	10	Andy Brady	Margaret McGauran	Fermanagh	NA	RC	*Superior*	NF
Peter Cavagan	10	Peter Cavagan	Mary Clarme	NA	Pierre Langis	RC	NA	NF
Catherine Connor	8	Patrick Connor	Bridget Sweeny	Mayo	Alex Rivard	RC	*Marchiness of Breadalbane*	NF
Mary Dempsey	9	Bryan Dempsey	Mary Queen	Kildare	Marie Grace	RC	*Lady Campbell*	NF
Patrick Hynes	12	James Hynes	Mary Hines	Mayo	Luc St Laurent	RC	*Rankin*	Family
Honora Kane	13	John Kane	Bridget McInanly	Mayo	George Lizotte	RC	*Sarah*	NF
Timothy Kane	11	John Kane	Bridget McInanly	Mayo	Hiliare St Laurent	RC	*Sarah*	NF
Ellen Leahy	11	Jacob Leahy	Ellen Heffernan	Tipperary	Pouliot Pilote	RC	NA	NF
James McGill	8	NA	NA	NA	Jean B Beaulieu	RC	NA	NF
John McManus	11	Hugh McManus	Catherine Skey	Tyrone	Mr Spencer	RC	NA	NF
Patrick McManus	8	Hugh McManus	Catherine Skey	Tyrone	Mr Kelly	RC	NA	NF
Thomas Boyle	?	Thady Boyle	Peggy Jennings	NA	Thomas Parent	RC	NA	NF

Honora Joice	18	John Joice	Sealy Joice	Galway	Dr Poulin	RC	St John	NF
Mary Joice	16	John Joice	Sealy Joice	Galway	Henri Martin	RC	St John	NF
Catherine Mahoney	7	Patrick Mahoney	Honora Kelly	Clare	Etienne Pineau	RC	Governor	NF
Mary Mahoney	13	Patrick Mahoney	Honora Kelly	Clare	Anton. Larouche	RC	Governor	NF
Patrick Shalloo	6	Patrick Shalloo	Ellen Hanarahan	Clare	Narcisse Banville	RC	Governor	NF
Anne Conray	14	Bernard Conray	Catherine Scott	Roscommon	Thomas Durette	RC	Georgiana	NF
George Cox	9	Martin Cox	Mary Maloney	Roscommon	Andre Gauvreau	RC	Virginius	NF
Mary Cox	7	Martin Cox	Mary Maloney	Roscommon	Andre Gauvreau	RC	Virginius	NF
Michael Hanley	12	Edward Hanley	Mary Egan	Roscommon	Germain Langis	RC	Virginius	NF
Bridget Holden	14	Henry Holden	Bridget Mahan	Roscommon	Auguste Lavoie	RC	Naomi	NF
Henry Holden	9	Henry Holden	Bridget Mahan	Roscommon	August Lavoie	RC	Naomi	NF
John Dalton	5	William Dalton	Onah Tierney	Roscommon	Pierre Coté	RC	Erin's Queen	NF
Catherine Prior*	9	Thomas Prior	Margaret McGinnis	Leitrim	Barth. Lemieux	RC	Superior	NF

Source: "O'Gallagher List"; Census of 1851–52, Canada East, District of Rimouski.
* Included are the twenty-four orphans from the O'Gallagher List and one foundling.

the county. Twenty-four Irish orphans, including the aforementioned Mahoney sisters, can be traced to their new placements in Rimouski, having remained in the region from their time of arrival in 1847 or 1848 to when the enumerators visited in 1852.[52] The Rimouski subset comprises about one third of the Irish children who can actually be traced within the first five years of their arrival in Canada.

The county of Rimouski is located about 300 kilometres northeast of Quebec City, with its northern boundary forming part of the southern shore of the St Lawrence River as it widens into the Gulf of St Lawrence. It is primarily hilly terrain, an extension of the Appalachian Mountain chain, punctuated by lakes and rivers which ultimately empty into the St Lawrence.[53] Given its potential as home base for fishermen and with the promise of some agriculture on the coastal plain and in the river valleys, the French Crown ceded this remote seigneury to Renée Lepage de Sainte Claire in 1688. The village, later to become the town of Rimouski, was founded in 1696 and soon became the primary centre of seigneurial life,[54] although its name remains controversial in terms of its origins: some say it is derived from the Mi'kmaq *animouski*, "land of the moose," or from the Malecite *lemouskeg*, "the place where dogs live."[55] Regardless of its etymology, Rimouski would become a place of Irish orphan settlement, as dozens of orphans were transported to the seigneury in 1847 and 1848 to live among the Rimouskois.

Because of its remote location, poor road connections with older seigneuries to the west, and perceived limited economic opportunities, Rimouski witnessed very slow population growth. In 1790, more than a century after its founding, Rimouski's population was only 333. Over the next thirty years, and with increased agricultural settlement, the population reached 1,963. At the time of the arrival of the famine orphans the region had a growing population of more than 3,600, about three quarters of whom were farmers.[56] The rise in population was certainly facilitated by the completion in the late 1830s of the King's Road from the village of Trois Pistoles, west of Rimouski. Ironically, when the Irish children arrived in the region local farmers were facing their own food insecurity: local harvests had been poor and there were critical food shortages in the county. The other, perhaps pleasant irony for the Irish children was that they would likely meet other Celtic settlers in Rimouski; a group of Scottish migrants had already settled in the Parish of St Germain.[57]

As was the case in other regions that had received orphans during the famine, the Roman Catholic Church in Rimouski had been instrumental in orphan placement. The Church had been a presence in the region since 1793, when the Diocese of Quebec established the first chapel for missionary priests.[58] When famine migrants overwhelmed Grosse Ile in 1847, Archbishop Joseph Signay of Quebec requested that a priest from Rimouski assist with the overwhelmingly Catholic refugee population flooding into the province. Antoine LeBel, the vicar or associate pastor of St Germain de Rimouski parish and a native of nearby Kamouraska, served on Grosse Ile for eight days between 3 and 10 August 1847. He witnessed the human devastation firsthand, burying at least 123 migrants during his short sojourn on the island. His encounters with the Irish also included the conversion and marriage of two sailors who wished to be wed to two young Catholic passengers from county Longford.[59]

His short time on Grosse Ile left an indelible impression on the thirty-one-year-old priest. With the assistance of Father Felix Cazeau, LeBel pledged to honour the archbishop's intention that Catholic families in the diocese take in the orphaned Irish children. LeBel himself took thirty Irish children to Rimouski and reported to Cazeau that he would return to Quebec for more to be placed among his parishioners.[60] This was not quite the dramatic commissioning of the "adoptions" as depicted in the *Heritage Minute* but a long journey by wagon and foot from the orphanage in Quebec City to the final destination nearly 300 kilometres away. Within the year, LeBel's superior at St Germain, Father Thomas-Ferruce Picard-Destroismaisons, reported to the archbishop that the Irish children were adapting well to their new surroundings, while keeping their Irish surnames although converting their Christian names to a French equivalent.[61] He added that many were learning French with some success, thus confirming the story of another orphan, Thomas Quinn, who became a priest of the Diocese of Nicolet and lost his English language skills entirely after his placement.[62]

While local historians estimate that as many as sixty Irish children were placed in Rimouski,[63] the O'Gallagher List indicates that fifty-seven children, or 13.6 per cent of the 406 traceable locations on the list, were relocated to Rimouski (see table 3.2). Of these fifty-seven children, only twenty-four were inscribed in the 1851–52 census. Admittedly at least four years elapsed between the placement of the Irish children and the taking of the census, which was completed in 1852. Much could have happened in that short time to account for the number of missing orphans. Children on the cusp of adulthood could have easily left their placements, seeking friends and relatives in other parts of British North America or the United States. Some may have left for other districts adjacent to Rimouski. Some may have died, although if they had done so their deaths occurred outside of the parish since the records of St Germain do not record any burials of Irish children during these intervening years. Nevertheless, the "disappearance" of these children from the public record, so soon after placement, casts considerable doubt on even their de facto adoption by French Canadian farmers. It would appear life on the frontiers of the future province of Quebec was merely a waystation for these Irish children, as they eyed independence and betterment elsewhere.

For the twenty-four children who stayed in Rimouski there were many life trajectories. The children had few common county ties except for the seven children from Mahon's estate in County Roscommon. Father LeBel may have met some of those from the Mahon estate because he likely buried the dead from the *Naomi* and the *Virginius*, after each ship's arrival at Grosse Ile in late July 1847.[64] There were four children each from Clare and Mayo, and the rest hailed from Fermanagh, Tipperary, Tyrone, Galway, Kildare, and Leitrim.[65] From disparate parts of north and west Ireland, these children were now bound by the trauma of the famine, loss of family, and transportation to a remote and seemingly wild place where few people spoke their language. All the children were placed in French Canadian Catholic homes, except for a few welcomed by some Anglo families in nearby Rivière de Loup. Of the twenty-four children, only one, Patrick Hynes, was listed as a family member on the census (see table 3.2),[66] confirming that there was no adoption per se but a living arrangement in which Irish orphans would help supplement the family workforce on the farm. Irish girls would assist French Canadian women with domestic and farm chores and the care of little children. Boys would work in the barns and fields. The census confirms that eight boys were listed as "journalier" or day workers or labourers, one child was permitted to go to school, one was listed as a servant, and one as a farmer. At least seven of the children were identified as having no occupation and three children were unidentified in terms of their work status. What is clear from the census, however, is that, in a fashion not atypical within nineteenth-century family life, these orphan children were expected to work. If they did not work and were of age, they found themselves in a French Catholic schoolhouse. The expectation that an orphan child ought to work or apprentice and be productive was not exclusive to Lower Canada. As one will soon see, the practice was already in play in Upper Canada as well.[67]

As has been made evident in the case of the Mahoney orphans, siblings did not universally benefit from being placed together in the same home. In this small sample from Rimouski, at least five pairs of siblings were placed in the same home, but others like the Mahoneys or the Shalloo brothers were not. Thomas and Patrick Shalloo were from Coolmean, County Clare and arrived at Grosse Ile in 1848. The elder Shalloo, Thomas (age thirteen) was placed with a Major Joseph Samson in Point Lévis, across the river from Quebec City, while his brother Patrick, who was only six, was taken to the farm of Narcisse Banville at Rimouski. The historical record leaves no trace if they ever met again. Honora and Timothy Kane, thirteen and eleven years respectively, were a little more fortunate. After their journey from Newport, County Mayo, Father LeBel took both children to Rimouski but placed them in different families. Honora was placed in the home of the town blacksmith, George Lizotte, while her younger brother, now listed officially as Thadée, worked as a farm labourer from Hilaire St-Laurent and his family. In addition to his work for the St-Laurent's, Tim was permitted to attend local school, which would have been conducted in French.[68] Most of the orphans identified in the census of 1851–52, are not recorded in the local census ten years later, a testament to immigrant mobility and children coming of age and seeking independence.

Reasons for the orphan disappearance from Rimouski in the official records after 1851 are many. Honora and Mary Joice were not long together; at eighteen and sixteen respectively they were close to marrying age; Honora was placed with Dr Poulin in Rimouski but appears to have left for Quebec City before 1851; her sister Mary had been placed with Henri Martin and his family in Rimouski, but she was no longer with the family in 1852 and had been replaced as a servant with Irish-born Anne Kane, who was nineteen years old.[69] Mary Joice may have moved to Chambly, near Montreal to work as a servant by 1851.[70] These young women probably represented a segment of the orphan population, who when coming of age, sought marriage, gainful employment, and less of a frontier environment to call home. Elizabeth Mahoney's life path took a different course. In 1858 she married Joseph St Pierre, a farmer in Rimouski at St Germain Parish and one of the families who had taken in one of the Mahoney sisters. Elizabeth and Joseph had ten children; Joseph died in 1911; the St Pierre's, by 1871, were living in the Saguenay region north of the St Lawrence and then Chicoutimi, where more abundant acreage was being opened for rural settlement.[71] Mary Dempsey's story is also different, perhaps unique in the sample. A native of Boldkell, County Kildare, she and her four sisters arrived at Grosse Ile in June 1847 on board the *Lady Campbell*. Two sisters Anne, six, and Bridget, four, died in the orphanage at Quebec, and subsequently Mary, age nine, and her sisters Hannah, eleven, and Elizabeth, ten, were placed in three separate Rimouski families: Rivard, L'Allemand, and

Grace. Although her sisters disappeared from the records after placement, Mary, listed in the census as Mary Damphery, in 1851, was living with a new family – Jean-Baptist Fiola, his wife, and two children. Mary remained in Rimouski, never married, and died at the age of twenty, 23 July 1858, from unrecorded causes. She was buried in the parish cemetery.[72]

Among the unsung Mahon orphans that could be traced there was George and Mary Cox, nine and seven years old respectively, who had been assisted off the Bumlin Parish on the Mahon estate in County Roscommon and had survived passage on the notorious ship *Virginius*. Their parents, Mary and Martin, who survived neither the voyage nor quarantine, had left them the modest sum of £1 2 shillings, the children's only means of survival, so they thought.[73] The Cox children were placed with the Gauvreau family in St Luce, in Rimouski County; Marie remained with the Gauvreaus, while George worked as a day labourer on the neighbouring farm of Eusèbe Lavoie.[74] Little remains recorded about them after 1852. Similarly, Bridget and Henry Holden, aged fourteen and nine, were orphaned after Grosse Ile, although their parents Henry and Bridget do not appear on the Grosse Ile registers as having died at sea or at the Quebec Marine Hospital. They were from Strokestown and had sailed on the *Naomi*, a ship with a notorious reputation only second to the *Virginius*; they were both taken by Auguste Lavoie, *dit* Samson, a farmer in Rimouski. They were listed as Olden, obviously a mistake made when the enumerator did not realize the children when pronouncing their names would not aspirate the "h" nor may have their "placement parents." In 1852 Henry was listed as a "journallier" – or day worker on the farm. The Holdens were among the few orphaned siblings that were recorded as having been placed in the same home.[75]

While Cazeau's intention that Irish children be placed together rarely happened, and Irish children retained their family names because of the absence of legal adoption, Signay and his fellow Catholics could take some satisfaction that these children had been placed in safe Catholic homes. The fear that these orphans might fall prey to Protestant proselytism was real in the minds of local Catholics. Reports coming from Dublin suggested that Catholic orphans in that city's slums were already the target of missionary efforts by Protestant clergy as were Catholic children in some of Ireland's Poor Law unions during the famine. Any Catholic clergy watching or reading reports in Quebec City's Anglican weekly newspaper *The Berean* would also be alarmed by the fact that its editor had been collecting funds for Protestant proselytizing efforts in Achill, County Mayo, and Dingle, County Kerry.[76] Known colloquially as "souperism" during the famine, some Protestant clergy would offer starving Catholics soup and food, providing they gave up their "Popish" religion.[77] While at times the practice of souperism, or cases of Catholics "taking the soup," have been exaggerated by contemporary chroniclers and historians, the fact still remains the Catholic clergy felt threatened by even a hint of such Protestant incursions among their people. Protestants in Quebec equally feared that Protestant children might be swept away by the omni-presence of Catholic clergy and religious at work in the hospitals, asylums, and fever sheds. The mutual fear and distrust between these religious groups on the ground led to the separation of Catholic from Protestant Children at Grosse Ile, Quebec City, and Montreal so that clergy from each Church could more easily deal with "their" orphans.[78]

Though small in terms of numbers, the Anglican Church was as concerned as the Roman Catholic regarding care for the orphans. Bishop George Jehoshaphat Mountain, who was administering the sees of Quebec and Montreal, took an active interest in both the famine in Ireland and the growing challenge of managing the refugees in quarantine at Grosse Ile. In the early stages of the famine, he had organized a relief fund that tapped many Anglican parishes in both his dioceses. By late May 1847, the bishop's relief fund had collected nearly £240 from parishes as far as Aylmer in the Ottawa Valley to Gaspé in the eastern most region of his Quebec diocese.[79] Like many of the aforementioned Catholic priests, Mountain spent a week on Grosse Ile, tending to all of the sick, but primarily presided over the burials of known Protestants.[80] He, like the Catholic priests working alongside him, wrote of the horrors he witness during his sojourn there: "Upon the whole, the impression produced upon my mind was that of the *hopelessness* of doing anything *effectual* to stay the consequences of such a visitation from the hand of God. A little abatement, a momentary breathing space, was followed by a thickening influx of squalid misery and fatal disease."[81] Mountain's son, the Reverend Armine Mountain, would spend the entire season on Grosse Ile. These experiences helped to set in motion Bishop Mountain's plans to assist the Protestant orphans left in the wake of the tragedy. Over the course of the summer, Mountain and some of his Anglican clergy gathered up more than one hundred Protestant orphans, of all denominations, from the Marine Hospital and the Prince Edward Street orphan asylum and sent many of these children to Montreal for further care and placement in sound Protestant homes.

Often hidden in the shadows of the coverage given to the prominence of Catholic priests and their efforts to assist the sick, dying, and orphaned Irish refugees, Anglican clergy were notable in their charitable work. The Reverend Charles Haersel, who also worked as the editor of the Quebec Anglican weekly paper, *The Berean*, served weekly at the Marine Hospital in Quebec.[82] His colleague the Reverend William Chadderton died at the hospital while in service of famine victims.[83] Likewise, three other Anglican ministers – C.J. Morris, Richard Anderson, and Charles Forest – all died of typhus during their service at Grosse Ile.[84] Similarly, Anglican ministers stationed upriver towards Montreal also gave their lives in 1847, including William Dawes who had been serving emigrants at St-Jean, south of Montreal, which was one of the principal access ways for emigrants to move south to the United States.[85] The Reverend Mark Willoughby died in Montreal in July 1847 while assisting in the fever sheds at Point St Charles.[86] Willoughby had been a career educator who had managed Anglican schools in Newfoundland and Quebec before moving to Montreal. Evidently, his selfless efforts in the fever sheds had caught the attention, and perhaps the admiration, of local Catholic clergy who laboured with him during Black '47 in Montreal.[87]

Such co-operation between Anglicans and their Catholic counterparts, however, did not necessarily mean that each side was willing to let down their sectarian guard. Anglicans, a minority in Montreal, were concerned that Protestant children not be placed in Catholic homes. The Reverend Charles Haersel at *The Berean* was unequivocal about the danger facing Protestants who were placed in Catholic hospitals and holding areas where "baptism and rites of the Church of Rome preparatory to death, [were] administered to them." He added that no Protestants should be exposed to such things "in their time of mental terror and bodily weakness."[88] In June and July 1847, Bishop Mountain and his Quebec City clergy managed to take responsibility for about fifty-six Protestant orphan children once they had been triaged out of the Catholic hordes. Before the end of the sailing season, Mountain had sent about sixty-nine additional children on to Montreal for care.[89]

Of the Quebec-based Irish Protestant orphan children, very little is known. The small sample of eleven children from this orphan cohort reveal fates similar to their Catholic counterparts. They were placed, picked up by extended family, or set to work. A native of Armagh, six-year-old Margaret Conlan lost her entire family on their journey from Liverpool to Quebec on board the *Achilles*. Her mother, Mary Blair from Tyrone, was left a widow, when her father John Conlan was swept overboard by a rogue wave. Her brother Benny died on board ship. Margaret's mother, who was pregnant, did not survive the quarantine on Grosse Ile nor did her older sister Mary Anne. Little Margaret was taken from Quebec to Montreal, where she was picked up by her father's brother, Benjamin Conlan, who had previously migrated to the Toronto area before the famine. Unlike the Conlan family, seven of the children of Mary Godkin and Gabriel Edmonds survived their journey from County Wexford to Quebec. When their parents died at Quebec after arrival in the city, the seven children, ranging in age from ten to twenty-two, were placed in the care of the Anglican Church. The three eldest – Alice (twenty-two), Margaret (eighteen), and Richard (seventeen) – were placed in service in Quebec City. In 1851, Alice was single and living in a boarding house but working as a nurse. The rest of the family scattered, although Alice's younger sister Deborah, only twelve when they arrived in Quebec, remained in the region, and Alice served as a witness at her marriage in 1854.[90]

In a third set of cases, Anglican clergy behaved very much like their Catholic counterparts in taking a principal role in placing children. The one twist to their agency was that as married clergy, unlike Catholic priests, it appears that Anglican ministers were able to integrate Irish children into their own households. The Reverend C.B. Reid of the Anglican Mission of Compton, near Sherbrooke, welcomed twelve-year-old Margaret Kirkpatrick into his and his wife Julia's home. At forty and thirty-three years old respectively, the Reids were childless, and although Margaret was chosen to assist with domestic work, the Reids included her officially as a member of their family.[91] In a different type of agency, akin to Father LeBel in Rimouski, the Reverend Dr John Cook of Quebec City collected Mary, Robert, and Sarah Ann Killock and placed them with "respectable families" in his congregation.[92] Similarly, Anglican cleric the Reverend Clogston placed James and Jane Alexander, both under the age of five, within his parish. In these cases, and more, Anglican clergy had followed a similar pattern to that of Catholic priests in ensuring that the faith of the Protestant orphans was maintained by placing them with Protestant families.

Perhaps holding a similar fear of Catholic influence as his clergy, Bishop Mountain removed the Protestant orphans from Quebec City and placed them in the Montreal Protestant Orphan Asylum. Established in 1822, the Orphan Asylum was a private charity intended to relieve poverty in the city of Montreal and avoid Catholic proselytizing of Protestant orphans.[93] Controlled by the wealthy middle-class Protestants and Anglicans of the city, the Orphan Asylum was intended to serve a place from which poor children could be uplifted, educated, and become productive members of society. The idea that such homes were ideal for formal instruction was not unique in British North America. In neighbouring Canada West, in 1799 the legislature made formal provision for the education of orphans in homes or asylums as a means of "reducing Juvenile crime."[94] In the early years of the asylum, there was little placement out,[95] although it appears that this policy was modified when there was a massive influx of children because of Bishop Mountain's plan. Like the Charitable Catholic Ladies in Quebec, the Montreal asylum managers kept a careful ledger of the orphans admitted to the premises, which recorded vital data and the names of those with whom the orphans were placed. It is with this ledger that one can reconstruct the work of the Anglican Church with the hundred or so Protestant orphans.[96]

Protestant children in the Montreal Orphans Asylum experienced similar fates as did their Catholic counterparts elsewhere in Montreal or Quebec City. Ten of the sixty-nine children died in the asylum. The youngest was John Millar, who at four months old died about eight weeks into his stay. The oldest to die, Margaret Corson, was hardly a child at twenty-two years of age. Other children were sent out to service. Mary Anne and Nancy Corson, both more than twenty, were sent to Trois Rivières to work as servants. Other teens were sent as servants to Toronto and Kingston, which appeared to be in keeping with the asylum's plan of retaining the younger children for education and training. There were some exceptions to this rule as was the case of the three Pickering brothers, William (fourteen), Andrew (ten), and John (nine). They were the lone survivors of their family who sailed on the *John and Robert* from Liverpool in June 1847, a ship that witnessed only thirty-four fatalities, just slightly less than 10 per cent of its passengers.[97] Yet, somewhere between Grosse Ile and Montreal the Pickering brothers lost both parents and were sent to the Montreal Orphan Asylum on 4 September, almost a month after their arrival at Quebec. Census data from 1852, suggests that an older brother, Francis, had survived the voyage and established himself as a farmhand with the Wideman family in Markham township, north of Toronto.[98] Shortly thereafter, his younger brother Andrew Pickering was no longer at the Montreal Orphan Asylum and had also found himself at work on Wideman farm.[99] The two other brothers soon followed their elders to Canada West and settled in Peel and Simcoe Counties.[100] The case of the Pickering brothers suggests the orphans themselves devised a plan wherein the oldest would move to the interior and seek work, the younger siblings would bide their time in the asylum, and then leave to join the older brother when they had the opportunity.

The six Scott children were all received by the asylum on 11 June 1847, among the first vanguard of Bishop Mountain's orphans. The Scotts came from the parish of Annen, County Cavan, and travelled to Liverpool where they departed for Quebec on board the bark *Ajax* in April 1847. By the time the *Ajax* had reached Grosse Ile, 36 of its 239 passengers had died at sea, including the forty-six-year-old family matriarch, listed only as Mrs Scott in the Grosse Il death register.[101] The *Ajax* would lose fifty-one more passengers as it sat at the Grosse Ile quarantine station.[102] Among the dead was fifty-year-old Thomas Scott, who was buried in St John's Anglican Cemetery by none other than the Reverend Charles Forest, who would soon succumb to typhus himself.[103] The *Ajax* was in quarantine for twenty-two days, and it appears that the healthy Scott children were dispatched to Quebec before the ship itself was released.[104] The surviving orphans ranged from Robert Scott at two-and one-half years old to Elizabeth, who at thirteen was the eldest of the orphans. They remained at the asylum for more than a month, during which time Thomas, age eight and his father's namesake, died. They were eventually removed by an uncle who took them to Kingston. The events surrounding the fate of the Scotts, Pickerings, and Corsons confirm that once landed under the watchful eye of the Anglican Church, Protestant orphan children fit the emerging general pattern of keeping children healthy, busy, and put to good use; if death did not claim them first, they were subject to instruction, collection by a relative, or placement in some sort of service to make certain they became productive members of society.

Montreal was sweltering hot in the summer of 1847.[105] Despite a cold snap in early June[106] accompanied by torrents of rain[107] Canada's largest city was to move from chilling dampness to a heat wave which would make the journey of Irish families up the St Lawrence miserable. Montreal was also unprepared for the onslaught of migrants. The waterfront was strewn with refuse, piles of lumber, and thin wharves and planks upon which tired and sick migrants would have to navigate if they wanted to come ashore.[108] It was not surprising that several migrants, including children, drowned while disembarking or treading along the faulty dock-works on the shoreline. Worse, those who had been infected by typhus, but had not shown symptoms either at Grosse Ile or Quebec City, were now getting sick in Montreal. Locals complained that the Irish wandered through the town in the evenings, looking for food, shelter, or work, and failed to keep the appropriate distance from Montrealers.[109] As a result of such close contact and the infectious characteristics of typhus, the city now faced a crisis of epidemic proportions. By the end of the sailing season, in the autumn of 1847, the city had created a fever shed "town" at Point St Charles, to the southwest of the downtown core and there as many as 3,579 people and their first responders died.[110] Montrealers, like their colleagues in Quebec, preferred to move the Irish along as quickly as possible so that they might become some other centre's responsibility. During the week of 19 July for instance, of the 2,790 migrants who landed nearly 1,800 were moved on to destinations west and south of Montreal at the government's expense.[111]

It was at Point St Charles, however, where the local Catholic and Anglican Churches formed the first line of assistance for those who were too sick to travel. The Soeurs de Charité de Montreal, or Grey Nuns, were the vanguard of the first responders in the fever sheds. Founded in Montreal by Marguerite d'Youville in the eighteenth century, the Grey Nuns were dedicated teachers, health care providers, and social service workers who moved with care, self-sacrifice, and expertise among the poor and sick of the city. The Irish summer, however, provided them with one of their greatest challenges to date, and they offered gripping first-hand accounts of what they faced daily in the sheds assisting the Irish migrants. As early as 7 June, the annalist for the Greys noted, "Our Mother was immediately led by an employee of the office to the main hospital (if we can give it that name). GOOD GOD! What a spectacle. Hundreds of people, most of them lying naked on planks haphazardly, men, women and children, sick, moribund and cadavers; all of this confusion hit the eyes at once."[112]

By the end of June there were more than 1,300 people in the sheds and overcrowding at the General Hospital run by the Greys.[113] By the end of July there were more than 1,600 people in the sheds and 187 had died just in the week of 20–25 July.[114] The work of the nuns became well-known across the colonies with the Halifax Catholic weekly paper *The Cross* commenting: "The ravages of this Fever in Montreal have been very great, not only among the unfortunate Emigrants, but the clergy and nurses who have attended them ... There are at the present moment 48 nuns sick from exposure, fatigue, and the attacks of the disease."[115] As a result of their dedication to what they considered their sacred duty to be "hands to the needy," ten sisters died of typhus and other illnesses directly related to their service in 1847.[116] They were quite simply overwhelmed by the disease and death all around them and gravely concerned about the fate of hundreds of Irish children who were now left orphaned after losing their parents and relatives in the sheds.[117] The nuns and the priests working with them were fearful that Protestant workers might take hold of the Irish orphans and deprive them of their Catholic faith. According to the annalist:

> The venerable M. Jean Richards, filled with compassion upon seeing the fate of these little innocents, the number of which was considerably increasing, and fearing that the Protestants would seize them, did not rest until the Commissary agreed to build a SHED exclusively for CHILDREN. He put them all together and, like a good father, tended to their more urgent needs. Realizing that these children were almost naked and that we did not have anything to change them, he allows the SISTERS to clothe them using rags that belong to orphans from the seminary.[118]

Thus, the construction of a separate space for orphan children served essentially two purposes: to isolate them from the sick and dying adults in the sheds and to preserve their faith from Protestant proselytism. While Protestant co-workers with the nuns in the sheds were welcome, they were not entirely trusted.

The relief of Irish orphan children began with the work of the Grey Nuns but did not end there. Bishop Ignace Bourget became directly involved in the orphan relief effort when it became clear that the Greys, the medical staff, and clergy working at the sheds at Point St Charles were simply exhausted and some overcome by the fever themselves. On 24 June 1847, Bourget issued a pastoral letter to the Catholics of Montreal asking them to support a refuge for the Irish children left orphaned at Point St Charles. He took his inspiration from a similar project that had been initiated in Marseilles, France, during an earlier cholera epidemic.[119] With the knowledge that the Grey Nuns were sick and succumbing to exhaustion in the fever sheds, he invited the Sisters of Providence to relieve the Greys and prepare to host the new orphan asylum.[120] The Sisters of Providence were a new order of women religious, founded four years earlier by a widow, Emilie Tavernier Gamelin. Bourget secured a house on St Catherine Street owned by the "Widow" Nowlan, which was assumed by Mother Gamelin and her sisters.[121] On 11 July, Bourget, accompanied by the Sisters of Providence, went to Point St Charles and escorted "by hand" 150 orphan children, taking them through the downtown streets to the fledgling St Jerome Emilien Asylum, an institution named after the Catholic patron saint of orphans.[122] That night seven children died.[123] Within four years a hospital, St Patrick's, would be established beside the asylum to treat the orphans who were sick – and there were many. Bourget reported that many died after arriving at St Jerome. From July 1847 to March 1848, the Sisters of Providence took in at least 600 children, of whom 332 died and 188 were placed in what Bourget proudly claimed were "homes of honour and charity." In retrospect he declared it "one of the most touching moments of his life ... one that he would be unable to forget."[124] In a similar fashion as both the Charitable Ladies at Quebec and the Grey Nuns in Montreal, Mother Gamelin's sisters compiled a comprehensive register of names and origins of each child who entered St Jerome and their subsequent placement either with local families, parish priests who replicated the placement of children as had been done in the Archdiocese of Quebec, or transfer to yet another religious order.[125] Good records also assured Bourget and the nuns that the government was dutiful in its per capita financial support for the sick and orphaned.[126]

In the summer of 1847, the Sisters of Providence were inundated beyond their asylum's capacity by the numbers of children entering their care daily and by the high mortality rate of their residents. In an effort to relieve this pressure, they enlisted the support of a small and equally new order of women, the Sisters of the Good Shepherd, to care for many of the Irish girls.[127] Beginning 18 August 1847 The Sisters of the Good Shepherd initially accepted eighty-seven girls ranging in age from two to twenty years from the St Jerome asylum. A letter circulated from the community explained that up to 160 girls arrived at their convent and that the nuns had scrambled to wash and feed them, the observation being that all of them arrived in a wretched state. The simple ledger kept of at least eighty-seven survivors lists most of them as "suffering" and little else is recorded other than their age. There is evidence to suggest that some of the girls may have been Protestant. Fanny (fifteen) and Jane (thirteen) Wadsworth were among the first two orphans on the list. Jane would end up in Belleville, Canada West in 1852, working as a domestic servant in the residence of a Free Church clergyman and listing her own religion as Wesleyan.[128] While it appeared the sisters and clergy were anxious to isolate and protect Catholic children, there was less oversight of Protestant children getting into the mix. In addition to the support offered by the Sisters of the Good Shepherd, the St Jerome Asylum also enlisted the aid of the cloistered order of women the Hospitallers of St Joseph, who admitted the sick to their hospital and placed themselves at risk of contracting typhus.[129]

In pastoral letters published in the summer of 1847, Bourget summoned every Catholic group in the city to action to relieve the distressed Irish and the orphans left at the fever sheds. This complete mobilization of the Catholic

Church in Montreal during the famine migration was immortalized in a piece of art that still graces the ceiling of the Notre Dame de Bonsecours chapel on the Montreal waterfront. Bourget commissioned Theophile Hamel to paint a portrait featuring the work of the Church in aiding the diseased newcomers.[130] "Le Typhus" depicts the Grey Nuns, Sisters of Providence, the Sisters of the Good Shepherd, and Bourget as they try to bring relief to the migrants. The painting not only underscores the critical role played by the Church in refugee aid in Montreal but it may be the only painting of its time in Canada to commemorate the horrific result of the Irish Famine migration. Bourget wrote a separate pastoral letter on 13 August 1847, encouraging Catholics to go on pilgrimage to the Bonsecours Chapel and pray to the Blessed Virgin Mary for relief from these harrowing times.[131] While Bourget saw the epidemic as an opportunity to reinvigorate the faith in prayer, the Anglican newspaper *The Berean* regarded the reintroduction of the pilgrimage as another of Catholicism's "delusive puerilities."[132] For the devout Catholics, prayer was seen as a necessity. Before the season was over Bourget would be stricken with typhus but survived. The mayor of Montreal, J.E. Mills, eight priests, including Bourget's vicar general, and thirteen nuns were not so fortunate.[133]

The situation at Montreal was simply dire for all concerned and this did not escape the Irish press. A correspondent to the *Armagh Guardian* reflected on the situation vividly:

> All is consternation here. Those who recollect the visitation of cholera here some sixteen years since, pronounce that day terrible, but was light compared to the actual occurrences and heavy forebodings of the present. Such is the mortality among the people in the emigrant sheds, that coffins can with difficulty be got made to cover or hearses to carry away the dead. I have seen a wretched looking native of Ireland with the remains of his deceased relatives on his back carrying them to the place of sepulture. And women may often be observed bearing the bodies of their children to the grave, with perhaps no-one to assist at the internment ... Business is dull, the dearth and disease having a most blighting influence on the full trade.[134]

Given the reports of death and disease coming from Montreal, it is not surprising that some newspapers warned that the orphans who survived the sheds and asylums of Montreal were potential vectors of infection. In a not-so-subtle warning, the *British Whig* retold the story of a French Canadian family who had taken in an Irish orphan and then had all died of typhus.[135] Toronto's *British Colonist* repeated the story under the title "Imprudent Benevolence."[136]

Nevertheless, at "ground zero" of the epidemic, Point St Charles, the Grey Nuns were the front line of the Church's response to orphaned and abandoned children. In 1848, when reporting to Bishop Bourget about the events of the previous year in the sheds, Elizabeth Forbes McMullen, Superior of the Greys in Montreal, submitted a list of 102 names of children that the nuns had rescued from the sheds. The "McMullen list" is less detailed than the records from the Quebec City asylum but what information is presented offers an interesting comparison with both the efforts of the Catholic Church in Quebec City and the Anglican Church across the province. The origins of the Irish children reflected the patterns discovered elsewhere; most, about 60 per cent, of the children came from the Irish provinces of Munster and Leinster, with county Tipperary accounting for the largest groups of children, sixteen, from any single county. Ten children were unidentified, and one child had Upper Canada listed as his place of origin (table 3.6). The Grey Nuns also placed seven children with French Canadian families but more than three times that number with families bearing Irish and Scottish surnames, which was the opposite of the placement pattern at Quebec. Perhaps, Montreal's burgeoning pre-famine Irish population offered a greater opportunity for the nuns to place Irish children among their "own kind." At least twenty-four of the children were collected by surviving parents or extended family members, thus confirming that there were several definitions of orphan, and in some cases parents used the Church institutions as a stop gap measure for childcare when they were desperate.[137]

Through the agency of the Grey Nuns one also notices that the front-line sisters readily used other agencies of the Church to care for the children. The Greys had fifty-four children on McMullen's list sent to the St Jerome Emilien Orphanage, where the Sisters of Providence would care for their general needs, offer convalescence to the sick, and place the healthy with other families. Notable, however, is the case of nine-year-old Bridget Brown from Galway, who was sent directly to the "Grey Nunnery." The record is clear that her father died at Point St Charles and Bridget was removed from her dying mother. Similarly, fifteen-year-old Philip Riley, neither whose parents nor county of origin are accounted for in the records, was sent to the "Brothers of the Christian Doctrine" in Montreal. The Greys also released at least one child, twelve-year-old Andrew Carroll, of Queen's (Laois) County, into the hands of a local parish priest, Father Kearen, who presumably did what his colleagues in the

Archdiocese of Quebec had done – placed the child with a family within his parish who had requested help.[138]

The pattern of Church institutions favouring other Church institutions for orphan placement was repeated once children arrived at St Jerome Emilien Asylum. The Sisters of Providence had at least 220 healthy or convalesced Irish children in their care in 1847, according to their ledgers. The Sisters sent twelve young girls to the Sisters of the Good Shepherd in Montreal and three more to a group of sisters at Longeuil. At least five more girls were retained at the Maison Providence, several of whom were identified in the 1851 census as having become domestic servants. Ten-year-old Anne Gaugher was the only girl placed with the Sisters of the Sacred Heart.[139] The placement of young girls in the care of other religious houses appeared to be entirely random, with age and presence of siblings not seeming to be relevant factors. The only coincidence is that all were moved from one institution or another on the same date, indicating that the placement was probably triggered more by a lack of capacity at St Jerome's than by any overarching plan. The same might be said of the twelve boys who, on 4 April 1848, were placed by the sisters in the Collège de Montréal. The Irish boys ranged in age from eight to fifteen years, indicating that they were of school age, but not destined for a single class, where there may have been a shortage. The Sulpician-run College was one of the finest Catholic boys' schools in the province, which had produced the likes of contemporary politicians George-Etienne Cartier and Louis-Hippolyte Lafontaine and Toronto's Bishop Michael Power.[140]

As a Francophone religious order, it is not surprising that almost all the placements of children by the Sisters of Providence were among Francophone laypersons. Perhaps the Greys with Elizabeth McMullen at the helm were more inclined to find Irish matches for Irish children. This is not to imply any neglect on the part of the Sisters of Providence because their acceptable placements included medical doctors, notaries, merchants, artisans, and farmers who lived outside of Montreal. Orphaned Ellen McMulty found herself on her way to Boucherville, for example, to take up residence with Dr J. Phénéas Proulx, the local physician. Proulx himself had also taken in fourteen-year-old John McCormick.[141] By far the most frequent agents of placement, as permitted by the Sisters of Providence, were two priests, Father Calixte Marquis of Béconcour, to the east of Montreal, and Jesuit priest Rémi-Joseph Tellier. Tellier had been one of the original members of the Society of Jesus, recruited by Bourget for his diocese. At the time of the massive migration, Tellier was the pastor of LaPrairie, the epicentre of early Jesuit activity in the diocese, hugging the shore of the south bank of the St Lawrence River, just across from Montreal. Tellier crossed the river frequently and became one of the priests who assisted the Grey Nuns at Point St Charles.[142] In the process he made frequent visits to St Jerome's and arranged for the placement of at least eight girls and ten boys, in private homes, schools, and local farms. Joseph-Calixte Marquis, however, was a curate in the parish of Bécancour, near Nicolet, and in November 1847 he brought ten children from St Jerome's to his home parish, although his total placements may have been as high as thirty-three.[143] Notable in Marquis's efforts were his ability to relocate siblings to his parish. The Cuthbert brothers, William (nine), Robert (seven), and James (four) were taken to Bécancour. In 1852, all three brothers were working on different farms, those of the Theriaults, Provenchers, and Crouteaus respectively; none of the boys was considered a family member, but like their fellow orphans in Rimouski, all were working for their keep and were in physical proximity to one another.[144]

The proximity of Montreal to major transportation routes to Canada West, New York State, and Vermont witnessed orphans travelling beyond the reach of the local churches. At least twenty-eight children were collected by family members from the Grey Nuns and transported to Canada West (Upper Canada), various centres in New York, Massachusetts, and Pennsylvania. Similarly, there were cases of children in the care of the Anglicans being sent to relatives outside of the province. Ann and Mary Hanton, for example, were collected by their father after their arrival in Bishop Mountain's group and then proceeded to Upper Canada.[145] Bartholemew Furlong (nine), his older brother James (thirteen) and sister Margaret were orphaned at Point St Charles after the deaths of their mother Mary Freeman and father Thomas Furlong. Natives of county Wexford, their uncle Harold Kennedy collected them and put them to work as labourers and servants on his farm in Lochiel, County Glengarry.[146] The cases of the Furlong and Hanton children underscore once again that the Montreal experience of the orphans reveals some aspects of emigrant agency, beyond families using the Church as a convenient childcare provider. Many Irish families who were fleeing the famine had some contact with relatives and friends who had already settled or were sojourning in British North America or the United States. Much like the Strokestown assisted migrants, other Irish travellers had a sense of where the opportunity was in Canada West, and, if they survived, they were intent to recreate their lives there. For those who had family on the frontier or in Canadian towns,

Table 3.6
Irish Catholic orphans in Montreal, 1847–48 (N=501)

Institution	Tracked	Dead	Not known	Total	French placement	Irish placement	Church placement	Not known
Grey Nuns*	21	1	47	69	7	22	3	37
St Jerome Females	28	1	90	119	62	22	35	0
St JeromeMales	47	0	54	101	63	20	17	1
S de BP	8	0	79	87				
Anglican	25	4	96	125	0	12	71**	32
Total				501	132	64	55	38

Source: The Canada Gazette, no. 345, Montreal, Saturday, 6 May 1848; APM, M 6 Registre des orphelins du typhus et Chroniques Hospice St-Jérôme-Emilien et Hôpital Saint-Patrice, 1847–52; AAM, Fonds Bourget, 525.103, 848-2. Category of the Orphans at Point St Charles, 12 March 1848; ASBP, "Names of the Orphan Children Entrusted to the Care of the Ladies of the Good Pastor, Montreal, 18 August 1847."

*The fifty-four transfers from the Grey Nuns to the Sisters of Providence are calibrated in the figures for St Jerome Emilien Asylum.

**Most (sixty-six) in the Montreal Protestant Orphans Asylum.

the children of those Irish refugees who died on route, continued their journey to a new life, once they were collected by aunts, uncles, older siblings, or family friends.

Not all experiences of the Irish children were the same. Orphans living in the St Jerome's Asylum seemed less likely to be picked up be extended family or travel beyond the Montreal region. Perhaps because they had already been triaged at Point St Charles and counted themselves among the truly alone or as Bourget might describe as children "relegated to a strange land, without parents, without friends, and ... reduced as well to horrible misery."[147] The exception were five young boys, ranging in age from eight to fifteen, who were collected by three Irish and two French Canadian farmers and taken up the Ottawa River to live on farms in Eardley Township, near Aylmer. Such placements merely confirmed the widespread demand for boys to engage in farm work, as had been the case with Daniel Tighe in Lotbinière or George Cox in St Luce. But Tighe's case was truly exceptional among the hundreds of orphans cast on Canada's shores. His lot was not that of a day labourer, tavern helper, domestic servant, apprentice, or farm hand. He did not move about searching for new work, a new country, or untraceable family members. His long journey from Lissonuffy ended at Lotbinière with a family, an inheritance, and a legacy. For other orphans, their Canadian journey was just beginning.

4

Catholic Orphans in Protestant Towns

Patrick Cox may have thought he was an orphan, but he was not. In May 1847, Patrick, his "widowed" mother Susan, and his six siblings set out from the townland of Culliagh[1] in the Parish of Bumlin and joined 270 other families from the estate of Major Denis Mahon of Strokestown on a journey that they hoped would bring them to a new life, free from hunger and disease, in Canada. During a harrowing voyage on board the *Virginius*,[2] Patrick Cox had taken ill, and local medical authorities removed him from his ship to the fever sheds at Grosse Ile with the hope that after his recovery he might eventually catch up to the rest of his family as they moved to the interior of Canada. In September, after almost two months had passed since his last sighting, Patrick's nearly frantic mother posted a notice in a local paper requesting any information about her son and directing any correspondence to Hamilton, Canada West, where the family was staying.[3] The Cox's were now over 900 kilometres to the west of where they last laid eyes on Patrick.

For his part, Patrick was alone and had to trust the officials that led him on to the steamer *St George* that his family had moved to the west, possibly beyond Montreal to a province they called Upper Canada. This made sense to him since that province had been the intended destination that Major Mahon's migrants had hoped might be their new home.[4] Whether someone had read the notice somewhere along his journey through Montreal, Kingston, and Toronto remains to be seen. What is entirely possible is that Upper Canadians merely assumed that this wandering Irish waif was just one more of the Catholic Irish orphans that had come flooding into their province during

Black '47. Patrick Cox might well have been an object of suspicion and derision: he was without parental guardianship, a Catholic in a Protestant province, an Irish refugee, and a potential vector of disease.

The efforts made to assist Irish orphans by both civil and ecclesiastical authorities in Canada East were not easily replicated in Canada West. The two provinces that had been fused into a single Province of Canada in 1841, differed in many ways, particularly in their linguistic, cultural, and religious composition. Whereas the Catholic Church became the dominant agent of orphan assistance in Canada East because of its social position in a predominantly Catholic society, it was not a given that the Protestant churches that dominated Canada West would enthusiastically rally to the aid of the large numbers of Irish Catholic orphans now emerging from the wharfs and fever sheds in the province's major towns.

Moreover, Catholics themselves might be concerned, as the Church had been in Quebec, that any Protestant advances might be for the purposes of proselytizing – in effect "offering the soup" to unsuspecting Catholic children. The question posed here is what happened to hundreds of Irish Catholic orphan children in other parts of British North America, where the Catholic Church was weak in terms of population, embryonic in terms of its infrastructure, and overshadowed by the dominance of Protestant churches in civic life. In 1847, in Canada West, Irish orphan children became an urgent public concern particularly in predominantly Protestant towns such as Hamilton, Kingston, and Toronto. Except for Bytown (now Ottawa), northwest of Montreal, none of these Canada West towns had a significant Catholic presence, as had been the case in Quebec and Montreal. While the Catholic Church in each of these cities had at least one church building and one or more separate schools, and in the case of Toronto and Kingston, bishops, Catholics possessed neither the influence politically nor socially when compared to the Church in Canada East, nor had Catholics a very highly developed institutional network to care for the numbers of Irish refugees and orphans as had Catholics in Montreal or Quebec City. This being the case, the burning question is what was to become of Catholic orphan children in Protestant towns, when the civic administration and provincial governments were overwhelmingly dominated by Protestants and, at times, officials with a profound anti-Catholic bias.

There is no simple answer to this question given the interplay of the churches in each of these colonial towns. Not surprisingly, Protestant churches would be active in placing the minority Protestant children, a precedent set by the Anglican Church in Quebec and Montreal under the leadership of Bishop George Mountain, which had taken responsibility for at least 6 per cent of the orphans who were Protestant.[5] As has been discussed, the Protestant community in Montreal established a Protestant Orphans' Asylum from which more than one hundred Protestant children were distributed to farms and business through a well-organized network of Anglican clergy.[6] Protestant Irish orphans in Montreal were sheltered in trusted Protestant homes, just as hundreds of Irish Catholic children were cared for and disbursed by the women's religious orders who placed the children in "good" Catholic homes.[7] This "Montreal" model appears to have been straight forward – each denomination took care of their own to assure the lasting faith of their children and resistance to placement where a child might be proselytized by the "other" religious group. The sheer numbers of Catholics in Canada East, supported by a powerful ecclesiastical infrastructure, assured Church leaders that there would be no apostasy of the young on their watch. Similarly, the Anglican Church, which despite its minority position in the province, was the "established" church, whose programs would be protected by the state. Outside of Canada East, however, it remains problematic as to how magnanimous Protestant towns would be in receiving hundreds of Catholic children, who were arriving under such troubling circumstances.

Close examination of the public and private records of the period, however, suggests that the Catholic Church worked cooperatively with local Protestant clergy, volunteers, civic officials, and first responders. Success in this inter-denominational concordat would depend on at least four factors from the Catholic perspective: firstly, the prominence and energy of the local Catholic bishop; secondly, the willing intervention of the local Catholic clergy, as had been the case in Quebec; thirdly, the presence of a women's religious order that was active in social service and health care; and, finally, an active, cooperative, and energetic cadre of local lay Catholic leaders. When most of these factors were in play, the Catholic Church was able to negotiate with Protestant civic leaders and heads of charitable institutions and direct the type of assistance and placement received by Catholic children. Without such a proactive approach with willing and cooperative Protestant leaders, the outcome for the Irish Catholic orphans would have been very different, as one might soon witness in Saint John, New Brunswick. Such co-operation in Canada West, however, did mask a fear of proselytism by the other, which did keep Catholics and Protestants on their guard, fearing the worst for "their children" should they not be fully engaged in relief efforts.[8]

Table 4.1
Orphan placement in Bytown, 1847
(N=56)

	Male	Female	Infant	Total	
Placed with mother or father	1	2	0	3	5.4%
Placed with relative	1	1	0	2	3.6%
Left on own	1	4	0	5	8.9%
Placed with French Canadian	16	19	0	35	62.5%
Placed with Irish Canadian	0	0	0	0	0.0%
Died in hospital	2	7	2	11	19.6%
Total	24	37	2	56	100.00%

Source: City of Ottawa Archives, Sisters of Charity (Grey Nuns), General Hospital Ledger, Bytown, 1847.

The citizens of Upper Canada, as Canada West was still known colloquially, were aware of the events transpiring in Ireland and Montreal, and on Grosse Ile and the high seas. Each of the major weekly and bi-weekly newspapers in the province carried Irish news directly from Irish and British newspapers, and they were updated on the events unfolding at Grosse Ile and Montreal from the major weeklies in those centres. Each week the *British Whig* (Kingston), *The British Colonist*, (Toronto), *The Globe*, (Toronto), *The Hamilton Gazette* and the *St Catharine's Journal*, among other news media, kept the literate population informed of the refugee tragedy unfolding all around them. In majors cities and towns, collections had been made for Irish famine relief, particularly among Irish expatriates. Churches, both Catholic and Protestant, took up relief for both Irish and the Highland Scots, who were also suffering from famine conditions. Donors also included Anishinaabe and Haudenosaunee peoples who donated to famine relief from their government annuities.[9] Upper Canadian Catholic were often directly in contact with Archbishop Daniel Murray of Dublin, who distributed Canadian monetary aid from Bytown, Kingston, and Richmond to his needy parishes across his archdiocese.[10] Even in the wild recesses of the upper Ottawa Valley, Father John McNulty, the missionary priest assigned to Mount St Patrick, collected funds from farmers, shanty men, lumberjacks, and parishioners throughout the Madawaska Valley. Donations ranging from nearly £30 to a mere few pence and shillings,[11] were gathered by the priest and then sent to Archbishop John McHale of Tuam, Ireland.[12] Nevertheless, such foreknowledge on behalf of Upper Canadian churchmen and civic officials did not necessarily translate into adequate local preparations to meet immigrant demand. As Irish refugees flooded into Canada West by June 1847, Provincial Secretary Dominick Daly would be inundated with requests for financial support for fledgling hospitals, sheds, and relief for widows and orphans.[13]

When Irish survivors of the sheds of Montreal moved farther into the interior, one of their options was to head up the Ottawa River towards Bytown (Ottawa) and beyond to the timber shanties and potential farmlands of the upper Ottawa Valley. In Bytown, Irish Catholic migrants would find that there was a rough infrastructure in place, with several active parishes in the vicinity and a group of Grey Nuns from Montreal under the leadership of Mother Élisabeth Bruyère who was only twenty-nine years old at the time. The Bytown area remained one of the largest Catholic enclaves in Upper Canada, where, according to Bishop Michael Power of Toronto, in 1847 6,662 of the total population of 8,100 inhabitants were Roman Catholic. He reported to Rome that this large Catholic proportion was bound to increase with the rise in Irish migration to the Ottawa Valley.[14] In June of that year Pope Pius IX created the Diocese of Bytown to respond to this growing need. Thus, Irish Catholics found themselves in a town dominated by an Anglo-Protestant elite but also where the Catholic Church constituted one of the largest Christian denominations and the only religious group for which an established health and social service infrastructure was operated by Catholic women religious.

The famine moment in Bytown, however, was characterized by co-operation between civic and religious leaders, Protestant and Catholic. Mother Bruyère and the Grey Nuns worked closely with local priest Father Antoine Adrien Telmond, OMI, chief medical officer Dr Edward Van Courtland, and emigrant agent G.R. Burke to accommodate the massive flow of Irish migrants disembarking at Bytown. During Black '47 the Grey's hospital accommodated 600 patients, at least 125 of whom succumbed to typhus.[15] Sixteen of twenty sisters serving there also contracted the disease, two young postulants very seriously, but none died.[16] According to Bruyère, they were simply overwhelmed and there were fears that the fever sheds on Barracks Hill were dangerous and perhaps too close to the sisters' main site of operations. Although now formally independent of the mother house in Montreal, Bruyère confided in Mother Elizabeth McMullen, the Grey Nuns' superior there, that she feared the spread of the contagion to their school, and it was hoped that the sick could be better isolated from the healthy. "Priez ma bonne Mère," wrote Bruyère, "pour cette bonne oeuvre ne nous échappe pas."[17]

The Grey Nuns also created an orphanage in their convent-hospital, accommodating just under sixty orphans in 1847.[18] Bruyère's sisters used the hospital as the principal site of orphan placement, especially for local French Canadian families who needed a young Irish boy or girl for domestic service or farm labour. Lacking in space, the sisters sought out local Catholic families where the healthy children might board until such time as they were placed or collected by relatives. Bruyère's initiatives to assist Irish orphans comes as no surprise, given that she herself was virtually orphaned when her father, Charles Bruguier, died at sea, and she looked after her two younger brothers when her mother went out to work.[19] In fact, one of Bruyère's first tasks after taking vows was the supervision of the Grey Nuns' Montreal orphanage.

The fate of the Irish orphans in Bytown demonstrates some strong similarities with those practices already in play for the children cared for by the churches in Lower Canada. Bytown, however, lacked the same procedures as other centres in separating Protestant from Catholic children. Of the fifty-six children who landed at the Grey Nuns' facilities in Bytown, only three were registered as Protestants, demonstrating both the overwhelming Catholic character of the migration and its orphans and that local Protestants, lacking in their own facilities, depended on the generosity of the Greys to admit all children, regardless of creed. As had been the case in Lower Canadian orphan asylums, however, the term orphan held many meanings; the sisters returned at least five children to family members, including mothers and fathers. Mortality rates were also very high, as had been the case in Quebec and Montreal, with close to one in five children dying while in the care of the sisters.

The one striking characteristic of the Bytown orphans, however, was that despite the high number of pre-famine Irish inhabiting the Ottawa Valley, none came forward to assist in "taking" in an orphan. The placements were entirely within French Canadian homes but limited to only five families. A certain Madame Labreche, for example, took twenty, or more than one third of the children. While there are no records surviving to substantiate the possibility that she kept them all, one suspects that she became an intermediary for the further distribution of the children in the community. Thus, it is possible that lay Catholic French Canadian women imitated the practices of clergy in Quebec by serving as the intermediaries between the Grey Nuns at the hospital and potential families for orphan placement. On 1 July, Mary McGuire and three of her siblings would have none of this. Identified as motherless, the eleven-year-old Mary likely took her younger siblings – Margaret (five), James (five), and Bridget (eight) – and simply left the home of Pierre Lavallee, where the sisters had boarded them, in an attempt to find their father.[20] There is no evidence suggesting they were successful in their search. Mary returned to Bytown alone, six weeks later, on 15 August but remained only two months before she left again and disappeared into history.

With poor census records for Bytown, for 1851–52, it is very difficult to determine what happened to these children. None of the French Canadian patrons who removed them from Mother Bruyère's care appear in existing census data for counties on either side of the Ottawa River. The search for these children is not helped by the fact that the Grey Nuns' hospital records for Bytown do not include such details as parents' names or Irish counties of origin. While lists at Quebec covered this data, including the names of ships that transported the Irish children earlier in the season, such information was not deemed relevant by local Canadians once Irish emigrants had ventured deep into the interior of Canada. The case of Philip Cahill (thirteen) does offer some clues. He had been admitted to the Grey Nuns' hospital on 2 September 1847 with his ten-year-old sister Catherine. By October both Philip and Catherine were placed in the care of Madame Perrault. There is no existing record for Catherine after that point, although in 1852 Philip appeared to have moved to Bagot Township, up the Ottawa Valley in Renfrew County, where he was apprenticing as a blacksmith with John Wilson. Cahill seemed to have landed within a Catholic enclave in the township and was learning a valuable trade on the frontier.[21] While Cahill provides only one case out of the forty-five children who survived Bytown Hospital, it does confirm patterns that orphan children may have had sufficient agency to seek out other Irish settlers and co-religionists and find work.

Bytown was only one point of refuge for Irish migrants after they left Lower Canada. On the route due west of Montreal, most Irish migrants would travel by steamship or Durham boat from Lachine to the St Lawrence River towns of Cornwall, Prescott, and Brockville. Each of these centres had boards of health and small hospitals run by doctors or by the local constabulary (police boards), but there are few records identifying the presence of Irish orphans left in those small towns.[22] The first major port of disembarkation in Canada West was Kingston, which was about a thirty-hour steamship trip from Montreal.[23] Between 1841 and 1844, it had been the capital of the new United Province of Canada, and it had benefited from an infusion of new residents connected with the legislature and civil service, new housing, roadwork, drainage systems, and capital.[24] Kingston was already the dominant agricultural market town, and its position as the gateway to the Great Lakes made it an important centre for steamships, shipbuilding, and the ancillary industries that accompany a thriving port. In 1847, Kingston would also be connected by telegraph service linking Queenston on the Niagara frontier and Montreal, revolutionizing regional communications.[25] Kingston was also served by the military garrison at Fort Henry, Canada's chief interior defensive work against a possible invasion from the United States. Although there had been a modest economic downturn, when the capital was moved to Montreal for the 1845 sessions of the legislature, "the Limestone City," with a population of nearly 10,000 in the late 1840s,[26] remained Canada West's second city, to Toronto, and the economic hub of the eastern section of what would eventually become Ontario in 1867.

In 1847, however, Kingston was overwhelmed by famine refugees, who had survived both the voyage and the deadly quarantines stations of Grosse Ile, Quebec City, and Point St Charles in Montreal. By 19 June 1847, one thousand Irish migrants had already arrived at the port, and local civic authorities scrambled to deal with the crush of sick and destitute migrants.[27] By year's end, it is likely that as many as 70,000 migrants passed through this eastern Lake Ontario port,[28] with estimates ranging between 1,200 and 1,500 for those who died in the sheds constructed at King and Emily Streets. The rector of St Mary's Cathedral recorded that its priests buried 1,234 persons that year, 989 of which were immigrants, of whom 289 were children.[29] Many migrants unknowingly carried typhus, which killed more than half the people who contracted it because medical officials were helpless to treat it effectively. The infection did not demonstrate symptoms for about ten days, during which time a carrier could look perfectly normal, avoiding most quarantine stations in Montreal.[30] At Kingston, the migrants were allowed to land at Brewer's Wharf, with the sick being moved to facilities operated by the Female Benevolent Society, which would eventually become the Kingston General Hospital, or to the overflow fever sheds located close to downtown at King and Emily Streets.[31] The healthy, or seemingly healthy, were quickly moved by water to ports farther west: Cobourg, Port Hope, Whitby (Port Windsor), and Toronto.[32] By October 1847, the numbers of newcomers to Kingston increased to crisis proportions, when the emigration agent for Canada West, Anthony B. Hawke, ordered that all migrants sheltered in Bytown, Prescott, Brockville, and Cornwall be accommodated in Kingston for the winter.[33]

The crowding of Kingston throughout 1847 demanded that religious communities work together. Roman Catholics in Kingston were well established and had forged a good working relationship with the town's Presbyterian mayor, Thomas Kirkpatrick. While there was some vocal resentment by locals to this massive Catholic migration, and the subsequent sights and odours of the fever sheds in the downtown area should not be underestimated,[34] the Catholic Church and Protestant civic and religious officials and volunteers worked together in a co-operative manner. The Catholic Church had been a fixture of the town since 1808 when Father Alexander Macdonell, the demobilized chaplain of the Glengarry Fencibles, established the first parish, St Joseph's.[35] In 1826, Macdonell, a fierce imperialist and Tory, was appointed the first Catholic bishop of Upper Canada and promoted the respectability of his Catholic flock.[36] After the rebellions of 1837–38, during which he publicly opposed William Lyon MacKenzie's rebels, the local Orange Lodges drank to his health.[37] His successor bishops, the sickly Remi Gaulin (1841) and coadjutor Patrick Phelan (1843) energetically expanded the Church's infrastructure in Kingston, including an invitation, in 1845, to the Religious Hospitallers of St Joseph (RHSJ), to establish a hospital, in Kingston.[38] Although cloistered and French-speaking from Montreal, the sisters successfully petitioned Phelan to allow them semi-cloistered status so that they could do their medical work more effectively within the community.[39]

In 1847, when Irish migrants flooded the port, the Hotel Dieu Hospital was still in need of a roof on its men's wing. During the crisis, the Protestant Female Benevolent Society, the board of health, and Mayor Kirkpatrick formed a partnership with the sisters, which allowed for materials support, food, and patient transfers between the Hotel Dieu and the fledgling predecessor to the Kingston General Hospital.[40] This co-operation included daily visits by the sisters to what they termed "the English Hospital" for supplies or to pick up Catholic children who had arrived at that facility.[41] The sisters also accepted aid from Miss Burnet, the daughter of a local Protestant minister, who generously delivered linens to the Hotel Dieu.[42] Facing this new crisis, the provincial government offered a subsidy of £1 per month per child to those institutions willing to open their doors to the great numbers of children who appeared orphaned in the local fever sheds.[43] Orphans were accommodated by the sisters prior to 1847, but local clergy ventured to the sheds and gathered up Irish children, who were eventually joined by other orphaned children, some of whom had been at the Kingston General Hospital. On Christmas Eve, 1847 Monsignor Angus Macdonell, nephew to the deceased bishop, delivered seventy-one more children to the sisters' makeshift orphanage facility. As the RHSJ annalist wrote, Macdonell did so "to save the poor children from misery and the danger they were in of losing their souls."[44] Such a statement reveals the concern the Church had for both the physical welfare of the Irish orphans and for the possibility that they might fall into the wrong hands in a Protestant town.

Even by the sisters' own admission, what greeted the children at the Hotel Dieu that evening was less satisfactory than hoped. The annalist commented that "Misery was depicted on the countenance of these poor little unfortunates several of whom had been sick and very much neglected or rather abandoned."[45] The walls of the institution were still un-plastered and there were less than half as many beds as would be needed by the seventy-one children. They also admitted that the beds were full of vermin. There was not even a sufficient eating facility as they gathered the children to eat their Christmas Eve supper. The sisters erected a makeshift table consisting of two barrels supporting a collection of loose boards from a bed. The annalist continues:

> The children had to sit down on the floor around the stove, they were chilled with cold and we served them by rows, as we had not sufficient dishes to serve them all at once, for the little girls, we got the dishes from the orphan girls ward, whom we had before the Emigrants came, and took the top of a bed, otherwise set on trestles for a table.[46]

The seventy-one children formed seven rows of ten to match the seven bowls, plates, and flatware made available to them. As one ate and cleaned the dishes, the next one took his/her place and shared the Christmas feast. After all the children had eaten, they retired to the ward, two and three to a bed, although the annalist commented that the sisters "were very sorry to put them in such disgusting beds."[47]

After Christmas, the sisters were in close contact with Protestant women in the community, who assisted in improving the conditions in the makeshift orphanage. The annalist reported that local women offered to sew new clothes for the children. The superior, Mother Amable Bourbonnière, evidently talented with a needle, worked throughout the night of Boxing Day (the Feast of St Stephen) to repair and remake clothing for the little girls, who comprised about half of the new batch of orphans. Several of the boys were reported to have been covered with scabs, but "they were hardly recognizable after they were better and were cleaned up." Mother Bourbonnière, whose talents also extended to pharmacology, prepared an ointment that proved effective on the sores and scabs.[48] Underscoring this entire effort at the Hotel Dieu was the co-operative spirit exemplified by the RHSJ and the leading Protestant women in Kingston. While the sisters might fear for the mortal souls of the children, they were very willing to accept the donations of food, clothing, and medicine provided by the Protestant women at the General Hospital.

Although the hospital sisters kept careful records of each child and their eventual placement, the census of 1851–52 is missing for Kingston and several surrounding townships and so one can only glean an incomplete picture of their placement. By mid-1848, most of the thirty-seven boys and thirty-four girls in the care of the RHSJ had been collected by distant relatives, immediate family members, or local families who were generous enough to open their homes and put the able-bodied children to work. Of the sixteen children that could be tracked in 1851–52, it appeared all were placed in Catholic homes, including ten with their own parents or family members. Although the census cannot confirm it, the sisters reported that at least two children were placed in Catholic rectories by the Catholic priests serving in Tyendinaga Township, near Belleville, and Camden, northwest of Kingston. This placement strategy seems consistent with the RHSJ's ongoing efforts to make sure that the Catholic faith of these Irish children was preserved; until placement, the orphan regimen consisted of regular confessions, Sunday mass, catechism classes, and visits to St Mary's Cathedral.[49] As for the orphans remaining at the General Hospital, no records survive. At the House of Industry, the fifty-seven Anglican orphans were accommodated by the local Anglican Church, with the rest, mostly Catholic, placed with local farmers or at the Kingston General Hospital.[50] For now, the paper trail ends there.

The curious result of the analysis (table 4.2) brings into question, once again, the very definition of what an orphan might be. As was discovered in the case of the Quebec orphans, there were really several characteristics of one's status as an orphan: a child without both parents; a child from a single parent family; a child with both parents still living but unable to care for them.[51] The ledger of the Religious Hospitallers at the Hotel Dieu reveals all three. In fact, among the children who were placed in the orphanage in 1847, at least half had parents who picked them up to continue the family journey in 1848. The ledger offers yet another twist on potential reasons for depositing children with the sisters. The orphanage itself appeared to serve as a temporary agency of care for destitute Irish families; when one or both parents could not nourish or care for their own children, they left them with the sisters in the autumn. In the spring, when the waterways and transportation routes were clear, when there appeared to be better prospects for employment, or when a parent had earned enough money to sustain the family unit, they simply returned to the Hotel Dieu to pick up their children. While this defies a common understanding of what an orphan is, this pattern of parental behaviour, at least in the Kingston area, suggests a higher degree of immigrant agency than has been recognized by scholars in the past. Similar practices were witnessed in Montreal and Quebec, where orphanages often became convenient short-term care agencies for impoverished parents.[52] Irish refugees recognized that they could not keep their families intact, in the short term, but relied on the infrastructures of the Church to serve *in loco parentis* until such time as surviving parents had the means to reunite their families.

Although half the children were placed with their parents, at least a third of the orphans, with both parents dead, were placed with local families in the Kingston area. Unfortunately, the sisters never did follow-up reports to ascertain how these children fared in their new "homes." The fragments of the census give a tiny glimpse as to where some of these children went and how they may have worked. Again, the sisters were careful to place the children in Catholic homes. Such was the placement of fifteen-year-old Patrick Grady in the Kingston home of Mr Cole, a Catholic. Grady remained in Kingston, working as a servant until his death in September 1856.[53] Patrick Flannigan, who was only eight years old, spent close to ten months with the sisters at the Hotel Dieu, until a widow, Anne Redmond, collected him to become part of her household in Northumberland County. In 1852, Patrick was still living with Mrs Redmond, her merchant son G.W. Redmond, his wife, and an "Irish girl," Mary Burke. While no occupation was listed for Patrick, he was not considered a family member so one suspects that, like other orphans, he was doing manual labour around the property.[54] Mary Ryan, who entered the Hotel Dieu among Father Macdonell's children that fateful Christmas eve, was collected at age six, nine months later, by a Mrs Hughes, who lived on Long Island, outside of Kingston. She remained in Kingston for fifteen years, working in 1861 as a hotel keeper for James Church.[55] Each case indicates that the sisters followed closely the practice of "placement" either with parents, extended family, and local Catholics. There is some evidence to suggest that the sisters may have had little choice in the matter.

The provincial government encouraged Kingston civic and religious leaders to place Irish orphans in good homes, as had been done in Quebec. With the sisters still trying to improve their hospital and orphanage facilities during the height of the refugee crisis, Bishop Patrick Phelan had requested that the Canadian government grant a regular allowance to the Hotel Dieu. He had heard that the government was remitting £500 to the City of Kingston for the

Table 4.2
Catholic children at the Hotel Dieu and their dispersal
(N=71)

Nature of placement	Number	Percentage	Traceable in census	Rural	Urban	Unknown destination
Placed with parents	36	50.7	8	7	1	28
Placed with sibling	3	4.2	1	0	1	2
Placed with relative	3	4.2	1	0	1	2
Died before placement	3	4.2	NA	NA	NA	NA
Placed with others	24	33.8	3	2	1	21
Runaway	2	2.8	NA	NA	NA	NA
Total	71	100.0		9	4	53

Source: RHSJ Archives, Register of Hotel Dieu Orphans, 24 December 1847; Library and Archives Canada, Census of Canada, Canada West, 1851–52. Online version.

care of the sick. The Hospitaller Sisters, Phelan argued, had cared for at least 144 patients and numerous orphans at a cost of more than £167 for which they had not been reimbursed. Moreover, the Sisters of Charity (Grey Nuns) of Montreal had been compensated per orphan accommodated during the crisis. The government refused.[56] Instead, Dominick Daly, the provincial secretary was quite clear in his directive to Bishop Phelan that orphans might be distributed to "families through the country ... as has been done in the Lower Province where a great number of orphans have been satisfactorily provided for in a way with little or no cost to the govt [sic]."[57] The following day Daly reiterated this position to the board of health when he asked for a report on the number of orphans in Kingston, including their ages, while suggesting that "country families" would take "the elder ones for their services in the same manner as has been done in Quebec, where a great number of them have been distributed to the neighbouring villages with little or no cost to the Government."[58] In other words, the government was unwilling to underwrite the costs of keeping Irish orphan children, if it could be done more cheaply by citizens themselves. Orphan placement had simply become a frugal and practical, if not parsimonious, government policy.

Some of the pressure on the overcrowding of the Hotel Dieu and the General Hospital was relieved when the City of Kingston opened its House of Industry in December 1847. With the consolidation of immigrant centres in the eastern region of Canada West at Kingston and the subsequent influx of Irish refugees it was important that that the long-discussed widow and orphans refuge be established.[59] On opening, the house admitted 144 migrants, mostly widows, children, and single men. By July 1848, it had housed 317 inmates, most of whom, 264 persons, were registered as Catholics (see table 4.3).[60] The fragments of the Irish families resident in the house had origins in many Irish counties but particularly from the counties of the provinces of Munster and Connaught, which mirrors the general famine migration patterns for 1847. The register kept by the House of Industry indicates that the guardians of the house followed the recommended pattern of letting older children and young adults be placed with local farmers and businesses. This was not always successful. In March 1848, fourteen-year-old James Mannion, an orphan from County Roscommon, refused to be placed with a local farmer and remained in the home. Some children, as has been witnessed at the Hotel Dieu, were collected by their parents in the spring of 1848, once gain underscoring the way Irish migrants used public and private institutions for childcare until the family was ready to move on.[61] Thus, those children who were suspected to be orphans were simply half-orphans, with at least one parent alive to collect them. A third type of departure from the house was characterized by a single mother taking the remnants of her family and simply moving on to the United States, which was not far from Kingston. Such was the case of one of the house's original inmates, forty-year-old Bridget Maloney, who took her surviving son Michael, age fourteen, with her as she left the house in May and simply was recorded as having "gone to States."[62]

The scene of local aid to immigrants in Kingston was not necessarily without certain sectarian anxieties. On 1 August 1847, a local priest stationed at St Mary's Cathedral, Father Bernard Higgins, was passing through Kingston, just having completed a visitation to a sick parishioner who was living at Fort Henry. He was approached by a young Irish woman who wanted him to visit her sick husband, who had been kept aboard the ship *Princess Royal* at Brewer's Wharf. When he boarded the vessel, he encountered many sick and asked the crew specifically for the young man in question. He was met unexpectedly with insults, including "to Hell with the Pope," according to his own testimony.[63] The ship's captain, Henry Twohey, ordered him off his boat and claimed the priest had no right to board it in the first place. The following day Father Higgins approached Kingston's head constable, who confirmed with the priest that he did indeed have a right to board the *Princess Royal* or any other vessel to administer to the sick and that Constable Greer himself would intervene

Table 4.3
House of Industry, Kingston by religion, December 1847–June 1848
(N=317)

Denomination	Number of children	Percentage
Church of England	47	14.8
Presbyterian	5	1.6
Roman Catholic	264	83.3
Unknown	1	0.3
Total	317	100.0

Source: Queen's University Archives, House of Industry, Kingston, Inmate's Ledger, vol. 1, 1847–1852.

on Higgins' behalf. Higgins left the constabulary to its tasks, and he proceeded across town to visit another sick parishioner. In his absence a mob attacked the *Princess Royal* as a retribution for its crew's treatment of the priest. One report had Higgins standing "on the wharf and shaking hands with the most violent of the ring leaders."[64]

A series of meetings between the board of health, the mayor, Bishop Phelan, Greer, Higgins, and Twohey, resolved the affair and exonerated the priest but not before local pundits had allowed the sectarian ugliness to spread.[65] While the quick resolution of the *Princess Royal* affair exemplified the high degree of co-operation that existed in Kingston during the famine, it none the less exposed the fragility of sectarian peace should it be seen that Catholics were over-stepping themselves in the public square. Moreover, such short tempers amplified the state of famine-fatigue in the colony, which would become more evident as the flow of refugees, the death of emigrants and local persons, and the public health risks at the fever sheds continued into the autumn. One writer commented that it would have been better had the emigrants landed on the "desert" shores of the Saguenay than in Kingston.[66]

Despite this singularly noteworthy incident, however, what is clear from the Kingston experience is that Protestants and Catholics co-operated in supporting the Irish orphans, including offering deference to Catholics to place their children in what would be a "secure" Catholic context. Like Quebec, the presence of an order of women religious, a proactive bishop in Phelan, assertive priests, and a tradition of diocesan loyalty to British principles made it easier for Protestant civic leaders, voluntary associations, and clergy to reach out to their Catholic counterparts. The Irish orphans were the focus of religious instruction by local priests, who offered Mass for the children regularly as a means of assuring they would not be lost to the Catholic Church.[67] It should also be noted that through this process it became clear to the sisters how bonded they had become to the children, having nurtured them through the trauma of the "sheds" and cared for their every physical and spiritual need. The annalist at the Hotel Dieu commented that when families came looking for a child, all the children were lined up for selection: "I assure you it was very painful to witness such a scene, when any of them heard their name mentioned, they knew they were going and began to cry and could not be consoled at seeing themselves separated from their companions in misfortune and from their mistresses, who also done [sic] their share of weeping."[68] As children departed the Hotel Dieu, more came to fill their places and the pattern was repeated until the facility was empty by April 1848.

The survivors of the Kingston experience generally moved west, taking steamer packets headed to the ports on the north shore of Lake Ontario, Hamilton, and the Niagara region. Landing in Cobourg or Port Hope offered Irish families the opportunity to move north into the "Great Pine Ridge" to pre-famine Irish settlements in Peterborough and Victoria Counties. Those sailing farther west might disembark at Whitby (until 1847, Port Windsor), looking for work in the farmlands of Ontario and Durham counties. Most moved on to the largest town in Upper Canada: Toronto.[69] Seven-year-old Mary Brennan was one such hopeful traveller. In August, she and her "feeble" grandmother, Mary Tobin, were the last survivors of her family. They were cleared by the Kingston Board of Health to move on to Toronto, but in her excitement to go, Mary was run over by a cart and her thigh bone was fractured.[70] Doctors in Kingston set her broken leg at the General Hospital,[71] but Mary soon appeared on a boat, essentially leaving the impression that further treatment would be left up to physicians in Toronto. When this orphan arrived at Rees's Wharf in Toronto and physicians discovered her pre-existing condition, there was outrage. The board of health even reported Mary Brennan's case to Dominick Daly as testament to the range of health concerns Torontonians had given what was coming up country to them from eastern Canada.[72] Worse for Mary, her grandmother was described as in the early stages of fever. Insulted by the accusations flying from Toronto, the surgeon in Kingston reported that the grandmother had disobeyed his order to keep the girl in the hospital and "absconded with her" to Toronto.[73] Mary's journey ended in Toronto, where she died on September 5; her grandmother survived and left the Convalescent Hospital eight days after the little girl died.[74] Mary Brennan's story speaks to Irish desperation to move to places where opportunity may be available to them, the less than adequate monitoring by authorities of emigrant travel, and the fact that for orphan children, their journeys could be perilous and, in this case, fatal.

Mary's story was merely one among tens of thousands of tales as Toronto's civic authorities and churches grappled with the immigrant and orphan challenges of 1847. Curiously, despite its reputation as the alleged "Belfast of North America,"[75] Toronto provided yet another variation of Protestant–Catholic co-operation in Canada's Anglo-Protestant cities. The initial "shock" of the famine migration appeared to bring Toronto's Protestants and Catholics together in a common cause. In the spring of 1847, the first of 38,540 migrants descended upon the former provincial capital of nearly 20,000 people.[76] Landing at Reese's wharf, the largely Irish crowds were triaged by local agent Edward McElderry, a Catholic who would die at the end of the sailing season;[77] the sick were sent to the Emigration Hospital (formerly Toronto General Hospital) and its annex of sixteen newly constructed sheds at King and John Streets.[78] The healthy were often given passage on steamers to Hamilton or Niagara-on-the Lake, or tickets to travel inland to Holland Landing, Newmarket, Barrie, and points west as far as the newly opened lands of the Huron Tract and Queen's Bush and other agricultural centres.[79] By the end of the year, 1,124 migrants and first responders were dead,[80] hundreds were sheltered in the convalescent hospital, and 627 had been admitted to the Widows' and Orphans' Asylum, of whom 523 were Catholic.[81] With more than 80 per cent of the refugees identified as Roman Catholic, Toronto became another Protestant British North American town with "a Catholic problem."

Most sources from the period agree that the situation in Toronto in the summer of 1847 was dire. With twice the city's population descending upon it in a single sailing season, it is not surprising that the medial facilities at the General Hospital were overwhelmed, including the sixteen hastily erected fever sheds on the hospital grounds. The local Catholic weekly, *The Mirror*, was unequivocal in calling citizens to aid the destitute Irish:

> Nine tenths of the community have been frightened, not only out of their wits – but, what is still worse, out of their humanity – by a bugbear, which has stood up before the distorted imaginations as grisly and spectral as the ghost of Hamlet's father. They think that because some thousands of poor wretches, who have been immured – or rather immersed,

for many weeks in the foul stench beneath the vessels in which they have been packed as close as herrings in a barrel – have contracted disease, or fallen as its victims, everyone who comes within hail of an emigrant must be smitten with pestilence! It is truly edifying to listen to the croakings of some of the screech owls who set the small hearts of the young sparrows fluttering.[82]

While the medical facilities were reeling under cases of typhus and the new Convalescent Hospital released patients back to the Emigrant Hospital when they relapsed, local authorities were perplexed by those who simply stayed in town or were released from the board of health's facilities and just remained in town, not availing themselves of the free transportation to other points in the province. *The Mirror* was particularly perplexed by "Emigrants [who] take up the business of beggars."[83] Aid to women and children who were facing destitution were of particular concern to both civic officials, clergy, and their congregations.

Given its later history, one might jump to the conclusion that Toronto might be indifferent to Catholic suffering and poverty. This assumption, however, would be an act of engaging in retrospective history of the worst kind. The Catholic population of Toronto was roughly 20 per cent and its diocesan status was new, having only been established in 1841. Its first bishop, however, a Nova Scotian of Waterford and east Cork descent, Dr Michael Power, was highly engaged in Toronto's civic life and was well respected by the Protestant community, counting Anglican bishop John Strachan and Methodist leader Egerton Ryerson among his friends.[84] Power, though supporting the principle of separate Catholic schools, served on the province's board of education, and was elected its first chair. His work among the Irish sick and poor was indefatigable, and he himself succumbed to typhus on 1 October 1847.[85] His priests, when healthy, were also engaged, and although there was no religious order in the city, until the arrival of the Loretto sisters from Ireland in September,[86] Catholic and Protestant clergy and laypersons could be found working together in the fever sheds, notably Dr George Grasset, chief medical officer and brother of the Anglican Archdeacon. Like Power, the doctor also died of typhus, as did his head nurse Susan Bailey.[87]

The establishment of the Widows' and Orphans' Asylum serves as a case when sectarian differences were set aside for the greater good amidst the public health crisis. The municipality had been accorded the right to manage its own social services and charities by the provincial government and, as such, was unique in its ability to create civic projects that assisted the pauper children and orphans of the city.[88] In July 1847, a public meeting of Toronto's citizens established a committee to set up the asylum. Its executive and commissioners represented Catholics and Protestants in the community, as did its attending physicians. Local businesses, both Catholic and Protestant donated furniture and food to the asylum, and Toronto's Irish Relief Committee gave nearly £760 for its maintenance. The asylum employed a superintendent and matron, Mr and Mrs McCausland, both with experience in England's Poor Law union workhouses, and a schoolteacher for the children.[89] One priority in Canada West was that asylums and orphanages were mandated with providing formal education to children. In Toronto Miss Julia Clarke was responsible for a curriculum consisting of "reading, spelling, writing, arithmetic, sewing and knitting." Grace was to be said before and after meals and it was generically Christian enough to give offence to neither Catholic nor Protestant clergy in the city.[90] Clergy were frequent visitors, particularly Catholic priests who would come to play a pivotal role in the placement of Catholic orphans.

Of the 627 inmates who passed through the Widows' and Orphans' Asylum, 197 were orphans who were destined to be placed in homes, as were their peers in Kingston and Bytown.[91] Sixty-nine children, or 35 per cent of the total, were placed by local priests, including Father Thaddeus Kirwan, who was active in placing Catholic orphans with "Men of good character and of industrious habits and in comfortable circumstances"[92] (see table 4.5). Most of the children, nearly 60 per cent, in the cohort of 197, were placed with farmers in counties neighbouring Toronto, while the rest were to find new homes in businesses, professional establishments, artisanal shops, or within the trades and service sectors of Toronto. From the published records of the asylum, cross-listed with the census data from 1851–52 and 1861, it appears that care was taken to place Protestants with Protestant families and Catholic children in Catholic homes. One child even ended up indentured to a professor at King's College, now the University of Toronto.

Most important, and clearly different from the placements that were recorded elsewhere in British North America, was the carefully spelled-out terms of child placement. Each orphan, unless in rare cases when collected by a parent, was expected to labour, but with the terms of financial remuneration, lodging, and board clearly laid out in the form of a contract. The agreements could also include the provision for a child to attend the local school or specify an allocation of clothing. The contracts varied in length with terminations often being specified at when the child turned eighteen or twenty-one; a few children were returned to the asylum, presumably having "not worked out" in their placement. One of Toronto's most noted Catholics, the Honourable John Elmsley, retained three children, Biddy Gilligan, Michael O'Brien, and John Gallagher, to work in his house and a local inn, in exchange for schooling, clothing, and board. In another case Father Thaddeus Kirwan brought nine-and-a-half-year-old Peter Kearns to farmer and bricklayer Michael O'Connor in Vaughan. While no terms of pay were disclosed, O'Connor was responsible for food and clothing "as long as he wishes to remain."[93] Kearns stayed for several years with the O'Connors, not as a family member, but as a servant.[94] In another case, but without the agency of a priest, asylum officials placed sixteen-year-old John Gallivan on 21 December 1847 with Richard Butler, a farmer and blacksmith in Whitby, to be bound as an apprentice smith for $25 for the first year, $35 for the second year, $45 for the third year, and $50 for the fourth year; by 1851–52 Butler was still in the census, but Gallivan was gone, likely having completed part of his contract, but now replaced by another Irish boy as apprentice.[95]

Such departures from their placements were common among the Toronto orphans. Census records from early 1852, just four years from the time of their placement, indicate that many of the patrons were still in their businesses and farms, but the children were gone. In some cases, the terms of the placement may have been over, but one suspects that the children fled to better circumstances as had the orphans placed in such areas as Rimouski. Maria Mooney is an interesting study of such disappearances. Mooney was fourteen when she arrived at the Widows' and Orphans' Asylum. On Christmas Eve, 1847, she was placed in the home of Isaac Waite, a Protestant farmer in Toronto Township to the west of the city. Her terms of indenture were clear. At the age of eighteen she was to receive a bed and "two suits of clothes."[96] When the census of 1852 was enumerated, Isaac Waite was still on his farm, but Mary was no where to be found. The register of the asylum suggests that she did not stay with Waite. Perhaps she had already reached her eighteenth birthday prior to the enumeration and had left with the promised bed and clothing. There is no record surviving to attest to this nor any follow up from the asylum committee, which had already disbanded. Equally puzzling was the placement of Mooney, a Catholic, with a Protestant. One can only speculate that Catholics on the asylum committee and priests like Kirwan and others had run out of eligible Catholic patrons. This would not be surprising since Catholics in the home district constituted only nine per cent of the population.[97]

Table 4.4
Widows' and Orphans' Asylum, Toronto, 1847–48, child placement by Catholic clergy and lay leaders
(N=197)

Name	Children placed	Percentage	Notes
Rev. Thomas Kirwan	24	12.2	
Rev. A Charest	20	10.2	Penetanguishene
Rev. S. Sanderl	11	5.6	
Rev. J. Quinlan	6	3.1	
Rev. Riley	5	2.5	
Hon. John Elmsley	3	1.5	Toronto
Subtotal	69	35.0	
Total orphans placed	197	100.0	

Source: *Report of the Managing Committee of the Widows' and Orphans' Asylum* (Toronto: Bowsell and Thompson, 1848).

Table 4.5
Widows' and Orphans' Asylum, Toronto, 1847–48, child placement locations by occupation
(N=197)

Occupation category	Children placed	Percentage
Professional	14	7.1
Private	9	4.6
Business	17	8.6
Clerical	6	3.1
Skilled/Artisan	18	9.1
Semi-skilled/labour	11	5.6
Farmer	118	59.9
Not given	4	2.0
Total	197	100.0

Source: *Report of the Managing Committee of the Widows' and Orphans' Asylum* (Toronto: Bowsell and Thompson, 1848).

The engagement of Catholic clergy with the Irish orphans provides some variation to the patterns established for orphan placement by the Widows' and Orphans' Asylum. Father Thaddeus Kirwan took the lead in placing Irish children. In April 1848, he placed sixteen children between the ages of four and six years with fourteen Irish farm families in the townships of Adjala and Tecumseh,[98] north of the city of Toronto. Neither the names of the children (of whom only five appear by name on his list) nor the names of the farmers involved appear in the asylum records. Presumably these children were drawn directly from the Emigrant Hospital or from families who had sojourned in the city, only to be faced with the loss of one or both parents over the winter of 1848. There is no documentation accompanying these children, as had been the case with the detailed contracts of indenture that were prescribed with all child placements from the asylum. The only document surviving was Kirwan's own report to the diocesan administrator, claiming that he certified that "the above-named men are of good character and of industriousness habits and in comfortable circumstances."[99] The letter does reveal several important elements involved in the placements. First, the fourteen farmers on the list requested the orphan children, thus confirming previous placement patterns assuring patrons that they would have additional help on their farms and businesses. From the Church's perspective, however, the patrons offered security to the children in terms of both the preservation of their Catholic faith and that they would live in "comfortable" surroundings. The note underscores that these children would also learn from and be mentored by Catholic gentlemen who demonstrated "industrious habits" thus underscoring the contemporary nineteenth-century idea that such placements were about teaching good work habits, industriousness, and skill for the edification of the child and the good of society. Unfortunately, the spottiness of the census records offers us no insight into what happened to these children after they were placed.

This clerical engagement in the placement process also signalled that Toronto became an important dispersal point for orphans across the central and western portions of the province (see tables 4.4 and 4.6). Kirwan had been key in placing some orphans on farmlands north of Toronto. His clerical colleagues, however, made contacts even farther afield, resembling the way French Canadian priests had removed children from Quebec and placed them in distant centres such as Nicolet and Lotbinière or on the frontier at Rimouski. Father Simon Sanderl, who served the German-speaking Catholic region which now forms part of Waterloo and Wellington counties, placed

Irish orphans in Guelph, Arthur, and Garafraxa, west of Toronto. Sanderl was careful, however, to make sure that the patrons to whom he delivered children were anglophones and mostly of Irish descent or birth. The work of Father Amable Charest, in this regard, was different. He transported twenty children to Simcoe County and to the largely French-speaking Catholic enclave of Penetanguishene, on Georgian Bay. Thus, when looking at the work of Kirwan and Charest combined, the Toronto orphans present an interesting parallel to those cared for by the Church in Quebec, beyond the vast territory that the priest-agents covered. The placement homes proved to be not just Irish but French Canadian Catholic. Finally, there are cases where the orphans who had been placed by the priests remained in the region, while the patrons themselves appeared to move. Such was the case of seven-year-old Anthony Loftus who had been entrusted to Father James Quinlan. The priest placed him in the Catholic home of Peter Mackey, a farmer outside of Paris, Canada West. By 1852, Mackey was not included in the enumeration of the census and had probably moved on like many of the mobile inhabitants of Canada in that era. Curiously, the then eleven-year-old Anthony was still working as a farm hand, this time to the Armstrong family living near Blenheim about 200 kilometres west of Paris.[100]

Adoption appeared not to be a legal option for the patrons of these children. In each of the cases originating from the Church or from Toronto's Widows' and Orphans' Asylum, Irish orphans were not adopted in the legal sense. Such adoption would not be the legal norm in Ontario until the 1920s.[101] As was the case with most Irish orphans in Lower Canada, the traceable orphans placed from Toronto were not considered family members in their new homes. There was one known exception, Catherine Ryan, a seven-year-old orphan who on 3 May 1848, was placed with Jane Hamilton, a widow and farmer in Chinguacousy Township. Catherine was the last orphan placed from the asylum and her placement included a contract that stipulated she would be owed a bed, bedding, a cow, and two suits of clothing when she turned eighteen. In the census of 1851–52, she is still living with the Hamilton family but now as Catherine Hamilton. Jane's twenty-something sons William and John worked the farm, and it appears all were members of the Free Kirk group of the Presbyterian Church.[102] This development would not have pleased Fathers Kirwan, Quinlan, and Sanderl who expressly engaged in the placement process to save the faith of the children. By mid-1848, and without Bishop Power at the helm, it appeared the unwritten rules of orphan placement, at least regarding religion, were no longer in play consistently.

Table 4.6
Widows' and Orphans' Asylum, Toronto, 1847–48, child placement locations by country
(N=197)

Country/City	Children placed	Percentage
Toronto	54	27.4
York	33	16.8
Simcoe	33	16.8
Peel	16	8.1
Halton	12	6.1
Wellington	12	6.1
Ontario	6	3.0
Dufferin	1	0.5
Durham	2	1.0
Welland	2	1.0
Lincoln	1	0.5
Wentworth/Hamilton	7	3.6
Brant	5	2.5
Huron	1	0.5
Gray	1	0.5
Oxford	1	0.5
Essex	3	3.0
Not Stated	3	3.0
Unknown	4	2.0
Total	197	100.0

Source: Report of the Managing Committee of the Widows' and Orphans' Asylum (Toronto: Bowsell and Thompson, 1848).

Less is known about the orphans after families left Toronto for points west and south. The board of health at Guelph, for instance, reported that there were numerous children in the area and at least twenty-one were being treated in the local hospital. Local officials, however, did not identify any as having been orphans.[103] Similarly, while at least 16,591 migrants, mostly Irish, landed in Hamilton, either directly from Kingston or via Toronto, there were no reports of an orphan problem in that city.[104] In Niagara, the board of health made monthly reports to the provincial secretary but nothing about orphans ever surfaced in the correspondence. While it has been acknowledged that young Roscommon-native John O'Connor had been orphaned at Queenston, this came because of the murder of his parents by Thomas Brennan, not because of illness contracted by his parents or their deaths in the local hospital run by the board of health.[105]

The Toronto case also demonstrated a high level of co-operation between Catholics and Protestants, perhaps in large part due to the networks of mutual respect and co-operation forged between Bishop Michael Power, Bishop John Strachan, Egerton Ryerson, and other religious leaders. The Widows' and Orphans' Asylum was evidence of how such cooperative relationships between the Christians of different denominations, could result in care and sensitivity in placing children where, in the minds of contemporaries they could be useful and productive members of society. One should not be surprised that these so-called "adoptions" anywhere in British North America were essentially relationships of indentureship between pauper children and families in need of assistance. While setting aside issues of exploitation and child labour, it should be remembered that, at least in Upper Canada/Canada West, pauper apprenticeship was considered a legitimate means of transforming potential problem children into productive citizens.[106] When clergy and churches became engaged, one could add God-fearing to that intended outcome.

Thus, when the major Protestant centres of immigrant reception are examined within the context of the famine migration of 1847 and 1848, the Catholic Church appeared to be able to make itself an effective partner to the civic authorities in Canada. In Bytown, Kingston, and Toronto the prominence and respect accorded to local Catholic bishops and women religious went a long way to forging effective partnerships in bringing relief to suffering families and children. Mother Bruyère was a formidable presence in Bytown, and her Grey Nuns had a proven track record of service for more than a century in Canada. Under her control, Catholic and Protestant orphans were cared for and then placed within local homes. In Kingston, local Catholic clergy had longstanding relationships with community leaders, and they were ably assisted by a fledgling order of women religious, the Religious Hospitallers of St Joseph, who constructed mutually beneficial cooperative arrangements with local organizations of Protestant women. In Kingston, Catholic leadership was engaged and respected. Toronto was different again, with its own special municipal status to engage in charitable aid and by the commanding respect of Catholic bishop Michael Power in local Protestant circles. He had proven himself to be a strong public advocate for immigrant aid and by October 1847 had become an acknowledged martyr of charity. The city's unique legal status gave Torontonians not only the flexibility to protect Irish orphans by means of rudimentary contracts of indenture, but there appeared to be social flexibility, allowing for Catholic and Protestant co-operation during the crisis. Thus, in 1847 one witnesses activities in Protestant cities with three variations on a theme. Such would not be the case elsewhere in the colonies. In Saint John, the opposite was true, with local clergy struggling to assert their needs and those of Irish Catholic children in the face of a Poor Law infrastructure that was stacked with lay Protestants. Moreover, the riotous climate between the Churches, evident in both Saint John and well up into the settlements the Saint John River valley, provided a context for sectarianism and the exclusion of Catholics. To this we turn next.

5

Assistance and Assimilation
Irish Orphans in New Brunswick

Ellen Mooney never met "Harry" Temple. They shared part of the same story, however, rooted in the Sligo estate where Ellen had been born and from where she had departed courtesy of Harry who had been her landlord. Better known as Henry John Temple, the Third Viscount Palmerston, Harry was too preoccupied with his job as foreign secretary in Lord John Russell's government at Westminster to pay very close attention to his 10,000-acre Sligo estates.[1] Though he once resisted efforts to assist indebted tenants off his estate, as a "cruel" practice,[2] by the onset of the worst years of the famine his agents continued a program whereby thousands of his tenants, in arrears of their rent, were transported to Quebec and Saint John, New Brunswick. Ellen had been one of these tenants herded on to the *Aeolus* with the hope of starting a new life in the British North American provinces. Upon arrival in Saint John in November 1847, Ellen aged twelve, her mother, father, and two siblings Anthony (fourteen) and Bridget (ten) and their shipmates were described by the *New Brunswick Courier* as "a destitute and helpless set ... They are penniless and in rags without shoes or stockings and lying upon the bare boards."[3] Kingston's *British Whig* added that "many of the females were in a state shocking to decency."[4] Ellen's father died and her mother, Catherine, became ill after landing. Ellen's new life would begin with her siblings at the Emigrant Orphans Asylum of the City of Saint John. Without her parents, friends, and the regular presence of Catholic clergy, Ellen, Bridget, and Anthony Mooney were alone in a new world, thanks in large part to the "generosity" of Harry Temple.

The reception, housing, and placement of Irish orphans in Saint John, New Brunswick, was patently different from what Irish children experienced in other parts of British North America. While there were great similarities between the New Brunswick-bound Irish migrants and their counterparts headed to Quebec, there were significant differences in the treatment of orphans. The city of Saint John, the principal receiver of the close to 17,000 Irish refugees in 1847, created a quarantine station akin to Grosse Ile at Partridge Island. From there the quarantine staff would triage survivors to the city's almshouse, hospital, orphan asylum, or permit them to keep moving through the province. Many Irish emigrants in New Brunswick, like their counterparts in Canada, elected to continue their journey to the United States.[5] In contrast to the interior provinces in British North America, where there appeared to be sectarian peace, in New Brunswick there was growing tension between Catholics and Protestants, which the famine migration helped to exacerbate. Unlike in Quebec or the western Catholic dioceses, the Catholic Church in New Brunswick was neither influential nor strong in term of its infrastructure and was unable to assert itself or defend its rights in the province. Bishop William Dollard was simply building a diocese from scratch, having only been in the new episcopal see since 1842.[6] As a result, Irish Catholic orphans were essentially at the mercy of a mostly Protestant-run asylum that had little regard for the religion of most of the children in its care. Thus, without the ability of both Catholic and Protestant churches elsewhere in Canada to place orphans with families or businesses where the child's religion might be preserved, there was little attention to such religious reciprocity in Saint John. Although placements were organized and well documented, the guardians of the asylum became agents of the assimilation of Catholic children into the Anglo-Protestant world of New Brunswick.[7]

People in New Brunswick were aware of what was happening with the crop failures, starvation, and death that terrorized Ireland after 1845. Local newspapers reported the worsening situation for the Irish cottiers in Connaught during the winter of 1847, and in Saint John it was reported that collections for Irish relief had "done well ... [for] the amelioration of the greatest sufferings on record in the annals of English history."[8] Colonial Secretary Earl Grey sent his thanks for donations to famine relief made by both the New Brunswick Assembly and Bishop Dollard, himself.[9] In 1846, there had been at least 9,000 Irish migrants to the province,[10] and the chief emigration officer for Saint John, Moses Henry Perley, anticipated that the sailing season for 1847 might bring even more migrants from Ireland as conditions there worsened.[11] The influx of more impoverished Roman Catholics would not sit well with local Protestants, particularly the Loyal Orange Order, which was growing in membership, for fear of being awash in Catholics. Such fears of a "Popish" invasion would only be enhanced by local newspapers publishing the comments of the general assembly of the Presbyterian Church in Ireland, which lauded its own relief work in Ireland given their observation that the Catholic priests had abandoned their people: "Erin, the green, is now a place of skulls, the angel of death has passed through her."[12] The prognostication of a Catholic wave of migrants became a reality as almost 17,000 Irish famine refugees set sail for the ports in New Brunswick, in 1847, of whom 800 died at sea and 1,300 more died in the local quarantine stations on Partridge Island at Saint John, Hospital Island near St Andrews, and Middle Island in the Miramichi River.[13]

There was no warm welcome for the Irish. The period leading up to the famine migration to New Brunswick had been marked by sectarian tension that had frequently erupted into violence between Irish Catholics and the Orange Order in major towns along the Saint John River valley. The religious and social climate was hostile to Catholics, who constituted one third of New Brunswick's population.[14] Acadian Catholics who lived in regions some distance from the Anglo-Loyalist population, appeared to offer no immediate threat to the Anglo-Protestant dominance of the colony. The Irish, however, who clustered in Saint John and environs or sought out farmland in the lush river valleys had yet to secure either social standing or political clout in a province where political representation and the franchise was rooted in land ownership.[15] Even a newspaper report of the building of a Catholic chapel, in this case in Fredericton in 1845, could elicit hostility from Protestant readers when it had been described to them as an event which exhibited a "spirit of good will and charity" for the Catholics and their Protestant guests.[16] The harsh realities of landlessness and unemployment also drew negative attention to newcomers. For many Irish Catholics immigrants, the promises of work on the proposed railways were unrequited,[17] as were possible jobs in the colony's timber industry. The sight of Irish vagabonds and beggars merely reinforced negative stereotypes of the Irish, as did their impoverished estate, sometimes slovenly appearance, and the "rumoured" potential for the Irish to transmit communicable diseases they may have contracted during their trans-Atlantic voyage. It is not surprising that with rising recruitment to the Orange Order,[18] Protestant hostility to the high numbers of new poor Irish Catholic migrants, and long-standing sectarian bitterness there were several "serious riots" in Saint John, Fredericton, and Woodstock in 1847.[19]

Amidst this sectarian bitterness, the Catholic Church possessed none of the institutional strength of the Church as witnessed in Quebec City, Montreal, or even Toronto. Bishop William Dollard was the Roman Catholic bishop of New Brunswick (later the Diocese of Fredericton in 1852 and now the Diocese of Saint John), but his residence was in the interior, up the Saint John River, at the capital, Fredericton. Despite frequent visits to Saint John, he was unable to keep a close eye on the migration challenges and give forceful Catholic leadership because civic officials, mostly Protestants, determined the fate of the immigrants, including care and relocation of the rising number of Irish Catholic orphans. By 1848, Dollard would have to take up residence in Saint John.[20] Worse still, unlike Archbishop Joseph Signay in Quebec, Bishop Ignace Bourget in Montreal, or Patrick Phelan in Kingston, Dollard had neither male nor female religious orders in Saint John upon which he could depend to give care to the children and the sick. Dollard had a handful of active priests that included Father Edmund Quinn, who gathered Irish migrants at Assumption Chapel, and Father John Sweeney, the future bishop, who served the Irish in the "front lines" at Partridge Island.[21] While Catholic migrants would also land at Middle Island in the Miramichi, at Shippegan, and at Little Hardwood Island (Hospital Island) near St Andrew's,[22] the majority of immigrants entered Saint John as their gateway to the province and where the Church's constant watchful eye was most acutely needed. With the absence of visible or residential episcopal leadership, few priests, and no religious orders, the Catholic Church was very weak in Saint John and lay persons, alone, could not flex strong enough muscles to stop the course of Protestant politicians, public servants, and volunteers.[23]

In the early nineteenth century and during the worst years of the famine, Saint John was second only to Quebec as British North America's greatest receiver of Irish migrants. With natural shipping connections to the Irish ports of Londonderry and Cork,[24] it should come as no surprise that the Irish migrants who elected to stay in the province, prior to 1845, were a strong mix of Protestants and Catholics from the Irish Provinces of Ulster, Connaught, and Munster. In 1832 a head tax was imposed on ship owners to underwrite the costs of the civic assistance.[25] It became clear over time, however, that this would be insufficient funding, as was the provincial Poor Law in paying for the expenses incurred in triaging, quarantining, and caring for migrants in Saint John. As was previously indicated, in 1847 Moses Henry Perley, the chief emigrant agent, focused the attention of local government on the strengthening of the quarantine station at Partridge Island in Saint

John's harbour. Perley's hope, and that of the medical staff and civic politicians, was that the spread of disease could be minimized by landing all ships at Partridge Island for inspection before allowing any migrant to set foot in the city or the rest of the province. In 1847 alone, eighty-one ships were inspected at the island. While most of the ship's landing during that sailing season could not be categorized as proverbial "coffin ships," there were too many exceptions that saw the island turn into an overcrowded fever hospital. Perley tended to blame the lack of inspections of malnourished passengers in the ports of origin for the outbreaks of ships fever, but such claims did not ease the pressure placed on the medical staff of the quarantine station. Dr James Patrick Collins was the first medical officer to contract typhus on the island and the first to succumb to the infectious diseases that abounded in the crowded quarantine station.[26] Chief Health Officer Dr William S. Harding also became ill but recovered, and in Collins' absence patients were attended to by Harding's brother G.J. Harding, MD.[27] By late summer there were 553 patients in the emigrant hospital, with more than one hundred new victims of disease arriving weekly.[28]

The case of the Foley family gives a glimpse of the tragedy occurring to many Irish families within the quarantine station at Partridge Island. Forty-one-year-old Edward Foley was a native of County Sligo living on the estate of either Robert Gore-Booth or neighbouring landlord Viscount Palmerston (the New Brunswick records are unclear). In the summer of 1847, he, his wife, and five children accepted the assistance of his landlord and, with 405 fellow emigrants, boarded the *Lady Sale* bound for Saint John. The ship arrived on 9 September and the conditions discovered aboard ship were among the most horrendous of all the ships that landed during that sailing season. Moses Perley described the passengers who disembarked as "an unusual proportion of aged men and women, widows and orphans, most miserable looking beings with scarcely sufficient clothing for decency ... I have never yet seen such abject misery, destitution and helplessness as was exhibited yesterday on the decks of the *Lady Sale*."[29] Of the 350 passengers on board, 21 died at sea, 19 in quarantine, and 44 were sent to the alms house, where 9 more passed away.[30] The Foleys were immediately hospitalized at the island. Edward Foley Sr died in quarantine as did three of his children: William (ten), Henry (seven), and Mary (six). His wife remained at the hospital, while two sons Edward Jr (twelve) and the eldest, Peter (fourteen) were removed to the mainland and eventually were placed in the Emigrant Orphan's Asylum. Young Edward would die on 1 December 1847, leaving only Peter, who was eventually collected by his mother in May 1848. From there the Foleys vanish into history. In the course of almost a year, this Sligo Catholic family of seven, hopeful of a new life in America, was reduced to only the mother and eldest son.[31]

Partridge Island was the first point of contact for famine migrants. From there, civic officials in Saint John directed the survivors from the voyage to temporary relief at the sheds on Lower St James Street, near the city barracks, and then to the Saint John City Almshouse. Loyalist migrants to New Brunswick established the earliest almshouse in 1784, but the current publicly funded facility dated from 1838 and the Almshouse Act.[32] By 1847, the almshouse commissioners welcomed white-only[33] paupers, who were required to clean, do their own laundry, and be "industrious," as was expected of the deserving poor. The almshouse also had a school for the children interred there.[34] The famine migration brought a crush of both healthy and ill emigrants to the almshouse, which quickly became a new vector for disease. In 1847, of the 2,381 emigrants housed there 560 died, as did 126 of the 610 local paupers from the "parish" of Saint John.[35] Because of the high numbers of orphans created by the horrendous conditions of the voyage, the quarantine station, and the almshouse, and in addition to the crush of numbers at the latter institution, on 28 September 1847 the commissioners of the almshouse established the Emigrants Orphans Asylum.[36] Until its closure in November 1849, the Orphans Asylum accommodated more than 300 Irish orphans of whom, 91 per cent were Roman Catholic, and most were from the west of Ireland.[37] Since New Brunswick was one of the few British North American colonies with an operative Poor Law,[38] local municipalities were legally obliged to underwrite poor relief, which cause increased anxiety among New Brunswickers that they were underwriting the neglect and callousness of Irish landlords.

There were several assisted migration schemes during the Irish famine period, including that of Major Denis Mahon, featured in chapter 2, Lord Lansdowne in Kerry, and that of Earl Fitzwilliam of Wicklow.[39] Two Irish landlords, Robert Gore-Booth and Viscount Palmerston, however, became frequent targets of the angry rhetoric of civic officials in Saint John and provincial politicians. Both Palmerston and Gore-Booth were prominent Sligo landlords, with the latter earning a reputation as an "improving" landlord who resided on his estate and was conscientious in the way he prepared his tenants for emigration.[40] Local Relief Committee authorities in Sligo lauded Gore-Booth for buying four boilers for the local soup kitchen, providing employment on his estate for his tenants out of his own pocket, and visiting tenants on his estate to assess and provide for their immediate needs.[41] Similarly, Gore-Booth had begun the migration scheme for his assisted tenants early in 1847, with the first batch arriving at Saint John, on board the *Aeolus* at the end of May, with about 500 passengers and no major incidents.[42] A committee of passengers actually wrote their landlord upon arrival thanking him and praising the captain, who "kindly treated" the widows, orphans, and the sick.[43]

Subsequent ships chartered by Gore-Booth, however, brought unwanted notoriety to his assistance scheme. Reports of the arrival of the *Yeoman* and *Lady Sale*, particularly the latter, elicited harsh criticism from New Brunswick pundits and politicians. In retrospect, the *New Brunswick Courier* reflected on the entire Gore-Booth project, beginning with the *Aeolus*, pointing out that migrants "were sent out at his expense, in order to clear the estate of its paupers, who would be chargeable upon it under the new Poor Law[44] which has recently come into operation in Ireland."[45] At least one editor slammed Gore-Booth, accusing him of sending 1,500 "pauper Emigrants" to the province: "it is a dreadful infliction not only on the benevolence of the Inhabitants of this Province but also upon the wretches thus exposed to all the sufferings and desease [*sic*] and poverty, without a home or friend save when the hand of charity, already overtaxed is stretched forth to relieve them."[46] By 3 September 1847, the Common Council of Saint John declared the arrival of the pauper Irish a "great public calamity," which had resulted from "a heartless system produced by some Irish landlords in shipping entire ship-loads of paupers from their respective estates for the purpose of relieving themselves from their undoubted and legitimate liability of providing the requisite support."[47]

Editors and civic officials, however, heaped worse scorn on Lord Palmerston, Gore-Booth's neighbour. Palmerston had engaged in assisted emigration projects well before the famine, but the preparations for most of the voyages and assembly of tenants was left to his agents in the firm of Stewart & Kincaid. There were several efforts to co-operate in these schemes with Gore-Booth, and at least two ships leaving Sligo contained passengers from both estates, including the *Lady Sale*. During the sailing season, Palmerston's agents assisted hundreds of migrants to Quebec and Saint John on the *Numa*, *Transit*, *Marchioness of Breadalbane*, *Richard Watson*, *Springhill*,[48] *Carricks*,[49] and the *Eliza Liddell*. The *Eliza Liddell*, for example, landed mistakenly at Shippegan, where there was almost no infrastructure to care for the 128 seriously ill passengers on board.[50] Several newspapers reported that there were forty-two orphans on board, having been placed there by "some workhouses in Ireland."[51] The passengers of the *Carricks* met a worse fate in May 1847 when the ship sank in the Gulf of St Lawrence with only one of every four passengers surviving.

The most notorious landing at Saint John, however, came well past the end of the shipping season and the scaling down of activities at Partridge Island. Just as officials were breathing a sigh of relief that the worst had passed, on 1 November 1847, the *Aeolus* landed in the province for the second time that year.[52] On this occasion the ship was packed with 428 of Palmerston's assisted tenants described as poor, dressed in rags, and likely to be completely dependent on public charity.[53] Moses Perley offered a shocking report to Provincial Secretary, John Saunders:

> There are many aged persons of both sexes on board, and a large proportion of women and children, the whole in the most abject state of poverty and destitution, with barely sufficient rags upon their persons to cover their nakedness; none of the younger portion of the inhabitants have either shoes or stockings; there is a great deficiency both of petticoats and trousers, and one boy about ten years of age was actually brought on deck stark naked. The arrival at this unusually late period of so large a number of destitute and naked emigrants is deeply to be regretted.[54]

When reporting back to Palmerston, in their own defence, his agents were apologetic about the condition of the passengers of the *Aeolus*: "we are very sorry to find that the authorities in St John's [sic] complain of their poverty and destitution and the late season at which they arrived."[55] They reassured the viscount that they had properly provisioned and clothed the tenants, who begged to leave the estate, but likely underestimated the harshness of the sea voyage itself as exacerbated by the "the inferior kind of clothing to which the inhabitants of the western coast of Ireland are accustomed."[56] Regardless of their intentions, civic and provincial authorities were outraged that, once again, the city and the province would have to cover the charitable expenses of keeping these emigrants alive.

Recently, there has been debate among historians about Palmerston's culpability in this mass assisted migration stream. Several historians have regarded Palmerston as one of Ireland's most notorious landlords for his "voluntary" assistance scheme,[57] while Desmond Norton has essentially argued that the schemes were arguably more the work of Stewart & Kincaid, Palmerston's agents, who prepared and executed the plans with the viscount paying the bills.[58] Nevertheless, despite Palmerston's comments in the 1830s that he would not indulge in such "cruel" practices, his public tone had changed by 1848, when reform of the Irish land system was one of the most urgent matters facing Ireland:

> Ejectments must be made without cruelty in the manner of making them; but it is useless to disguise the truth that any great improvement in the social system of Ireland must be founded upon extensive change in the present state of agrarian occupation, and that this change necessarily implies a long continued and systematic ejectment of Small Holders and Squatting Cottiers.[59]

Regardless of his intention, Palmerston's tenants were a burden on the Province of New Brunswick, felt most acutely by local citizens who, in the absence of any major private Church-run charity, were taxed through the Poor Law to pay for what they considered to be someone else's problem. Based on Perley's scathing assessment of Palmerston and the conditions on the *Aeolus*, Saint John Mayor John H. Partlow and the city council resolved that "the Clergy be requested to use their influence in inducing these distressed people to accept passage to Ireland."[60] While the clerk of the council sent the resolutions to the Crown, who also received similar denunciations of Palmerston from Canadian parliamentarian Adam Ferrie,[61] the emigrants remained in New Brunswick and in the care of the almshouse and Orphan's Asylum.

With the casualties being so high on the ships landing in Saint John, filled with assisted tenants from the Gore-Booth and Palmerston estates, it is not surprising that the largest group of orphans left in port hailed from Sligo. Of the 302 orphans that can be logged in the register of the Orphan's Asylum, only 270 can be identified by their county of origin. Of these, 131 children, or 48.5 per cent, were from County Sligo. The only other county coming close to this proportion of Irish orphans was County Galway at fifty-two orphans, or far less than half of the total from nearby Sligo. Of those whose counties of origin have been recorded, three quarters of the orphans came from Connaught.[62] That the Gore-Booth and Palmerston estates had become orphan mills for New Brunswick was identified by Dr W.S. Harding as he boarded the *Lady Sale*, where he saw "chiefly widows and orphans and large helpless families depending on one man's exertions. I noticed in one instance 16 children so to be dependent, probably grandchildren."[63] All of these children

Table 5.1
Irish counties of origin of the Saint John orphans
(N=270)

Country	Province	Number of orphans	Percentage
Sligo	Connaught	131	48.5
Galway	Connaught	52	19.3
Cork	Munster	19	7.0
Mayo	Connaught	18	6.7
Donegal	Ulster	12	4.4
Limerick	Munster	7	2.6
Kerry	Munster	6	2.2
London/Derry	Ulster	5	1.9
Tipperary	Munster	5	1.9
Tyrone	Ulster	4	1.5
Louth	Leinster	3	1.1
Fermanagh	Ulster	2	0.7
Offaly (King's)	Leinster	2	0.7
Clare	Munster	2	0.7
Antrim	Ulster	2	0.7
Down	Ulster	1	0.4
Clare	Munster	1	0.4

Source: Peter Murphy, *Poor Ignorant Children: Irish Famine Orphans in Saint John, New Brunswick* (Halifax: D'Arcy McGee Chair of Irish Studies, St Mary's University, 1999). All calculations were derived from the published "Ledger" in the volume, 32–75.

except two at the asylum were Roman Catholic.[64] In total, 41.4 per cent of the 302 Irish orphans housed in Saint John's Emigrant Orphan Asylum were from either the Palmerston or Gore-Booth estates: twenty-one from the *Yeoman*, thirty-nine from the *Lady Sale*, and an incredible sixty-five from the *Aeolus*. The anger of the local officials at Palmerston is made palpable by the fact one ship from his estates produced one in every five orphans supported by the public purse in 1847–48.[65]

When Irish orphans entered the new orphan asylum in October 1847, there were mighty expectations of them. Upon entry the children were stripped of their clothing, given new garments and headwear, and were assigned beds and blankets. Local officials regarded the asylum as a place where its inmates could become useful citizens and avoid adding to the growing population of vagrants and crime-oriented children already trolling the streets of the city. Such beliefs about instilling "honesty, industry, and virtue," were common throughout Britain and its colonies.[66] These same principles motivated civic officials in Toronto and the school promoters of that era[67] – social uplift in the asylum was to be carried out under the auspices of a formal education. According to historian Koral LaVorgna, a proper education of these children would correct "idleness" and give them skills to make something of themselves in their new home.[68] While the keeper and matron of the asylum were a Catholic couple, James and Annie Cunningham, the teacher retained for the orphans was a New Brunswick teenager of Irish Protestant descent. Seventeen-year-old Alice Minette was the daughter of a local surveyor who had left Ireland in 1818 to set up his practice in the province.[69] Alice was to run a school for the youngest children, which made sense given the need to build good foundations in the youngest emigrants, while also acknowledging the reality that the older children were her peers and some were even older. Michael Feeney, who had disembarked from the ill-fated *Lady Sale* was twenty-two, while Ellen and Bridget Gillen, from the *Aeolus*, were nineteen and twenty years of age respectively.[70] There were many teens among the orphans and with this age group, the commissioners considered placement with New Brunswick families and businesses to be a more effective means of saving these Irish children from a life of vagrancy. Here the commissioners varied little in their assumptions about progress, discipline, and social uplift from their contemporaries in the other British American provinces.

The ledger of names for the orphans asylum reveals similarities in the patterns of emigrant behaviour, and orphan life, in Saint John when compared to similar institutions in Quebec, Montreal, Bytown, and Kingston. As has been indicated, an overwhelming number, more than 90 per cent, of the children were Roman Catholic, which stands to reason given the preponderance of counties in Connaught as their places of birth.[71] A second similarity with the other British North American orphan refuges was that about 53 per cent of the children were "half-orphans" with one identifiable parent still alive.[72] Such was the case of the aforementioned Peter Foley, who had lost his entire family except his mother, which he likely only discovered when she came to retrieve him from the asylum on 10 May 1848, after she had recovered from her illness. Peter, however, had spent six months in the asylum,[73] a period of stay which exceeded the average of only twenty-nine days.[74] Lawrence Coyne was not an orphan at all. He and his four siblings were placed in the asylum, after their voyage on the *Aelous*, while their parents recuperated in hospital.[75] Other stories of true half orphans, however, have less than happy endings, as was the case with "infant Flaherty." The unidentified baby was left by his father in November 1847, perhaps with another passenger from the *Aeolus*, but only survived until 28 December 1847[76] – ironically the Feast of the Holy Innocents, commemorating the slaughter of baby boys by Herod's soldiers in Bethlehem. Young Flaherty was only one of the forty-one children who perished in the asylum.[77] Another similarity with children detained elsewhere in British North America, was that some inmates took the first opportunity to escape from the orphan asylum. James McGivinn, for example, was a thirteen-year-old survivor of the *Yeoman* from the Gore-Booth Estate. With his father dead and his mother ill in the sheds, James lasted six days in the asylum before he bolted and was never heard from again.[78]

One significant difference from between orphans at Saint John and those elsewhere is that at least eight children were recorded as orphans who actually sailed from Ireland as orphans. Such was the case of Mary Clarke, a fifteen-year-old girl from County Mayo, who was permitted to board the *Midas*, with the officials in the port of Galway City knowing full well that her parents were dead in Ireland and she was travelling alone.[79] Similarly, fourteen-year-old Alexander Blackburn from Londonderry was allowed to board a ship in Donegal, his parents having died, but little is known of his fate because he ran away from the asylum shortly after his arrival there in March 1848.[80] While there were cases of Poor Law unions assisting orphans from Irish workhouses with the hope of these girls finding domestic employment in Canada,[81] there is no evidence that orphans were shipped out in other assisted migration schemes such as that of Major Denis Mahon in Roscommon or Earl Fitzwilliam in Wicklow.[82] At least two of Palmerston's orphans from the *Aeolus* appear to have been travelling on their own: Mary and Margaret Conway. Both, however, were older than twenty and would be treated as adult women.[83] This could not be said for the Foley sisters – Mary (thirteen) and Bridget (fourteen) – and two Foley brothers – Bartholomew (ten) and Mick (twelve) – who were permitted to board the *Lady Sale* from the Gore-Booth estate, despite the fact their parents were dead in Ireland.[84] The presence of these unattended youth on board ships like the *Lady Sale* and *Aeolus*, when compounded by the numbers of orphans created during the voyage itself, may have prompted Perley's comments about the sight of so many orphans on board these ships when they landed.

For older youth sent to the asylum, "placement" with New Brunswick families was their usual fate. In the absence of any adoption laws, which were not introduced into New Brunswick until 1873,[85] there was no legal obligation by a farm family or business to incorporate these orphans as family members. Other similarities with Canada included the fact that children who survived the ordeal of migration were split up from their siblings. Furthermore, as was graphically the case in the other provinces, orphan children who were placed were expected to earn their keep. The McNamara family may serve as an illustration of both points. Originally from the estate of Lord Palmerston, the McNamara family, two parents and five children, boarded the *Aeolus* late in the sailing season and suffered all the indignities of the voyage and quarantine as previously described by Moses Perley. Both parents died in the emigrant hospital sometime after the arrival of the ship in November 1847. The five children left the almshouse and were admitted to the orphan's asylum in March 1848. By June, eight-year-old John died and his death was followed by the placement of his two elder siblings, Ellen (fifteen) and Patrick (twelve). Ellen was placed with Elijah Spragge, a farmer in Springfield, King's County, presumably to work as a domestic for a wage of five shillings per month. Patrick ended up with Robert Jones in Greenwick, Kings County. Ten-year-old Michael McNamara was placed with farmer Henry Scovill in Springfield Parish, King's County, in November 1849, more than a year after his older siblings had left the asylum. The youngest child, Hugh, aged only five when he entered the asylum was sent back to the almshouse in 1849 when the asylum closed.[86] It was not until 1851, when Hugh was likely eight years old, that James E. Northrup, collected the boy to take to his property in Hamstead, Queen's County. There is no record of any of the children in the 1851 census nor any evidence that they ever saw one another again.

Joining the McNamaras on board the *Aeolus* were the Coyne family, also from the Palmerston estate. Although Mrs Coyne died in the Saint John hospital, the father appeared to be still alive but sick when his five children – Bryan (sixteen), Andrew (fourteen), Michael (twelve), Lawrence (ten), and Bessy (five) – found themselves in the asylum about a week after their ship arrived. Because of her age, Bessy seemed to remain at the asylum until it closed in November 1849 whereupon she was transferred to the almshouse. Dr Leslie, of Annapolis, Nova Scotia, collected her six months later; three of her older brothers, Bryan, Andrew, and Michael, were placed in farming communities at Shediac, Little River, and Annapolis respectively. At this point the tale of the Coyne family looks little different from that of the McNamaras in terms of children being used for employment across the province. Peter Murphy's findings, as confirmed by census results when available, suggest that half the children were sent to rural areas and about one third sent to professionals and businesses in the city of Saint John.[87] In the mind of the commissioners of the asylum "placement" became a remedy to filling up the Irish ghetto in Portland (near Saint John),[88] an antidote to the vagrancy and delinquency believed by locals to be out of control,[89] and an action perfectly in keeping with contemporary notions of forming these Irish children into useful, law-abiding, and productive citizens.

The experience of Lawrence Coyne was a little different. He was taken to Dorchester by A.L. Palmer, a local lawyer. In 1851, Lawrence was enumerated by census takers in Dorchester as Lawrence Cowan, a servant of Irish birth still living in the Palmer household.[90] Palmer had at least three servants, two of whom were identified as Acadian and Lawrence who was also listed as an apprentice.[91] To be listed as a servant was not necessarily unique to Coyne. His fellow traveller from the *Aeolus* Patrick Flannagan also reappears on the 1851 census as living as a servant in the house of Stephen Burpee, a farmer in Sheffield.[92] At first glance Coyne, his siblings, and Flannagan appear to confirm what one suspected: that Irish orphan children were a cheap source of labour for New Brunswick and, in some cases, Nova Scotian families. What made Lawrence exceptional was the fact that Palmer may have seen a spark in him that prompted his patron to help him in his barrister's practice. While Lawrence Coyne vanished thereafter into history, his double classification as both servant and apprentice suggests that some Irish children may have begun as cheap labour but over time may have advanced into a life scarcely imagined when digging potatoes on Palmerston's estate.

The placement process in Saint John when considering a child's religion, however, differed significantly from placement procedures in the other provinces. In a Protestant town like Saint John, child placement was under tight Protestant control. The asylum's head commissioners were Protestant men: Henry Chubb, the owner of the *New Brunswick Courier*,[93] and Alderman William O. Smith, a Presbyterian originally from Nova Scotia.[94] There was only one Catholic representative on the Board.[95] As a result of such numeric superiority, Commissioner Smith despatched orphans to where and to whom they were wanted, including potential labourers to his farming interests in the Annapolis Valley in his home province. This is likely how Bessy Coyne ended up in Annapolis. Without a well-organized network of Protestant and Catholic clergy to collect and place orphans, as was the case in Canada, the commissioners of the asylum took to advertising in local papers for "prosperous persons" to take healthy children.[96] The religious identity of the placement homes is difficult to track because, in New Brunswick, one's religious affiliation was not included on the census until 1861. While the ledger for the asylum is still helpful as a detailed record of each child, the orphans are impossible to identify by the religion of their new "placement families" in 1851. According to Peter Murphy, 127 placements were made and 88 per cent of these were Protestant. Of the sixty-four placement households identified over two censuses, it appears only nine placement families were Catholic, thus providing evidence that Catholic children were indiscriminately shipped out to the farms and businesses of the colony's Protestant population.[97]

There may be some truth to the comment that the commissioners of the orphan asylum used orphan placement "as a vehicle of religious and cultural assimilation," although the reality of Catholic child placement may be a little more complex.[98] While there was an increasing number of Irish Catholics in the province, many had arrived recently and had not yet become well established in business or in farming. Many of the prime agricultural lands in the southern counties and in the fertile valley of the Saint John River had already been surveyed and occupied. Rioting at Woodstock was perpetrated by local Protestant farmers who wished to keep potential Catholic farmers out.[99] Thus, had commissioners sought a large pool of ready and willing Catholic farmers in which to place Catholic children, they would have been sorely disappointed. It is also true that there was a growing Irish Catholic middle class, merchants and shopkeepers, that had emerged in the cities of Fredericton and Saint John. Many of the men engaged in these activities were pre-famine migrants, who had built strong roots in the local community, but once again this was a very small pool for potential patrons. Furthermore, the evidence in actual case studies of placement are not conclusive about Protestant proselytization, although Peter Toner does suggest that the rise in the number of Irish Baptists, a Christian group that is not an extensive one in Ireland, may point to some conversions from Catholicism.[100] Nevertheless, the census data does not readily yield the proverbial "smoking gun" of a Catholic child, as a rule, adopting the faith of their Protestant patron as a "normal" practice. Three factors make this kind of hypothesis problematic: first, religion is not indicated in the census of 1851; most children are unaccounted for a decade later in the census of 1861; and, finally, when girls came of age and married, their surname changed and they become extremely difficult to trace. Worse still, the results of some census districts are lost or become, according to Peter Toner, "casualties of time and indifference."[101] Several case studies, however, may reveal, the nuances of religious fidelity or apostacy.

The story of orphan Bartholomew Foley illustrates how Catholic children could be placed without reference to their religion. Bart's parents had died in Ireland on the Gore-Booth estate, and he and his brother Michael sailed on the *Lady Sale* as two unattended orphans. He and his brother were both in the almshouse but were later admitted to the emigrant hospital, where Bart's brother, Michael, died on the 26 December 1847. Within a week, on 4 January 1848, the ten-year-old Bart arrived at the asylum. His stay was remarkably short at the home because after only five days William Smith placed him with Calvin Luther Hathaway of Maugerville, in Sunbury County.[102] Hatheway, was the son of Loyalist settlers and a surveyor and author of a popular history of New Brunswick. His son George Luther would become premier of New Brunswick in 1871.[103] Hatheway's given names certainly betrayed his Protestant roots. Nevertheless, a young Irish Catholic Bart Foley seemed to have landed in the arms of New Brunswick gentry. In the census of 1851, however, the enumerator discovered Bart living in the Parish of Maugerville, working as a servant on the farmstead of Martha Dow, who was a neighbour of Hatheway. Dow was a thirty-five-year-old single mother, with three daughters under seven years old, which probably prompted Hatheway to loan her his Irish ward. Bart was the youngest among three servants working on the Dow farm.[104] Despite the fact that there was no Catholic Church in Maugerville in the 1840s, with the closest being St Dunstan's in Fredericton, Foley still identified himself as a Catholic. In 1861, he declared to the enumerator that he was Catholic and continued to live in Maugerville working as a lumberman and living as a lodger with an Anglican (Episcopalian) family.[105] Evidently, in the case of Bartholomew Foley placement with Protestant families and living in the predominantly Protestant Maugerville did not seem to loosen his attachment to the Church of his birth.

The Hurley family, however, demonstrates many of the limitations of assessing the impact on Catholic children within Protestant families. The Hurleys set out from Galway, on board the *Midas* and landed in Saint John on 27 August 1847. They were admitted to the emigrant hospital where the father (unnamed) died, leaving thirty-four-year-old Mary, sick and responsible for their three children: Mary (thirteen), Patrick (thirteen), and Bridget (twelve).[106] All three children were discharged from the hospital, with both Patrick and Bridget ending up in the orphan's asylum, presumably as half orphans, since the records appear to indicate that their mother, Mary Sr, was still alive. The younger Mary, who was probably fourteen or fifteen when discharged, simply vanished from the record.[107] Within two weeks of entering the asylum on 4 November 1847, William Smith dispatched Patrick to George Scribner, an Episcopalian (Anglican)[108] resident of Gagetown. But Pat Hurley, like many other orphan children, did not remain long in his placement. By 1851, at the age of sixteen, he was living and working as a servant in the household of the Widow Eletha Smith in nearby Barton. The widow was a Congregationalist whose daughter Sarah was married to William McLean, an Irish Catholic, who also resided in the house. Despite the presence of McLean, Smith was still listed as the household head.[109] In this environment, with the potential support of McLean, Hurley would not have been a fish out of water in his Catholicism, perhaps suggesting that the placement of Catholic children in Protestant homes might not have always encouraged apostacy.[110]

Patrick's sister Biddy or Bridget was also sent to a Protestant home. On 9 March 1848, more than three months after her arrival in the asylum, she was collected by Silas Marven, a farmer and proprietor in Springfield, King's County. When enumerators came to take the census in 1851, Bridget was still on the farm, working as a servant. Marven was an Episcopalian (Anglican),[111] so it was clear that she was placed in a Protestant home, but the 1851 census would not indicate if she was Catholic or Protestant or whether she would have even been supported in her faith. There would not be a Catholic parish in the area until 1877, so she would be without a chance to attend Mass even if she had wished it.[112] She was listed as aged thirteen, which can also be problematic for the researcher.[113] As a young woman, it was highly unlikely that she would have remained in the home for the next ten years in order to be captured by the census of 1861. At twenty-three she may have moved elsewhere, married, and had a different surname, which would make it extremely difficult to track Bridget down. Given the proclivity of many Irish migrants to New Brunswick to head to the "Boston states," it is not beyond the bounds of probability that, when she came of age, Bridget headed to the United States or perhaps sought out her brother Patrick who was also unrecorded in the census of 1861.

The available records provide little proof of Protestant proselytization of their Irish Catholic wards, since many of the orphan children, like Bridget Hurley, are just not present in the homes of their original patrons in 1861. The case of Thomas Kelly is, however, a little more perplexing. Like so many children, Thomas was left an orphan because of the disastrous crossing of the *Aeolus* in November 1847. With both parents dead, he was sent to the almshouse shortly after the ship landed and then transferred to the asylum in December 1847. At only five years of age, there was little urgency to place him, and he likely found himself in Miss Minette's Infant School. When the asylum shut down, young Thomas was transferred to the almshouse, whereupon he was placed in the care of the Widow McLeod, almost a year later.[114] Jemima McLeod lived in Long Reach with her two children and Thomas next appears with William McLeod, possibly a relative of Jemima's, and the "six" year old is listed as an apprentice.[115] Ten years later, in 1861 in nearby in Greenwich, King's County, one finds Thomas "Kelley" working as a servant. Jemima McLeod's entire household is listed as Episcopalian, but Thomas has no religious identification. Perhaps he was far too young to have consciously retained any religious affiliation and, as a servant, may not have been included in family social gatherings, such as Sunday services. If the McLeod's had expected him to be "Godly" it is plausible he attended the Anglican services with them but was never formally invited to be a member of the congregation.[116]

The case of John Moran presents another scenario of how Irish Catholic orphans survived the placement process. The Moran family had been part of the group of assisted tenants from the Gore-Booth estate, who set sail for New Brunswick on board the *Yeoman*. John's father died during the journey, but his mother survived. The *Yeoman* arrived on 21 August 1847, but John did not show up at the orphan asylum until 21 January 1848. There were no siblings accompanying this twelve-year-old boy upon arrival and no indication that his mother was deceased. One can only speculate on what happened to John during this five-month gap between his disembarkation and dispatch to the asylum. Perhaps his mother was well enough to take care of him, but, as was the case with many half-orphans, she turned him over to the care of the asylum until such time when she had the means to resume her parenting of John. The commissioners wasted no time in placing John. The day after he arrived, John found himself with John A. Morrison, a merchant and pre-famine Irish migrant living in Saint John.[117] Morrison's religious affiliation is not recorded in 1851, and he does not appear in the 1861 census.[118] In the latter year, however, John Moran appears with his mother Mary, who is listed as head of the family, living in St Mary's, York County and working as a general labourer.[119] Both are listed as Catholic. So despite being a half orphan and placed quickly, John's mother found him and was able to reunite the fragments of her family. The Morans present yet another twist in the complicated tale of the Saint John-based orphans.

Finally, Timothy Purcell, presents the rare case of an Irish Catholic child, who actually was placed in an Irish Catholic home. Tim was one of the few children in the asylum from the Irish province of Leinster. James Purcell was sixty years old when he set out from Dublin with his two young children, Tim (eleven) and Sally (nine); it appears that no other family members made the journey with them. James died in the emigrant hospital of fever and dysentery, and the two children were placed in the orphan asylum on 25 October 1847. William Smith placed Tim with Patrick Ryan, a Catholic farmer in Sussex, King's County, who had arrived in New Brunswick in 1825. Tragically, Sally was left behind in the asylum and died there in March 1848.[120] Tim, however, was still with Ryan in 1851 and presumably working as a hand on the farm with four other young Irish persons, three of whom arrived in the colony during Black '47.[121] A decade later, Patrick Ryan at age sixty-five was still farming in what appeared to be a Catholic enclave in Sussex, and he was assisted by several hands but not Tim Purcell. Now in his mid-twenties, Purcell left to seek his fortune elsewhere and vanished from the printed record.

It must be admitted that the evidence of what happened to Irish orphans in Saint John is fragmentary at best, and that which does exist presents a complex set of relationships between patron and orphan. Thomas Kelly presents the case of a child too young to know what religion he was and certainly appeared to be happy enough staying with his placement much longer than his fellow orphans from the asylum. While it is entirely possible that placement from the orphan asylum resulted in some children leaving the Catholic faith of their birth, the evidence presented here suggests that the children may have been more resilient than had been originally thought. It appears that children who were placed with Protestant families departed within three years, which would have made assimilation to Anglo-Protestant social practices and religious mores difficult to take root. It should not be forgotten, as was the case of John Moran, that many of these children were half orphans and were collected by their Catholic parents, presumably continuing their previous religious practices. Quite simply, if commissioners like William O. Smith, himself a Presbyterian, had intended to use the process of orphan placement as a means of reducing the number of "Papist" children in the province, the available evidence suggests that the plan was unrequited.

No doubt the sectarian tensions that existed in New Brunswick made it easy for the Protestant supervisors at the asylum to make arbitrary decisions about placement. The Catholic Church in Saint John certainly was not strong, but it was not entirely supine either. Bishop William Dollard was not resident in Saint John but was living in the episcopal see of Fredericton and thus he had little direct influence on day-to-day decision making at the asylum nor does it appear did his local priests. Shortly after the famine migration, the diocese would relocate to Saint John, which was essentially the social, economic, and demographic hub for the colony's English-speaking population. With a Church essentially battered in the streets, unwanted by the charter population, without effective local leadership, and without a male or female religious order to assist migrants the position of the Catholic Church and its majority Irish congregations in Saint John was dire. The orphans were treated accordingly, and their case, although similar in their eventual indentureship, was remarkably different from the Catholic-led relief efforts in Quebec.

While lacking the infrastructure of Catholics elsewhere in British North America, the Catholic Church in Saint John remained as active as it could be to take care of Irish emigrants and especially orphans. Central to the Catholic effort was Father Edmund Quinn, who created an unofficial charitable hub at his mission outside the then city limits of Saint John, in which the current parish of Our Lady of the Assumption is located. In 1848, when writing to her parents in Ireland, Catherine Hennegan credited Quinn with housing her: "when you write, direct to the care of the Revd Edmund Quinn CC forwarded to the Neal Quinn Church land St John N.B."[122] Quinn not only cared for emigrants at his church, he raised money within the community for the care of the Irish orphans when they were in the almshouse and later when they were re-located to the emigrant orphan asylum. Given the surviving lists of his donors and patrons, it appears that Quinn was able to affect some ecumenical co-operation at a time in the province's history when such concord was in short supply. In December 1847, he publicly thanked donors for the gifts of bonnets, hoods, and outer garments for the orphan children in the city. Notable among his thanks was that to Mrs Charles Johnston, the wife of the high sheriff of Saint John.[123] Earlier in the month Quinn's list of benefactors, though bearing mostly Irish surnames, was headed by Lady Colbrooke, wife of the lieutenant governor, with a donation of £5. Second on the list was Bishop Dollard himself, who matched Lady Colebrook's donation.[124] Quinn also organized "The Ladies of Saint John" to meet at the Temperance Hall to make clothing for the orphans and collected £21 6s 4d, proceeds of a Charity Ball, "for procuring clothes for the poor children attending Catholic Sunday-Schools."[125] While Quinn was a major Catholic figure in orphan relief in Saint John, he did not possess the influence or political clout of fellow clergymen – Cazeau in Quebec, Macdonell in Kingston, or Kirwan in Toronto – to co-ordinate the placement of Irish Catholic children in Catholic homes and businesses.

The Catholic infrastructure in Saint John would improve within a decade of the famine migration. In 1851, William Dollard died and was succeeded the following year by Thomas Louis Connolly,[126] an Irish-born Franciscan. His consecration on 4 May 1852 coincided with the creation of the Diocese of Fredericton, replacing the Diocese of New Brunswick. Under Connolly's watch the Catholic Church created St Vincent's Orphanage in 1854, and that same year he oversaw the formation of the Sisters of Charity of the Immaculate Conception, which would provide the social services and educational facilities so desperately needed by the growing Irish Catholic population.[127] With so much Church activity focused in Saint John, shortly after Connolly's elevation to the office of Archbishop of Halifax the Vatican translated the episcopal see from Fredericton to Saint John in 1860. Perhaps, this development was too late for the famine migrants of 1847–48, but it was a tangible reminder of how important the famine migration was for the evolving presence of the Catholic Church in Saint John.

Little Ellen Mooney did not live long enough to witness these many changes in her new home. With her father dead and her mother scrambling to fend for her children, on 30 November 1847 the Mooney siblings were admitted to the asylum. They were another example of half orphans being placed in the care of the public purse while a single parent either struggled to recover from illness, find money, or both.[128] On 2 May 1848, the commissioners placed fourteen-year-old Anthony Mooney with Mrs Cecilia Ranney, an English widow who ran a boarding house in Saint John. Ellen died on 9 June and her mother came to collect ten-year-old Bridget, the youngest of the Mooney children, ten days later. The Mooney's journey did not end there but the official, routinely generated records of them did. While Cecilia Ranney can be found in the New Brunswick census of 1851, Anthony is no longer with her. Perhaps he joined his mother and youngest sister and tried to make a new life in America. Such was the fate of many who were left at the mercy of Harry Temple's largesse.

6

Brave New World

Edward Nealon did not encounter the same reception in Quebec as did Molly Johnson of *Heritage Minute* fame. He was not part of the Black '47 migration, having arrived at Quebec in June 1848. In that year there were far fewer ships bound for Canada from Ireland, with most Irish migrants electing to travel to the United States. Moreover, the Canadian government had raised the fines for landing sick passengers and now had taken control of emigration and relief by raising the per capita fees charged on incoming migrants. Young Edward would have known none of this. At eleven years of age, he left Coolmean, County Clare and boarded the *Governor* at Limerick with his father, James Nealon, his mother, Honora Moylan, and his older brother James. Both parents died on the journey leaving Edward and James Jr in the care of the Charitable Society of Catholic Ladies at Quebec City. Both boys were sent to Ste-Catherine, outside of Quebec, with James being placed with Dennis McCarthy and young Edward with Cornelius McCarthy. The thirty-six-year-old McCarthy (McCarty) was from County Cork and had been in Ste-Catherine since at least 1843. He and his wife Ann Driscoll had four young sons ranging from one to eight years old. Their neighbours were mostly Irish hailing from counties Kilkenny, Cavan, Offaly, and Tipperary. By 1851, Edward, listed as Neilon, had been with the McCarthys for nearly four years and as a fifteen-year-old was likely labouring in the fields, tending the wheat crop, with Cornelius.[1] However, like most of the Irish orphans, he was not considered a member of the family.[2] Unlike Molly, there was no romantic sense of a union of peoples with an Irish placement among French Canadians; the

Nealon brothers were separated but landed in the same community with a pair of Irish brothers and their families.[3]

While Edward's own life appeared rather ordinary, his descendants would make quite a splash. For the next decade Edward continued to live in the countryside working as a lumberjack in Portneuf and, by 1861, was married to Alice Irish.[4] Alice was from a neighbouring farm in Ste-Catherine, and, although she was born in the area around 1835, her parents hailed from counties Waterford and Monaghan.[5] Edward obviously had become smitten with Alice while living in this Irish rural enclave in Portneuf. By 1891, Edward Neilan (census spelling) was living in Montcalm Ward and working as a carter. He and Alice were living next to their daughter Nora and her husband Michael Dinan. Edward Neilan's granddaughter Johanna Dinan, called Josie by her friends, married Harry Quart. Josie would have a remarkable career and was one of two women named to the Canadian Senate in the 1950s. She was "famed for her uncanny ability to spot Bolshevist tendencies ... A strikingly handsome woman, Josie was known for her big floppy hats, her Lauren Bacall voice and partisan exuberance."[6] As a senator and honoured as a member of the British Empire, her journey stood in stark contrast to her grandfather's flight from misery and hunger in County Clare.

Edward Nealon's (Neilon) life was not unique among the Irish children who lost one or both parents and then were forced to face a new world bravely on their own. His placement family, the McCarthys, were pre-famine Irish who gave him sufficient opportunity that he gained a modest living as a blue-collar worker, married, and raised a family not far from where he landed in Quebec. The most exceptional feature of his story is that of his granddaughter, who embodied the social advancement of many children and grandchildren of emigrants. But Nealon's settlement and adaptation to Canada was but one of a variety of life trajectories for the famine orphans. After having been placed, there were several pathways that orphans followed, pursuing a new life away from Ireland. Many decided to keep moving, instead of remaining sedentary as Nealon had. The most common destination was the United States, where there were prospective family, friends, and perhaps fortune already awaiting them. Other children searched for their relations in British North America, tracking them by travelling inland from Quebec and following the Irish settlement grid that was already in place in Canada prior to the famine. Others fell in love and married someone from their placement family or someone on an adjoining farm or in a nearby street. Such marriages between Irish and French Canadians were not unusual nor were partnerships between famine orphans and pre-famine Irish settlers. A fourth group embraced the life of priests and nuns, emulating those who had tended to them in the fever sheds or with whom they had taken shelter elsewhere. Noting the benefits of a religious life, Irish orphans joined the ranks of the Quebec clergy or the Grey Nuns. A fifth group pushed forward into the farming frontiers of British North America, particularly into the Saguenay region of Quebec and the vast lands of the Huron Tract, managed by the Canada Company in Western Ontario. Still other orphans moved to the frontiers where there was work available, notably the canal works of the Niagara Peninsula, which had the bonus of being in proximity to the United States. When the demand for canal labourers dried up, they could simply cross the border and pursue opportunities in the republic. New groups of orphans, primarily young women from Irish workhouses who emigrated to Canada under the Earl Grey scheme, after 1849, would find themselves as domestic servants and potential wives for Canadian men. Thus, Nealon was not alone in trying to make his stand in the brave new world, but the life paths chosen by the orphans were as varied as the children themselves.

Perhaps one of the most common journeys for Irish orphans was setting out to see if they could make a better life for themselves in the United States. In the ledger of the Charitable Ladies of Quebec, several orphans were identified as being sent to the United States. On 26 October 1847, for example, Mary Brennan, who hailed from the Mahon estate in Roscommon, and had survived the horrendous conditions on the *Naomi* was described as having "left for Brooklyn."[7] No other notations were made, leaving one to assume that there may have been extended family on Long Island among the growing Irish community in the New York City area.[8] Similarly, Matthew Carroll of Clonakilty, County Cork was sent to Pittsburgh, evidently to live with an uncle who had previously settled in Pennsylvania.[9] He was still is Pittsburgh in 1850 when enumerators of the United States census found him living with his Uncle Andrew in Ward Six, Pittsburgh, in Alleghany County.[10] Little is known of what happened to him later in life, although there is some strong evidence that he, like many Americans of his generation, moved west and settled in Wisconsin. In 1870, a Matthew Carrol matching his description, Irish birth, and age is discovered married, with two small children, and working as a miner in Hazel Green, Grant County, Wisconsin.[11]

The familial connections to the United States also pulled orphans away from their temporary lodgings in Saint John, New Brunswick. Having lost both parents in the course of their migration from County Galway, the Mitchell orphans – Catherine (ten), Mary (five), and Michael (three) – were placed with John Burns, who was presumably charged with taking them to Boston and then to Cantonville where they could live with their uncle.[12] There were no details as to who underwrote the cost of their voyage from Saint John to Boston or whether or not John Burns completed the task. Nevertheless, the Mitchell children appear to confirm a pattern of families merely planning to use British North America as a way station, as a part of a larger plan to rejoin family in the United States. Having articulated these intentions to their guardians at their point of entry, it appears that the children provided some agency in carrying through the family plans despite the death of their parents. Local religious and civic figures in Canada and New Brunswick somehow took the time to investigate the familial ties in the United States and then made the appropriate arrangements to reunite the separated families. Given the stresses and financial strains of the time, and the frantic circumstances in ports, the guardians should be credited with not taking the path of least resistance and just placing these children, willy-nilly, in the most convenient local shelter.

The case of Bartholomew Furlong, however, describes another trend in the pilgrimage of orphans from Canada to the United States. When he arrived at Montreal in 1847, nine-year-old Bartholomew Furlong was the youngest of three siblings taken into the care of the Grey Nuns. Originally from Adamstown, Wexford, the Furlongs had become orphaned before leaving Ireland, and their passage may have been one of the rare cases of children who sailed alone or were accompanied by a relative who disappeared from the historical record between departing Ireland and the Furlong children's arrival at Montreal. The three were placed with Harold Kennedy, a Scottish Catholic farmer in Glengarry County, in Upper Canada but not far from Montreal. Little is known about what happened to the eldest child, James (thirteen), but his sister Margaret, two years his junior, was working as a servant on the Kennedy farm in Locheil Township as late as 1851. Margaret remained in Glengarry, eventually working for Alexander Macdonell, a merchant, and his wife Isabella. The couple was evidently childless, so it appears Margaret Furlong remained with them to keep house. Her youngest brother Bart, who seems to have eluded Glengarry census takers in 1851, did appear that year working near Fenelon Falls with another small group of Irish Catholics in the newly developed back county of Victoria, Canada West, although he listed Lochiel as his official place of residence.[13] At that time it seems he had joined Margaret in Lochiel, using it as a home base for pursuing more lucrative employment as a manual labourer on the frontier.[14]

Bart had a wanderlust about him. He left Glengarry and became naturalized as a US citizen in New York City sometime before 1871. Furlong continued to move, and by 1880 he was in Cameron County, Pennsylvania. There he married Mary O'Rourke, a woman twenty years his junior, who was an immigrant of Irish origin but of Scottish birth. Evidently the O'Rourkes had migrated first to Glasgow, like many Irish, and then made the trans-Atlantic crossing. Bart and Mary had seven children, one of whom appeared to be named after Bart's missing brother James.[15] At the time of Bart's death in 1891, he and Mary had moved to Sterling Run, Pennsylvania, where they ran the "Alpine House," a successful local tavern.[16] Unlike many of his fellow orphans who seemed to move south to the United States on a rudimentary form of family chain migration, Furlong appeared to be a lone wolf, seeking his fortune wherever it would come: Upper Canada, New York, and Pennsylvania. In some ways he more resembled the wandering settler of the period, akin to the famous Irishman Wilson Benson,[17] seeking opportunity where it could be found and often eluding civic enumerators in the process.

With the number of orphans who simply disappeared from their Canadian placement homes by the time census takers were mobilized in 1851–52, it might be assumed with some degree of confidence that many orphans simply made their way to the United States. Few appear in Canadian censuses thereafter, and orphan girls are extremely hard to track since many took their husband's surname upon marriage. Given the evidence provided by the samples in this study, including Bart Furlong and so many others, it appears that the United States offered the promise of greater opportunity in its eastern cities which then were teaming with Irish migrants and in the American Midwest, which was rapidly opening for settlement. Whatever the case, the trail of the orphans in the United States quickly runs cold, not just in identifying young women thru the decades but also pinpointing such identifying markers as religion, which was not recorded in the decennial census in the United States.

Whether the children moved on to the United States or not many of the surviving orphans suggest a higher degree of agency than previously considered by historians. The lure of America, or the search for stability and security in Canada, was often combined with a child's own connectedness with family and friends in the new world who had left their townlands in Ireland before the failure of the potato. Some orphans demonstrated that their families had had some "plan" in mind as they made the decision to leave Ireland during the famine. While parents may have died on route to their final Canadian home, the children left behind carried out the family's original intent with varying degrees of agency. Such was the case of Margaret Conlon, who was introduced in chapter 3. Born in County Armagh in 1842, young Margaret set out with her father John, her mother Mary Blair, and three siblings on board the *Achilles*, which sailed from Liverpool in April 1847. The trauma experienced by this family over the next six weeks is heart-rending. While standing at the bow of the ship, John Conlon was swept overboard by a rogue wave. Benedict Conlon, Margaret's brother, died at sea. Mary Blair was pregnant and left to tend to three young girls, hoping that she would arrive in time at Quebec and then travel to Toronto to meet by her dead husband's brother, Benjamin, who had already settled in Upper Canada. In a letter written on board ship, she related her sad tale to this brother-in-law, hoping that the remnants of her family could hold on: "I am destitute if you do not meet me ... I do not intend stopping at any place until I reach Toronto and if you meet me there neither I or the children will be any burden on you."[18]

Such hopes were unrequited. When the ship landed at Quebec, only five-year-old Margaret survived, with her mother and sisters dying at Grosse Ile. As an Anglican child, Margaret was taken into the care of Anglican Bishop George Mountain and delivered to the Protestant Orphans home in Montreal. It was there that her Uncle Benjamin, the farmer from York County, collected her and she began a new life in Ontario. In 1868, she married Hiram Dewitt, a farmer, and they began a new life in Saltfleet Township. They had four daughters and a son, and Margaret lived to the grand old age of eighty-six,[19] having outlived her husband by more than thirty years and having the great opportunity of enjoying generations of Dewitts with whom she could share her story of the famine pilgrimage.

The six Sheridan orphans also had a plan. In a remarkable story of fortitude, siblings Catherine (twenty), Mary (nineteen), Anne (fifteen), Owen (fourteen), Ellen (twelve), and Patrick (ten) had all survived the voyage of the *Naomi*, one of the four ships commissioned by Major Denis Mahon to assist some of his tenants to Canada. As recorded earlier in chapter 2, the list of the dead was lengthy on board the *Naomi* and two of its victims were James Sheridan and his wife Mary Connor. Their children became wards of the orphanage in Quebec City the first week of September 1847, but they did not stay long. Within a month, the register recorded only that they had "left for Lockport Oct. 2."[20] Presumably the older siblings, Catherine and Mary, took the lead and had a plan. Lockport was on the Erie Canal in upstate New York and been a hub for trade and for canal works. Naturally, there might be the attraction of employment, although there were several other canal towns, Lachine, Beauharnois, even towns along the Rideau Canal, which all would have been closer to Quebec and were teaming with Irish sojourners and settlers. Lockport, to the chance observer, seemed to be a little too far off the beaten track for six orphans on the loose in North America for the first time. Upon closer examination, it appears that the itinerant Catholic priest working between Lockport and Elmira was a Father John Sheridan.[21] In 1848, he founded the first Catholic Parish, dedicated to St Peter and St Paul, in Lockport. While the presence of Father Sheridan in Lockport does not answer definitively why these children would abruptly leave Quebec for the Finger Lakes District of New York, it is too strong a coincidence, suggesting perhaps family ties between the children and this priest. Further evidence of the connection is offered by the US census which records, in 1850, Father John Sheridan living in Elmira with a young Ann Sheridan, presumably serving as a housekeeper.[22] While the evidence is not foolproof, the Sheridan story does suggest a strong sense of agency in migrating families trying to reunite with former friends and family in the new world. The Sheridans, just as Margaret Conlan, had a plan to connect with family members who had migrated prior to the famine.

Not far from Lockport, on the Canadian side of the Niagara frontier, orphan John O'Connor was trying to make sense of a new life in Upper Canada that had gone horribly wrong. His father and mother, Patrick and Mary O'Connor, had left the Mahon estate in Roscommon before Major Denis Mahon put the assisted migration scheme into play in April 1847. The O'Connors did not have the benefit of being subsidized by their landlord so they only brought son John along, leaving two daughters behind in Lissonuffy with Patrick's brother William.[23] The O'Connors travelled as far as the Welland Canal area of the Niagara Peninsula, where there was employment on the upgrades to the original canal and a fair number of Irish countrymen from their native province of Connaught.[24] Patrick had made considerable money and appeared poised to pay for the passage of his daughters, creating yet another link in the migration chain forged between Niagara and Roscommon. As was recounted in chapter 2, these plans would remain unfulfilled. In early 1848, Thomas Brennan, another tenant of the estate and a participant in the Mahon scheme, ventured to Niagara, grieving the loss of his wife and one child at Grosse Ile. He and his teenaged daughter took lodgings close to the O'Connors, and he began drinking and cavorting with the family. In May he murdered Patrick and Mary, stole their money, and attempted to kill young John by throwing him off the Niagara escarpment near Queenston. John survived but was unable to testify in court against Brennan, who had been captured in Toronto with a large sum of money and Mary's clothing in his possession. Brennan was hanged for the crime and buried in the churchyard of St Vincent de Paul Parish in Niagara-on-the-Lake. With the assistance of the court, John O'Connor was taken in by a local Mennonite farmer.[25]

The story of John O'Connor appears to be yet another anomaly in the stories of orphan adaptation to Canada. First, unlike his peers from both his estate and among all those fleeing famine from across Ireland, he does not lose his parents on the first leg of the journey, at sea, or at Grosse Ile or Partridge Island. His misfortune came to pass as old neighbours renewed conflicts that had begun in the old world on the Mahon estate. John was still a famine orphan none the less, and he remained within proximity of fellow Connaught migrants at Niagara. He never gave up trying to find his two older sisters, who had been part of the family re-unification plan dreamed by his father. As late as 1871, John was still searching for his sisters and writing to the *Irish American*, in New York for any information leading to their discovery. According to the notice, written by a third party: "The little boy, only, by God's providence, miraculously escaped sharing the same barbarous fate [as his parents]. This boy, arrived at manhood, now resides in this City, and wishes most earnestly to obtain such information as will enable him to find or communicate with his sisters."[26] Like many other Irish youth, John had ventured to the United States but still with the hope of restoring what may have been left of his family.

Eliza Hetherton (Herington) presents another variant in the movement of Irish orphans to the United States. She arrived in Montreal in November 1847 and became a resident of the St Jerome Emilien Orphange. As has been mentioned before, Father Calixte Marquis transported many of these orphans to the parish of Béconcour, east of Montreal. Eliza (also known as Helen) had been placed with the Lamontagne family but was not considered a family member when census takers posed the question to the Lamontagnes in 1852.[27] In 1856, at age eighteen, she married Joseph Lamontagne and continued to reside in Bécancour until at least 1880. At that time her family, like so many French Canadians in the period, had relocated to New England, pursuing work in the various mill towns in those states in proximity to Quebec.[28] The Lamontagnes remained in Maine until 1901, and that is where Eliza died.[29] Her journey as an orphan was not to complete the intentions of their parents but was part-and-parcel of her having becoming a member part a French Canadian family, subject to the economic lure of the United States and the limited opportunities in Quebec.[30]

As great as the urge may have been for some orphans to move on from their initial ports of entry or venture to another "land of dreams," there were those who never moved far away from their initial point of Canadian contact. These children may have not been party to a family plan, a migration chain, or in a financial or physical situation causing them to venture far from where they had landed. Some may have been simply too young to know of such attempts to reunite with former neighbours and kin, or they may have been simply too old and well employed to think about moving on, even in the short term. Alice Edmonds, much like Edward Nealon, never moved far from the Quebec City area, where she had landed with her six siblings in 1847. Her mother Mary Godkin died in 1844, in Gorey, County Wexford, and her father Gabriel Edmonds opted to leave Ireland during Black '47, with the remnants of his family: the youngest, Maria, was only eight years old. Gabriel survived the voyage but died in Quebec on 15 August 1847. This left Alice, the eldest sibling at age twenty-two, hardly a child at the time, in charge. As Protestants, the Edmunds children were all listed as being under the care of Anglican Bishop George Mountain, but Alice, her sister Sarah (eighteen), and her brother Richard (seventeen) immediately began to work to support all the children. The bishop's register of orphans listed all three as being "in service." In 1851, Alice was living in a boarding house in Quebec City, working as a nurse.[31] Three years later she married Joseph McLaughlin at Holy Trinity Anglican Cathedral in Quebec and remained in the city. She and Joseph had four daughters and a son between the years 1854 and 1865. Alice Edmunds McLaughlin died of pneumonia on 3 March 1884 at the age of fifty-six having been predeceased by her husband. She was buried at St Peter's Anglican Church in Quebec.[32] Alice represented a whole cohort of orphans who found work and family where they landed and simply never left.

Steady work was often a motivation for children just to stay put. Introduced in chapter 3, John and Patrick McManus, eleven and eight, from county Tyrone, both ended up in Rivière de Loup, a town southwest of Rimouski on the south shore of the St Lawrence. They were among the few Irish children in the region placed in a non-Francophone environment. John lived with the Spencer family and worked as a labourer; by 1861 he was still living in Rivière de Loup, working as a barkeeper and married to Elizabeth who was five years his senior. His younger brother Patrick had been placed with the Kelly family who kept an inn in the town. Another Irish orphan, Jane Harvey, who is not counted among the 619 on the O'Gallagher List, appears to have been living in the inn as well, as does a fifteen-year-old orphan named Cornelius O'Keefe. One suspects that Mr Kelly took the opportunity to "employ" some Irish orphans as workers in his hotel. In Rivière de Loup, the McManus brothers found employment, love, and a small Irish community, so they stayed.

One cannot underestimate the longing for companionship and stability as a child's motivation for staying where they were placed. Perhaps the storyline that seems most compatible with the "Molly Johnson" vignette is the migration of orphans to Quebec's rural hinterland and the intermarriage between Irish orphans and the relatives or friends of their placement families. Given the previous discussion of disappearing children and the more common flight of such children to the United States, the fairy tale type ending was not normal among the orphans placed in rural communities. This having been said, there were several cases where orphans, particularly young women, decided to stay on the farm. Records from churches, censuses, and newspapers indicate that there were cases of Irish women marrying and settling down with French Canadian farm boys. In those cases, the young women appear to marry into the families in which they were placed or wed young men from adjoining farms. In some cases, these blended Irish–French Canadian families remained in the same region for generations.

Perhaps the case of Catherine Kennedy resembles most closely what has passed into Canadian lore as the mythical life trajectory of a female Irish orphan at the time.[33] John Kennedy and Margaret Howe (Haugh) left Burr, Tipperary and sailed on board the *Sir Robert Peel* out of Liverpool, England. During their fifty-one-day journey, having arrived at Quebec on 19 September 1847, the ship lost forty-nine of its 480 passengers, more than 10 per cent, either in quarantine or at sea.[34] It is likely that three of the victims on the voyage were John, aged forty, Margaret, aged thirty-eight, and their infant son Patrick, who was only a year old.[35] Catherine, aged twelve, and her younger brother John entered the orphanage in Quebec City on 6 October. Although they were split up, their placement families were both in L'Islet, with Catherine residing with the family of Clovis Caron and John taken in by the neighbouring Bélanger family. Both families listed the Kennedy children as family members when they were enumerated by census takers in 1852 – an unusual circumstance when compared with other orphans.[36] The "Molly Johnson" model continued to be manifest in L'Islet among the Kennedys. In 1853 Catherine married Louis Léon Caron, a nephew of Clovis, and they had seven children:

three girls and four boys. The family sojourned briefly in Maine where the sixth and last daughter, Lea, was born in 1874, but they soon returned to Quebec, near Nicolet. A photograph preserved by the family represents Leon and Catherine seated with their children and Leon holding a rifle, resembling a French Canadian version of the famous painting *American Gothic*. Catherine died in Nicolet in 1876, shortly after the birth of her seventh child, Joseph,[37] but her story would seem to bear out that some orphan children not only embraced their placement families but became a part of the fabric of rural Quebec and French Canadian Catholic society.

The case of the Mahoney sisters, however, raises several different scenarios for "orphan" children including the nuptials between Elizabeth Mahoney and Joseph St Pierre of Rimouski. As was described in chapter 3, John Patrick Mahoney and his wife Honora Kelly lived in Coolmean, County Clare with their six daughters. In 1847, Honora died and Patrick decided to start a new life in Canada with his six daughters. Sailing on the *Governor*, the Mahoneys landed in Quebec in late May 1848. While at the quarantine station at Grosse Ile, five-year-old Ellen Mahoney died and was buried on the island. Patrick took his surviving five daughters and, as a near destitute labourer, placed three of his girls, Bridget (twelve), Mary (eleven), and Catherine (seven) in the orphanage run by the Charitable Catholic Ladies.[38] He evidently kept the baby of the family, four-year-old Nancy, with him, as he did Elizabeth (thirteen), the eldest of the sisters, who was likely charged with the care of her baby sister and father. The orphanage sent the Mahoney sisters to Rimouski: Catherine was placed with farmer Etienne Pineau, Mary resided with the family Anton Larouche, and Bridget went to Johnny Mavinon. The pattern of priests settling Irish orphans with their parishioners seemed typical here.

The Mahoney case, however, provides two interesting twists to the commonly accepted historical myths about the Irish orphans.[39] First, Patrick did not die, and his daughters were essentially half-orphans. He also illustrates how some parents, without the means to support their children, placed his three pre-teenage daughters in the care of the Charitable Ladies, so that he could have an opportunity to earn some money and perhaps reclaim them at some point. It is at this stage of the family's life that things become even more intriguing. By 1851–52, one discovers that Patrick himself is sojourning in Rimouski on the farm of Hubert Levèsque and his wife Genevieve Ruest. Both he and eldest daughter Elizabeth are listed as non-family members of the household, and the forty-seven-year-old Patrick appears to be working on the farm. The Mahoney strategy is unique in how Patrick strategically put his daughters into care and then followed them to their French Canadian placements – even to remote Rimouski – to restore what remained of his family. Two daughters, Catherine and Elizabeth, would marry into the community. On 15 February 1858, Elizabeth Mahoney married Joseph St Pierre, a local farmer, at St Germaine Parish in Rimouski, and several months later, Catherine wed Joseph Pineau, a member of the family in which she had been placed.[40] The fact that Catherine signed the marriage register in her own hand attests to how she had acquired a modest education, like other orphans in Rimouski, over the previous decade. Equally as interesting is that fact that her father, Patrick, remained in the region and was living in L'Islet working as a merchant. At least in the short term for the Mahoney's, their new lives were proving fruitful in ways not seen in the cases of other orphans and their families.

The story of Elizabeth St Pierre (nee Mahony) did not end in Rimouski. While it appears that the newlyweds remained in Rimouski early in their marriage, by 1871 they had moved to the Saguenay region, north of the St Lawrence River, where agricultural settlement was growing in the late nineteenth century. Census records show that they lived in Escoumins, Milles Vaches, and Bersimis, all near the growing industrial town of Chicoutimi. From 1858 to 1879 they had ten children, six girls and four boys. All of the children appear to have led long lives. It should be noted that in later censuses, Elizabeth St Pierre always identified English as her first language, although likely had to have learned French by necessity having migrated to a predominantly Francophone region of Quebec. Joseph St Pierre died in Bersimis in 1911. Elizabeth died on 7 June 1916 in the family home. Evidently, the story of Elizabeth's voyage during the Irish famine was not lost on her descendants. One great-great-granddaughter has written, "her family left Ireland during the great famine for a better world. Such great suffering for this family. She lost her mother during the journey, was separated from her sisters, she did not speak the language [French]. What courage she had this builder."[41] It is obvious that Patrick never saw his daughter and her large family thrive in the Saguenay; he died at the Hotel Dieu in 1871 and was buried in St Patrick's Cemetery in Quebec City.[42]

Other children also decided to stay rooted in their new placement families. These orphans would have been a minority among the close to 1,700 famine orphans who were left to fend in Canada and New Brunswick in 1847–48. Census and parish registers do indicate that some children eschewed the wanderlust of travelling and became rooted in the land. When we last left Daniel and

Catherine Tighe, they had been safely deposited on the farm of the Coulombes in Lotbinière, on the south shore of the St Lawrence. François Coulombe and his wife Marie were childless and had only wanted a boy to help François work the farm, but after the loud cries and protests of Catherine, who feared separation from her last living relation, the Coulombes had generously taken them both. Catherine presumably worked around the house with Marie, while Daniel worked in the fields as had been the Coulombes' initial plan. Though Daniel and Catherine were never formally adopted, still not possible under Canadian civil law, François Coulombe arranged that a notary draw up papers to award Daniel the Coulombe farm upon François's death. This was remarkable among the known fates of the Irish orphans, in so far as none of the others have been recorded as having this opportunity of inheriting the property upon which they were placed. Although the story of Daniel Tighe's success is well known today in his native Strokestown Ireland, what is less known is that his case was an anomaly among his fellow orphans.

Daniel was true to his fortune and remained on the farm his entire life. In 1871, at the age of thirty-eight, he was married to a local French Canadian girl, Virginie, and they had two small children, Joseph and Maria. It is important to note that in the twenty-four years separating his arrival in Canada and his management of the farm, Daniel would become fluent in French and the family name of "Tighe" would be Gallicized to "Tye," as it remains today.[43] Catherine Tighe never married and after living with her brother's family on what would become the "Tye" farm, she moved to the parish of St-Croix in Lotbinière where she resided with the local priest, E.O. Coté, and his family. She served as Father Coté's housekeeper and likely tended to the needs of his elderly father who was also living in the rectory.[44] She died in 1898 and is buried in the St-Croix parish cemetery.[45]

Daniel's family continued to grow and prosper. In 1921 Daniel was still alive at eighty-six years of age, and Virginie was also alive. Although the census enumerator lists Virginie as unilingual French, it appears that Daniel had maintained his native English and was bilingual. While three of his sons moved to the United States, the farm was evidently run by their adult son Alphonse, age forty-seven, who also was married and had several teenaged children living at the farm. While at first appearance the family seems to be thoroughly French Canadian, the Irish spark was still alive and being passed from generation to generation, something a census is hard pressed to reveal. One of the youngest of the Tye clan was Leo, who at age sixteen was particularly close to his Irish grandfather.[46] According to Leo's own testimony, recorded years later to historian Marianna O'Gallagher, Daniel regaled Leo with his stories of growing up in Ireland during the famine, the terror of crossing the ocean, the loss of his mother and uncle, his and Catherine's placement with the Coulombes, and his new life as a farmer in Canada. Irish businessman James Callery, founder and owner of the National Famine Museum in Strokestown, was party to that conversation in Lotbinière and was responsible for bringing the Tighe/Tye story full circle. In 2013, with Leo having passed away, Callery and the people of Strokestown invited Leo's son Richard to join the town for "The Gathering," a special Irish commemoration of migration and the return of descendants to Ireland from across the Irish diaspora. Richard and his wife, both unilingual Francophones, accepted the offer and became the first Tighes to return to Ireland, since Daniel and Catherine's ill-fate voyage on the *Naomi* in 1847. In this one case, an exceptionally fortunate orphan gave rise to a proud French Canadian farming family whose descendants were able to make the return journey to Lissonuffy and reconnect with the descendants of the same family who remained during Black '47. While it is important to note the Daniel Tighe story as exceptional among the orphans of the time it is undeniably remarkable in that the Tighe story has had such an epilogue.[47]

While many of the orphans escaped the historical record and vanished into the mists of history, there are some who, unlike the Mahoney sisters, Catherine Kennedy, or Daniel Tighe lived quiet and unremarkable lives in the places of their original placement. Anne Kilmartin came from the same parish as Daniel Tighe, Lissonuffy, on the Denis Mahon estate at Strokestown, Roscommon. Her parents Thomas Kilmartin and Catherine Gaherty died on board the ill-fated *Virginius*. Anne found herself placed with Jacques Bourgeois and his family at St-Gregoire, near Nicolet. Kilmartin may have been treated well by the Bourgeois, given the fact that they embraced her as a family member in addition to their other four children. Perhaps this is why she stayed in the region, although never married, and ended up working as a day labourer twenty years later for Zephin and Agnes Brassard and their seven young children. According to the census, Anne never learned to read or write but appeared employed as a caretaker to the Brassard children.[48] Similarly, Mary Dempsey, from County Kildare, ended up being placed in Rimouski where she lived with the family of Jean-Baptiste Fiola. She remained on the farm, never married, and died at the age of twenty, having never left the region since her placement.[49] From the surviving records it is difficult to ascertain why Anne or

Mary did not venture forth to explore their new country, as had so many other orphans, but they are a testament to the varied responses of Irish orphan children to their new environment.

Some children, however, found their vocations within the local Catholic Church and became rooted in the pastoral life of their parishes or the charitable works of the convent. In the several documented cases of Irish orphan children embracing the religious or clerical life, the pattern appears to be similar. When placed by priests with families that had close ties to the Church, a vocation to the priesthood was a career option. Similarly, young girls often remained with the women religious who were their initial caregivers, either as lay workers or as vowed religious. Given the dominance of the Grey Nuns, the Sisters of Providence, and the Sisters of the Good Shepherd in Montreal, it is not surprising that orphan girls often were drawn to the routines and charism of the sisters. In 1847, Brigid Brown, a nine-year-old refugee from Galway, found herself in the care of the Grey Nuns after her father died in the sheds at Point St-Charles and her mother was unable to care for her. Several years later, in 1852, Bridget, was still living with the Greys and assisting them with their care of about 113 orphans and children born to unmarried women.[50] Fanny Armour was a half orphan from Cork. Although she was originally cared for by the Greys, the sisters despatched her with dozens of other orphans to the St-Jerome Emilien Orphanage. In 1852, at the age of fifeteen, Fanny was a student at the College de Sacre Coeur in Terrebonne near Montreal, presumably discerning a potential vocation.[51] She appears not to have taken vows with either the Sisters of Providence or the Grey Nuns but relocated to Windsor in Canada West where she worked as a servant in a private home.[52]

Some Irish girls did remain in the convents long enough to study and profess their vows. Bridget Carter was only eight years old when she arrived in Montreal and was placed in the care of the Grey Nuns. The sisters sent Brigid to their boarding school in Montreal and afterward Brigid continued her studies at the Collège de Sacre Coeur in Terrebonne. In 1881 she was a living in Montreal as a member of the Grey Nuns.[53] More famous among local historians were the Reilly sisters Helena (twelve), Bridget (seven), and Mary (five) who arrived in Quebec on board the *Avon*, which had sailed from Cork.[54] Although the three Reilly sisters hailed from County Roscommon they were not among the assisted migrants of Major Denis Mahon. Their parents Thomas Reilly and Mary Barry died between the time of their arrival at Grosse Ile in July 1847 and the arrival of the girls at the orphans' shelter in mid-August that same year.[55] The girls were listed as having resided in the general hospital where their father had been taken before he died. In 1860, Bridget left the hospital and married Astreul Samson, a local man. Helena, however, took vows as a Hospitaller Nun, becoming Sister Saint-Felix.[56] Although primarily a nursing sister at the hospital she was also an accomplished writer, penning a biography of Bishop St-Vallier, the second bishop of Quebec, during the Ancien Regime. One can only speculate on what motivated these young Irish girls to take vows with French Canadian orders; the fact that they had been cared for by sisters in their time of need and wished to repay the kindness is one possibility. Perhaps they were inspired by the witness of the women religious generally. It is also possible that the convent provided them a sense of security after the trauma of the famine and the voyage to Canada.

The orphans who opted for the Catholic priesthood received even greater notoriety in a Church dominated by male clerics. Unlike many congregations of women religious, whose charism publicly downplayed the work of individual sisters in favour of maintaining a strong, humble community image in society,[57] priests were constantly in the public eye. As pastors and curates in parishes and often the most educated men in rural parishes in Quebec, priests were prominent, respected, and authoritative leaders in their communities. Church records and local newspapers recorded the work of priests often, and, in the world of Ultramontane Catholicism, priests were launched into the public sphere as models of a living witness to Christ in the world.[58] While the records available in diocesan archives and the collections of men's religious orders assist greatly in building a profile of the orphan boys who embraced the clerical estate, the task of finding them has been made easier by record keepers, particularly in Quebec, who many years after the children landed, noted on the orphans register that they had "become a priest."[59]

Robert Walsh was one such orphan. Much of his entry in the registers kept by the Charitable Ladies of Quebec is blank. Walsh arrived in the orphan asylum in July of 1848 at the age of seven, but it is not noted where he was from or on what boat he sailed. He was taken to St-Gregoire, near Nicolet, by Joseph Pavre. His older sisters Anne (eight) and Margaret (ten) were placed with the families of Pierre Poirier and Joseph Prince, respectively, also in St-Gregoire.[60] Similar to what was witnessed elsewhere in the placement of orphans in Quebec, the siblings were separated but kept near one another in the same village. Ironically, in 1860 Robert's sister Margaret, then around twenty-three years old, married another Irish orphan who had been placed in St-Gregoire: Thomas Davy of county Kildare.[61] Their marriage is one of the few recorded in this study between the orphans themselves.

The happenstances of Robert Walsh, however, would be shrouded in mystery until the 1860s. Had it not been for the research undertaken by John Francis Maguire for his *Irish in America*, we might know nothing more about Walsh. The Irish priest was teaching at the seminary in Nicolet in the 1860s when Maguire was doing his research in Canada, although they evidently never met.[62] After completing his religious formation at Nicolet and prior to his ordination, his superiors sent Walsh to St Michael's College, Toronto in 1863 and 1864 to learn English.[63] Walsh reported to Maguire that his mother died at Grosse Ile, that he spoke only Irish as a child, and remained mute for two weeks after losing his parents on the journey to Canada. Robert, however, had the last wishes of his dying mother – that he be placed under the protection of the Blessed Virgin Mary – as his motivation to pursue the priesthood. He assimilated into his French Canadian community, spoke only French, and was encouraged in his vocation by his adopted parents. The theme of French Canadian agency emerges here as in other stories passed down by some orphans, in so far as their faith was valued and nurtured in their new home, making the possibility of embracing the priesthood an option for their life's work. Walsh also held out some hope that he could find another sister who had been left behind in Ireland. Robert Walsh died in 1873, having failed to find the long-lost sister who he mistakenly thought might be in Kilkenny. Recently, historian Jason King has discovered what Walsh could not. King found evidence that Walsh's younger sister Honora had been living in the Killee estate near Mitchelstown in north Cork, a place where, ironically, Robert's father had been employed prior to migration.[64]

There was a similar vocational trajectory for two brothers from Roscommon. Patrick and Thomas Quinn had been passengers on board the ill-fated *Naomi* in 1847. Their parents James Quinn and Peggy (Margaret) Lyons, who had agreed to become part of Major Denis Mahon's assisted migration scheme, left the parish of Lissonuffy but perished before they set foot in Quebec City. Two Quinn daughters, Mary (nine) and Catherine (one) also died at Grosse Ile.[65] When reflecting on the experience later in 1914, Thomas Quinn, although he had only been six years old at the time of the crossing, remembered passengers piled up in the hold of the ship, most of whom were infected with typhus.[66] Quinn recounted that he was placed with the family of George Bourque, while his brother, Patrick, who had been recovering from typhus, eventually was placed with the family of Joseph Geoffroy. Eventually the boys were reunited in the Bourque household, on the grounds of the seminary of the Diocese of Nicolet. In his reflection at the age of seventy-three, Thomas referred to the families as "adopting" him and his brother, perhaps hinting at the kindly way in which they were treated by their French Canadian hosts.[67] Both Quinns sought ordination to the priesthood, with the elder brother Patrick ordained in 1862 and Thomas embracing Holy Orders two years later.[68]

The Quinn brothers would serve with distinction in the Diocese of Nicolet. Thomas Quinn taught for three years at the seminary of Trois Rivières and then assumed a career in parish ministry across the Diocese of Nicolet.[69] He laboured in Francophone parishes and effectively became a Francophone priest. He died in 1923 at the age of eighty-two and was eulogized by colleague Father Elzéar Bellemare as "l'exile, le patriote, et le prêtre."[70] Bellemare described his friend Quinn as having embraced the French Canadian people, who had offered hospitality to him and his brother, being as thoroughly educated as a French Canadian priest would be, and as having served with great distinction until his retirement to Nicolet. In 1912, Bellemare related Quinn's speech at the Congress de la Langue Français, held at Montreal, where he vociferously defended the use of the French language, particularly against those Irish in Canada who would limit its use. In his speech, it was quite clear that Quinn was expressing his opposition to the policies of Irish Canadian Bishop of London Michael Francis Fallon and that prelate's support for the elimination of French-language instruction in Ontario schools after the second grade.[71] In Bellemare's words, Quinn stood in solidarity with Canada and the French Canadian people who embraced him: "Bien qu'il fut natif de l'Irlande, nul ne pouvait-redire avec plus conviction et de verité cette parole sortie du Coeur d'un patriote célèbre: 'O Canada, mon pays, mes amours!'"[72]

Meanwhile, his older brother Father Patrick Quinn served fifty-two years in the Catholic parish at Richmond, Quebec before his death in 1915 in his eightieth year.[73] The elder Quinn was noted as a skilled administrator, and he eventually served as councillor to Antoine Racine the first bishop of Sherbrooke in 1874. In the new diocese, while serving at Richmond, Quinn oversaw the expansion of the parish network in the growing townships now included under the jurisdiction of Bishop Racine. As far as one knows, in 1887, Patrick Quinn may have been the first of the orphans who settled in Canada to return to Ireland to visit family members who were still living in County Roscommon. One relative, Mary Quinn, returned to Canada with him and evidently remained a member of his household until Quinn died.[74] In 1912, a year when his younger brother was publicly advocating French Canadian language rights, Patrick was well ensconced in his Richmond parish, celebrating his fiftieth anniversary of ordination to the priesthood. In September, and in the presence of Bishop Paul Larocque of Sherbrooke, Quinn's brother Thomas, dozens of priests of the diocese, and two thousand parishioners, Patrick Quinn was celebrated by colleague Father J.C. McGee: "Your parishioners vie with one another in their praises of your sterling qualities of your indefatigable labour among them." But McGee also used the occasion to thank the Quinn brothers' parents for instilling in them the Catholic faith, and "the members of this good French Canadian family for adopting and training these two priests ... How many souls are in Heaven to-day, and how many will go there in future through their charity to these two exiled orphans."[75]

The lives of the Quinn brothers are not just another trajectory of what became of some of the famine orphans; their story enriches a specific reading of the orphan event within the context of Canada's polarized history of its two "founding settler peoples." The historical memory crafted around the Quinns was curated in a way that, in their own time, they became symbolic of the possible solidarity that could exist between the Irish and French in Canada, sometimes against a common enemy. Patrick Quinn's obituary was fairly explicit on this point, explaining that their "adoption" by French Canadians was "a deed which the beneficiaries have ever been grateful for and which has made them constant friends and defenders of the French Canadian race in all concerns and vital interests."[76] The Quinns did not forget. Bishop Bourget's reminders to McGee and the parishioners of St Patrick's in Montreal in the 1860s were not needed in Nicolet and Richmond. Fathers Bellemare and McGee were convinced that the Irish survivors in Quebec owed the French Canadians a debt for their kindness and welcome – a slight twist on the future provincial motto "je me souviens." Such reminders of the sacrifices of French Canadians in nurturing the Irish became *au courant* at a time when French Canadians regarded their language and culture under siege across Canada. Contemporaries fashioned a nationalist narrative linked to two Irish orphans. Boys of faith who, in their orphaned state, were rescued by French Canadians who formed them into pillars of the Church and defenders of the nation. Sometimes it is not surprising how the drama of "Molly Johnson" captured the notion that the Irish and French Canadians were natural allies and that the Irish formed a natural bridge between Canada's "two solitudes."

Many of the children would leave their Canadian and New Brunswick placements to try and eke out a living in the growing industrial cities of central Canada, the canal works in places like Niagara and Beauharnois, the rich resource and timber areas on the colonial frontier, or on the steadily opening farmlands in western Upper Canada or the Saguenay Valley. Trying to find these orphans in census and assessment roles is difficult and nearly impossible for the young women who would marry and take the name of their husband. Routinely generated records, therefore, are limited in their utility as the hunt for orphans becomes an exercise akin to trying to find the proverbial needle in a haystack. Sometimes obituaries, newspaper reports, and family histories yield some results. Of the close to 1,700 Irish orphans who arrived in Canada and New Brunswick, very few leave a clear trail like the Quinns, Mahoneys, Tighes, or Nealons.

The Pickering brothers – William, Andrew, and John – however, were not content with staying put in Quebec and came to represent a group of orphans who embraced the challenges of the Canadian frontier. As introduced in chapter 3, their parents, William Pickering and Matilda Wilson, were Protestants from Aughrim, Woods Chapel, in County Derry/Londonderry. Neither parent died on board their ship, *John and Robert*, which sailed from Liverpool to Quebec in late June 1847 with 346 passengers in steerage.[77] By the time it arrived at Quebec after five days in quarantine, thirty-three of its passengers had died. None of the Pickerings were among that number, but it seems likely that both William and Matilda died of typhus or a related communicable disease as they moved inland with their children. By the time they reached Montreal, the three boys became wards of the Anglican bishop in the same way that Alice Edmonds and Margaret Conlan had. Like Conlon, the Pickering brothers were housed at the Montreal Protestant Orphans Asylum, where they awaited placement in willing homes and businesses. There are gaps in the story, but all three boys eventually found themselves on the farming frontier of what is now in Ontario. Andrew joined his older brother Francis, who was working on a farm run by the Wideman family near the town of Markham. In 1881, while in his mid-forties he married Hanna Greer and settled in Whitchurch, not far from Markham. He died of apoplexy at the Forks of the Credit in 1917, at the age of eighty-two, and was survived by six children. His brothers William and John both worked on farms near Sunnidale, Simcoe County.[78] John also spent time with his brother Francis on the Wideman farm and married Mary Jane Wideman in 1868 and had seven children.[79] William resided on a farm near his brother and died there in 1908.

Once again, despite the appearance of the Pickering brothers charging out on to the frontier to make their fortunes, there is a powerful sub-narrative of chain migration at play here. Their choice of mid-central Ontario was no accident. They had an older brother, Francis, who had already made a life for himself in the farm country north of Toronto. It appeared each brother used the Wideman farm as a diving board into new lives for themselves. John Pickering characterized what happened to several female orphans in Quebec, like Elizabeth Mahoney or Catherine Kennedy, when he married a local and remained close to his wife's community. In this case it was young Protestant men from Ulster who quickly adapted and appeared to prosper in a province where Irish Protestants were among the largest settler-colonist groups in the mid-nineteenth century.[80] These orphans appear to have fit right in to the prevailing religious and cultural ethos of the region.

One magnet for Irish migrants in the early nineteenth century was the Huron Tract in western Upper Canada. In 1826, Lord Goderich, the British chancellor of the exchequer, engineered the passage of legislation through the Westminster Parliament that formed a joint stock company: the Canada Company. This new corporation would administer and sell the 1.1 million acres recently "acquired" from the Chippewa (Ojibwa') First Nation on the Huron Tract, and 42,000 acres of the Halton Tract near the current city of Guelph.[81] The Canada Company was headed by a London-based commission of directors (after whom all the townships were named), although the chief administrator on the ground was John Galt, a Scottish-born novelist, historian, and entrepreneur, who, from his headquarters in Guelph, Canada West, was tasked with surveying and allocating the lands of the Huron Tract.

Although thousands of Irish migrants were to settle the tract, the Canada Company struggled to meet its lofty objectives. Competition from cheaper lands in the American Midwest and bordering territories in Canada West provided serious challenges for the Canada Company, and subsequent failures to attract large groups of settlers had directors and parliamentarians questioning the continuation of its charter.[82] In 1839 Galt's successor Frederick Widder adopted a new strategy: advertise the lands more effectively in the provincial newspapers and create a lease-to-own scheme, which might be more attractive to prospective settlers. A new extended lease period of ten years was created, with no down payment required.[83] Fifty- and one hundred-acre lots were available for five pence per acre rent per year with 6 per cent interest. Average annual rent would amount to around three pounds. The settler could fix the final price in advance and could be awarded the deed once the balance was paid. The lands were widely advertised in the major ports of entry and by word of mouth.[84] Irish immigrants, particularly famine migrants, would have been aware of this deal awaiting them on the Canadian frontier either through word of mouth or the many advertisements in local newspapers.[85] Moreover, with the established presence of some pre-famine Irish in the region, there may have been personal links pre-existing between famine migrants and those who had gone before them, simulating the characteristics of chain migration.

The Woodlock children must have been aware of the land to be had in what is now Western Ontario. Originally from Goulden Parish, County Tipperary, David Woodlock and his wife Mary Gorman, left Cork, Ireland on board the *Saguenay*, landing at Grosse Ile and Quebec City on 22 August 1847 after a harrowing sixty-four days at sea and fourteen in quarantine. Of the 466 passengers who embarked at Cork, 167 (36 per cent) did not live to see their final port of call in Canada.[86] Neither David nor Mary survived the journey and left behind eight children – Thomas (twenty), John (eighteen), Margaret (fifteen), Edward (twelve) David (fourteen), Bridget (eight), Mary (seven), and Kate (six). As has been witnessed already with large groups of siblings, the Woodlocks, presumably led by Thomas, left the orphanage as a group with the intent of joining their brothers (Patrick and Michael) near the Huron tract area of Upper Canada.[87] While there is little more than circumstantial evidence to suggest it, it appears that the Woodlocks were part of a family migration chain, with older brothers setting out prior to 1847 on order to secure land in Middlesex County. In 1851 several of the Woodlocks were employed as farmers or farm labourers in Adelaide Township.[88] Patrick Woodlock had fifty acres, about half of which was under crops and the other half under pasture. His brother Michael lived on the same concession and held a hundred acres of land of which only eight acres was cultivated.[89] Both were growing wheat, which was one of the more lucrative crops at that time but subject to boom bust cycles depending on the weather and markets.[90] Nevertheless, the Woodlocks persisted in the county. John Woodlock, for example, was still farming in the township as late as 1911, and he was assisted by his wife Mary and two adult children, Joseph and Helena.[91]

The Woodlock family history confirms patterns already witnessed among some of the clusters of orphan siblings arriving at Quebec. There appears to have been a family plan from the outset of their departure from Ireland to join family members who were already in Canada. By 1851, Patrick Woodlock appears to have been farming for enough time to have cleared half of his fifty acres, while it seems Michael was just beginning the process. Clearly the arrival of the siblings in 1847 was a boon to the older brothers who needed additional farmhands to increase their acreage under cultivation. With Edward and Thomas having worked on other nearby farms, there appeared to be no shortage of work for the Woodlock orphans. The family had a plan. The eldest boys availed themselves of the cheap land near Lake Huron, and the rest of the family planned to join them. Even with the death of their parents, the children continued their trek to the Canadian frontier, demonstrating a significant dose of agency in how they were going to live their lives.

There were other attractive beacons for potential Irish workers. Labourers were needed on the Niagara Peninsula to work on repairs of the original Welland Canal and continued construction on a second canal.[92] Irishmen from Munster and Connaught were notable in their sojourning in the area seeking canal work. In fact, Corkmen and Connaughtmen, including many from Roscommon, competed for the manual labouring positions when they became available. On the Niagara Peninsula prior to 1849 if there was a dust up between Irish workers, it was less likely a matter of the Orange versus the Green but a donnybrook with Irish Catholics from different regions using fisticuffs to secure employment.[93] The Niagara, as has been seen in chapter 2, was a particular draw for Roscommon migrants, some of whom, such as Thomas Brennan, used his new home to settle scores begun in the old country. Canal jobs near "the Falls" were known in Ireland and families appeared to create necessary migration chains in order to earn a living before the next job opportunity presented itself.[94] Andrew Connor, for example, was the ringleader in the successful plot to assassinate Major Denis Mahon, near Strokestown, in November 1847. He eluded authorities, travelled to Canada, and sojourned in Port Robinson, finding work alongside his brothers who were already navvies on the canal in 1848. While not an orphan, Connor was a prominent example of chain migration and emigrant agency, which has already been witnessed among orphans who carried the dream of their parents forward.

There are many stories with a tragic and frustrating beginning but whose end is still unknown. One such case may have been Thomas Boyle. Originally from Onagh, in County Galway, fourteen-year-old Thomas was the son of Thady Boyle and Peggy Jennings, who evidently did not survive the journey on the ship *St John* in 1848. Thomas and his seven-year-old brother Edward were placed in Rimouski with two different families. Thomas appeared to have been shuffled around, first sent to Clement Hins at St-Henri and then to Thomas Parent in Rimouski in August 1848.[95] Evidently, the placement with Hins did not work out; the Charitable Ladies left no reason for his return to Quebec and his need for a second placement. Things may have gone better for Thomas in the second placement. The record reveals few details other than that he was still in Rimouski in 1851, listed as a day worker but not as a member of the Parent family.[96] Like so many of the orphans who did not fit into the categories that have been outlined here, their stories are lost to history.

What is clear is that there is no single story for the famine orphans who landed in British North America in 1847 and 1848. Their brave new worlds took many forms. Some resembled the "Molly Johnson" stereotype of living with a French Canadian family, retaining their Irish names, and making contributions to their local communities. Others had the itch to find something better, greater autonomy for themselves, and better opportunities. Many departed for the frontiers of Canada and the United States. Through these individuals' stories one discovers that, even as children and strangers in a strange land, many appear to have had considerable agency in deciding their next steps after leaving the orphanages. In the interior of the continent, they connected with family and friends, resumed their farming past, dug canals, felled trees, worked in factories, or went into business for themselves. Surely Bart Furlong was not the only orphan who in adulthood opened a tavern. Other children found themselves heading for the priesthood or vowed religious life. There they paid tribute to the Catholic clergy and religious who had cared for their suffering families and allowed parentless children to take refuge in their orphanages and homes. Many married and had families, some with French Canadians, some with New Brunswick Protestants, and others with Irish men and women who had already settled in America or who had travelled with them and were orphaned as well. Their progeny tended the soil, fought in the American Civil War, or entered politics. The stories of the Sheridans, Daniel and Catherine Tighe, or Edward Nealon could not have been more different from one another. As is often the case, the complexities of history are not easily condensed into a minute-long sound bite for television.

Conclusion
Finding Molly Johnson

Among the more than 1,700 Irish orphans researched for this study, no Molly Johnson was found. Molly was simply a child created by the producers of the *Heritage Minute* in the early 1990s. Her name signalled the engagement and welcome offered by French Canadians to the Irish. After all, two future Liberal premiers of Quebec would be named Daniel Johnson (father and son), and a leader of the opposition for the separatist Parti Québécois would be Pierre-Marc Johnson. Molly's little friend Kathleen Ryan, embraced and carried high in the air by Archbishop Signay, would also give rise, presumably, to future statesman Claude Ryan. Patrick O'Neill, the third child identified in the *Heritage Minute*, may have reminded viewers of Louis O'Neill, son of Thomas O'Neill and Alexandrine Lafontaine, who served as a member of René Levesque's Parti Quebecois government from 1976 to 1981. He was a well-known journalist of mixed Irish and Quebecois decent, then serving as minister of culture in a sovereigntist government. The selection of the Irish children's names seems something beyond coincidence.

In a time of political turmoil and constitutional unrest between Quebec and other Canadian provinces, and between French Canadians and those who spoke English or other languages, Molly represented an olive branch. She was a creation, a bridge between Canada's two founding settler peoples. Molly was an impoverished Anglophone girl, left destitute on Canada's shores, only to be warmly embraced by *les Canadiens* who were self-sacrificing in their hospitality. Her broken French would develop into fluency, and she would be the mother of Irish descendants who would thrive amidst their French Canadian Catholic patrons. They would succeed. Here was a model for na-

CONCLUSION 171

tional healing and reconciliation, true to the Biblical adage that the "little children would lead them."

Although fictional creations, Molly and her on screen cohort become a portal through which the lives of Irish children in mid-nineteenth century Canada may be explored and understood. The world of the Irish orphan in 1847 and 1848 was far from the romantic and idyllic scenes that followed the French Canadian acceptance of Molly's entreaties. They did not surrender their Irish names because of the largesse of their hosts but because of the simple fact that they were never legally adopted. Families had no intention of stripping them of their Irish names, substituting French or other Irish surnames in their place, and then allowing them to inherit the land. This was a far cry from the Biblical invocation that the meek would inherit the earth. The realities of the nineteenth century were less friendly, even to children. In British North America, children were expected to pull their weight in society, lest in their idleness they lapse into indigence, dependence, or, at worst, criminal activity. In the Church- or state-run orphan's homes they were to be educated and then moved to places of industry – farms, artisanal shops, businesses – to ensure they become good and productive citizens. Thus, the young girls found themselves doing domestic work, caring for the children of their placement families, or doing scullery work in hotels and taverns. Boys found themselves working the fields on farms, generally with their only wages being a roof over their heads and food in their bellies. On occasion a few of the children adopted the religious life as priests or nuns and served the French Canadian Catholic Church. There were exceptions to unregulated child labour, however, particularly when civic officials in places like Toronto made certain that the contracts of indenture were clearly spelled out and children were duly compensated for the indentured service to which they were bound.

Alas, such expectations were not universal across the provinces, although cases of child abuse were often left unrecorded in this period. It is from future emigration assistance schemes that brought orphans and "waifs" to Canada, such as the "Barnardo children" of the late nineteenth century, that suggest that domestic violence may have been part of the lived experience of orphans in their placements. Horrendous reports of the Barnardo children's working conditions, diet, and death amplified the need for greater oversight by the state to assure that children were not abused and enslaved by placement families.[1] While not attempting to read backwards into history, it is not impossible to imagine that the abuse experienced by "Barnardo Boys and Girls" in the late nineteenth and early twentieth centuries was a new feature of child placement. Although a difficult subject to tackle because of the available sources, it is certainly worthy of examination.

Similar stories of other Irish orphans in the famine period have yet to be fully explored. There was one more group of orphans who have received very little attention in Canadian history: the workhouse girls. In 1848, Secretary of State for the Colonies Earl Grey initiated a scheme that would relieve pressure on Irish workhouses by removing young women and orphans and shipping them off to Canada and Australia as domestic servants.[2] While the Earl Grey scheme between 1848 and 1850 has been well documented in Australia and forms the central motif of the Famine Memorial at the Hyde Park Barracks in Sydney, the Canadian side of the story is far less examined. Australia, however, has archived an impressive collection of records on the 4,114 young women,[3] who were removed from the workhouses, educated on board ship, and landed in New South Wales as potential servants for families and wives for Australian bachelors.[4]

The Mountbellew Poor Law union in Galway, with the encouragement of Tyrone native A.C. Buchanan in Quebec, gathered orphans, young women, and those considered abandoned by their families for an assisted migration to Canada. Buchanan was convinced that domestic servants were needed, particularly in the cities of Montreal, Toronto, and Bytown (Ottawa). In 1852 Canada was the recipient of about sixty Galway girls who arrived in Montreal and were cared for by the Sisters of Charity. One of the great problems in tracking these young women is the fact that they arrived just after the census had been taken, they were moved to the Ottawa Valley, and those who married after their arrival could only be traced if their maiden name was included in the marriage register.[5] A few of the young women, however, can be traced, including Ellen Egan, who at fifteen years of age upon departure, had already spent six years in the Mountbellew workhouse. Ellen appeared in the 1861 census listed as a bread-maker in Toronto but one year later was married to William Parker. Ellen ended up on the Parker farm in Renfrew County where she and her husband raised five children. The couple retired to Guelph where Ellen died in 1915. There is a great need of more research to be done to uncover the fate of Ellen's other companions from Galway.

The workhouse "domestics" arrived in all Canadian ports from different Poor Law unions in Ireland. In 1850 about 122 young women arrived at Quebec from Dungannon in County Tyrone. They were provisioned in Quebec before travelling to Kingston, where they were met by Anthony Hawke, the emigration agent. Hawke saw to it that the women were placed in homes to work as

CONCLUSION

domestic servants. One commentator observed that Hawke's action "speaks volumes for the kind-heartedness of the people, for many, doubtless were taken where their services were not absolutely required."[6] Similarly, Waterford workhouse women and girls arrived in Montreal in 1851, and Cork Poor Law Guardians send young women to both Quebec and Saint John. Given the anger of New Brunswick officials after the "dumping" of Irish emigrants and orphans on them, particularly from the estates of Gore-Booth and Lord Palmerston, it is surprising that Poor Law Guardians thought New Brunswick a wise option. According to historian Gerard Moran, it is entirely possible that the Cork Guardians figured they would see a departure of most of these women to the New England states, as had been the migratory pattern out of Saint John for most Irish. The important thing to these Guardians was that they relieve the over-crowded conditions in their own workhouse; orphans and young women could make do once they arrived in "America." There is still much work to be done in this dimension of young adulthood and assisted immigration. Hopefully the current study of Irish orphans can provide guidance both methodologically and historiographically for those researchers who might pursue the fate of "Earl Grey's Girls" in Canada.

In retrospect, the Irish orphans' plight brought out both the best and the worst among British North America's Christian denominations. At a time when governments lacked a social safety network to which Canadians have now become accustomed, Protestant and Roman Catholic Churches stepped into the breech. The Churches provided immediate aid at the ports of entry and the quarantine stations, offering spiritual and medical assistance to Irish refugees in the fever sheds, hospitals, and houses of refuge. In the process, numerous women religious, Catholic priests and Protestant ministers sacrificed their lives for the sake of the adults and children who were placed in their care. Churches and their members also established orphanages and hospital to care for the children and took time and care in making sure that children were placed in homes and business where their Catholic or Protestant faith would not be jeopardized. There were exceptions to this benevolence and charity, as in Saint John, New Brunswick, where the Catholic boots on the ground were few, the voices of Catholic leaders less robust, and where Catholic children were placed in homes and farms indiscriminately without thought to their faith tradition.

Across each of the colonies, some children were content to stay where they were placed. They found themselves in schools, learned a new language, and made new friends. These orphans grew into young women and men and often married local youths with whom they had become familiar during and after their placement. This type of new life was the one anticipated in the *Heritage Minute*, where in Quebec there would be a union of two "races" and therefore a bridge between Canada's two charter settler groups. One example is Daniel Tighe who passed on the stories of his Irish youth and the famine tragedy but was fortunate enough to inherit the Coulombe farm and chose to Gallicize his name, perhaps to publicly confirm that he had elected to stay among those who had demonstrated to him such kindness. The churches that played such a pivotal role in the care of these newcomers would also benefit from the enlistment of several orphans into schools and seminaries that would prepare them for consecrated religious life or a vocation to the Catholic priesthood.

Many children had no such attachment to their new homes in New Brunswick or Canada. They moved west and south, demonstrating a sense of agency – that they would be the architects of their own future. Some might be fulfilling their family's intention through the emigration process; others might have seized the opportunity to strike out for what appeared to be a better life in the United States or Canada West; others still may have known the whereabouts of extended family and friends and chose to take their chances with them. Most orphans simply eluded the records taken routinely at the time and vanished into history without leaving much of a story to be recovered. Above all, the stories of many of the "rediscovered" orphans reveals a high degree of immigrant agency. Many families had a strong sense of where they were going and which friends and family, already settled in Canada or the United States, would welcome them as sojourners until they could establish themselves more securely in the new world. Even when children lost their parents on route to Canada they held on to the family plan, and groups of siblings like the Sheridans or Woodlocks continued their pilgrimage until reunited with families. While the *Heritage Minute* depicts a rather sad train of hopeless urchins uncertain of their future, the stories of many of these children reveal a sense of agency that might surprise their contemporaries. Perhaps this agency caused many of them to flee their orphanages and placements, knowing their families had planned something different for them. Even Molly expresses her own assertiveness when Signay suggests that their names would change and they would be Canadian now. Her brazen interjection in the face of the archbishop reveals that some of the children had their own plans.[7]

The Great Irish Famine was the "perfect storm" leading to the worst catastrophe in Ireland's modern history. The combination of an inequitable landholding system imposed by its colonial masters, food insecurity, dramatic climate shifts in 1846–47, an unbreakable belief by the Imperial government in *laissez-faire* capitalism, and the rapid spread of infectious disease among the starving masses created Europe's worst refugee crisis of the nineteenth century. Of Ireland's eight million people on the eve of the famine, one million died and 1.5 million more simply left by 1852. The population of Ireland, to this day, has not recovered. While the famine sparked the high-water mark for Irish migration to British North America, in 1847, it also sparked a crisis in how those British provinces would cope with the thousands of refugees arriving in such adverse conditions. At the eye of the storm were hundreds of children – orphaned, abandoned, and ill – who had to be cared for within a colonial context where social safety nets were not provided by the governments of the day. New Brunswick had a Poor Law in place, but it was completely inadequate to meet the challenges posed by the migration of Black '47. Through the agency of the Churches, with some per capita government support and makeshift civic relief initiatives, the children were gathered, fed, schooled, and then placed. In this drama Molly Johnson becomes an amalgam of the lives of survivors, children who did not give up, and, when able, left their mark on the society that "adopted" them.

Notes

INTRODUCTION

1. Historica Canada, *Heritage Minutes*, DVD, Heritage Minute #16 "Orphans," CRB Foundation, 1991–2012.
2. O'Gallagher, *Grosse Ile: Gateway to Canada*, appendices. O'Gallagher's list is transcribed from the ledgers of the Charitable Ladies at Quebec and is not without problems in the spelling of surnames and Irish townlands. In her excellent MA thesis Marie-Claude Belley uses O'Gallagher's list and additional information gleaned from the *Canada Gazette*, which places her number of orphans at 702. Belley, "Les orphelins Irlandais á Québec en 1847–1848," 28–9. For the analysis in this book, the O'Gallagher list is being used because of the comprehensive nature of its data as compared to what is offered in the *Canada Gazette*.
3. McGowan, "Rethinking the Irish Famine Orphans in Quebec, 1847–1848," 95–122.
4. Note that about 125 orphans were Protestant out of a cohort of 702. The *Canada Gazette*, Number 345, Montreal, 6 May 1848, "Names of Emigrant Orphans," submitted by A.C. Buchanan.
5. Roche, *L'Adoption dans la Province de Québec*, 21–7.
6. Strong-Boag, *Funding Families, Finding Ourselves*, 11. British labouring children are the subject of Parr, *Labouring Children*, 14–23
7. McGowan, "Rethinking the Irish Famine Orphans in Quebec, 1847–1848," 114–17.
8. Peikoff and Brickey, "Creating Precious Children and Glorified Mothers," 29.
9. Ibid, 37.
10. Ibid, 42.
11. The practice of child placement was common in the United States during the same period. Sutherland, *Children in English Canadian Society*, 5.
12. McGowan, *Michael Power*.
13. Prunty, "Battle Plans and Battle Grounds," 119–43.
14. Wilson, *Thomas D'Arcy McGee: Volume 2*, 301–3.
15. King, "Remembering Famine Orphans," 115–40.

16 Maguire, *The Irish in America*, 138.
17 Quigley, "Grosse Ile: Canada's Irish Famine Memorial," 195–214.
18 Scally, *The End of Hidden Ireland*.
19 Rees, *Surplus People*.
20 Lee and Jenkins, *Shoeboxes*; and Lee, *Coollattin*.
21 Moran, *Sending Out Ireland's Poor*.
22 Dunn, *Ballykilcline Rising*.
23 Anbinder, "From Famine to Five Points," 351–87.
24 McMahon, *The Coffin Ship*.
25 The Australian records, likely inspired by the reports required to process convict migrations, is extensive and detailed. See https://irishfaminememorial.org/orphans/. The database covers the famine period and beyond for Irish women who were sent from Irish Poor Law Unions to New South Wales to work as domestic servants (and hopefully become potential spouses for the male population.
26 O'Gallagher, *Grosse Ile: Gateway to Canada*, appendices. For the purposes of this book, only the orphans on the O'Gallagher list are included in the calculations. It was also coincidental that orphans from Roscommon accounted for the highest number of orphans from any single county, among the 360 orphans who had a county recorded beside their name on the list. After those declared dead were removed from the data sets, the researchers proceeded methodically to search orphan names through a variety of sources: the Canadian census, beginning in 1851–2 and continuing to 1921, the census of the United States, beginning in 1850, the databases at Ancestry.ca, FamilySearch.com, and parish registers and records for British North America. There were eight categories that would measure a match: 1. Surname; 2. Given Name; 3. Irish birth; 4. "Adoptive Family"; 5. Approximate Age; 6. Timing based on age and birthplace of children (for later censuses); 7. Location of place of Settlement; and 8. Religion. The latter category (8) was problematic when using the American census, since religion is not recorded. Four colour-coded categories were created: Green (6–8 matches), Blue (4–5 matches); Orange (less than 4); Yellow (did not find). The team met weekly to discuss their findings and every month a new colour-coded master list was created, based on the revisions and additions up to that point. The research project lasted just over three months and has provided a relatively clean data set of names and location upon which a historical narrative might be constructed and the prevailing ideas about "orphan adoption" tested.
27 Belley, "Les orphelins Irlandais á Québec en 1847 et 1848."
28 His thesis can be found online at https://library2.smu.ca/xmlui/handle/01/22486.
29 Gagan, "Enumerator's Instructions," 355.
30 Kinealy, King, and McGowan, *Hunger and Hope*, chapter 6.

CHAPTER ONE

1. Mangan, *The Voyage of the Naparima*.
2. Mitchel, *The Last Conquest of Ireland (perhaps)*, 219.
3. In fairness to Mangan, in the original published version in 1982, he does acknowledge that the diary was "fictionalized." Mangan, *Voyage*, 15.
4. Library and Archives Canada [hereafter LAC], Robert Sellar Fonds, MG 30 D314, vol. 10, "*Gleaner* Tales – Summer of Sorrow," file 16.
5. O'Driscoll, *The Untold Story*, 1:152.
6. McGowan, "Famine, Facts, and Fabrication," 48–55; Hill, "From Famine to Fraud," 8; Jackson, "Famine Diary," 1–8. The real events can be traced to a series of essays by James M. O'Leary, published in *The Catholic Record* (London, Ontario), 9, 16, 23, and 30 April 1892.
7. Miller, *Emigrants and Exiles*. Irish nationalists in the United States, whose experience was likened to a state of "exile" from their homeland, were pronounced in their use of the famine as a justification for the use of physical force to rid Ireland of British rule once and for all. See Brundage, *Irish Nationalists in America*, 83–7; Campbell, *Ireland's New Worlds*, 105–7.
8. Gray, "Memory and the Great Irish Famine," in *The Memory of Catastrophe*, 46–64; Mark-Fitzgerald, *Commemorating the Irish Famine*; McGowan, "Contemporary Links between Canadian and Irish Famine Commemoration," 267–84; and McGowan, *Creating Canadian Historical Memory*.
9. The standard volume on the famine is Smith, *The Great Hunger, 1845–1849*. Revisionist views include Ó Gráda, *Black '47 and Beyond: The Great Irish Famine in History, Economy, and Memory*; and Daly, "The Great Famine in Irish Society," 3–20. Post-revisionist works include Kinealy, *This Great Calamity*; Donnelly, *The Great Irish Potato Famine*; Gray, *The Irish Famine*; and O'Murchadha, *The Great Famine*. One of the few scholarly tomes on the famine, and one promoted by the Irish government, is the useful Edwards and Williams, *The Great Famine*.
10. Edwards and Williams, *The Great Famine*.
11. Smith, *The Great Hunger*.
12. Ó Gráda, *Black '47 and Beyond*; Mokyr, *Why Ireland Starved*; Daly, *The Famine in Ireland*.
13. Coogan, *The Famine Plot*, 229–30.
14. Ibid., 231.
15. Kennedy, *Unhappy the Land*.
16. Ibid., 119.
17. Ó Murchadha, *The Great Famine*, 197–8.
18. Gray, *The Irish Famine*, 19–20 and 22–3; Kelly, *The Graves are Walking*, 19–22; Kinealy, *This Great Calamity*, 5–6.
19. Mokyr, *Why Ireland Starved*, 278–94.
20. Ó Gráda, *Black '47 and Beyond*, 126–34.

21 Ibid., 17–18; Kinealy, *This Great Calamity*, 32.
22 Kinealy, *A Death-Dealing Famine*, 38.
23 Donnelly, *The Great Irish Potato Famine*, 8–10.
24 *Globe*, 19 August 1845.
25 McGowan, "A Tale of Two Famines," 57–68. Also, Morgan, *Early Cape Breton*, 136–52.
26 Donnelly, 47; Gray, *The Irish Famine*, 35.
27 Kinealy, *A Death-Dealing Famine*, 41–8.
28 Crawford, "Food and Famine," 62–3.
29 Gray, *Famine, Land and Politics*, 94–101; O'Neill, "The Organization of Relief," 212–22.
30 Gray, "Ideology and the Famine," 89–90 and 102–103; Donnelly, *The Great Irish Potato Famine*, 69–70; Kinealy, *Death-Dealing Famine*, 60.
31 Kinealy, "'This Great Agony of the Empire,'" 43–55; and MacAtasney, *This Dreadful Visitation*.
32 See chapter 6.
33 Conacre farmers lived from annual lease to annual lease, usually on a single acre of land, which provided nourishment through the cultivation of potatoes. Conacre farmers were often employed as labourers by middlemen and small lease-holding farmers.
34 Kinealy, *This Great Calamity*, 205–10; Ryan, "Commissioners, Guardians, and Paupers: Life and Death in the Limerick Poor Law Union, 1838–1850," 2–12 and 195–9. Ryan's detailed study focuses on the Limerick Union, which was the third largest in Ireland.
35 Ibid, 153–4 and 171–9.
36 Sen, *Development as Freedom*, 168–70.
37 Kinealy, *This Great Calamity*, 93–4 and 102–6; Donnelly, *The Great Irish Potato Famine*, 81–92.
38 Ó Gráda, *Black '47 and Beyond*, 85; Kinealy, *A Death-Dealing Famine*, 151; Donnelly, *The Great Irish Potato Famine*, 169–71.
39 Ibid., 118; Gray, estimates that £8.1 million was spent on famine relief with about £1.1 returned from government loans, *The Irish Famine*, 94–5; Ó Gráda estimates about £10 million, *Black '47 and Beyond*, 83; Donnelly estimates the cost was about £7 million, *The Great Irish Potato Famine*, 118–19. There is no unanimity on a final number for the government expenditure; nevertheless, the expenditure was considerable considering the times and the state of the British Treasury.
40 Gray, *The Irish Famine*, 94–5. For information on the famine in Scotland see Devine, *The Great Highland Famine*.
41 Gray, *Famine, Land and Politics*, 108–25: Kinealy, *Death-Dealing Famine*, 53–65.
42 Ó Gráda, *Black '47 and Beyond*, 26–7; Kinealy, *This Great Calamity*, 190–1; Ryan, "Commissioners, Guardians, Paupers," 153–66.

43 Kinealy, *Death-Dealing Famine*, 98–103.
44 Donnelly, *The Great Irish Potato Famine*, 132–68.
45 Ibid., 158.
46 Hamrock, *The Famine in Mayo*, 76–9.
47 Ó Gráda, *Black '47 and Beyond*, 70; and Donnelly, "Irish Property Must Pay for Irish Poverty," 60.
48 Cited in Stout, "The Geography and Implications of Post-Famine Population Decline in Baltyboys, County Wicklow," 31. For her compassion see Delaney, *The Great Irish Famine*, 141–2 and 145–9.
49 Reilly, *Strokestown and the Great Irish Famine*, 14–23.
50 Reilly, *John Plunket Joly and the Great Famine in King's County*.
51 Trinity College Dublin, Stephen De Vere Famine Diary, MS 5061, vol. 1 29 April–1 December 1847 (my thanks to Dr Jason King for providing me with a transcription); Mackay, *Flight from Famine*, 266–7; McGowan, "Famine, Facts, and Fabrications," 53; King, "Famine Diaries." Delaney, *The Great Irish Famine*, 219.
52 Kinealy, *Charity and the Great Hunger in Ireland*, 160–1.
53 James, *John Hamilton of Donegal*; Delaney, *The Great Irish Famine*, 169.
54 Rees, *Surplus People*; Lee and Jenkins, *Shoeboxes*; Lee, *Coollattin*, 201–74.
55 Daly, "The Great Famine and Irish Society," 4.
56 Kinealy, *Death-Dealing*, 82–3; Ó Gráda, *Black '47 and Beyond*, 135; Somerville, *Letters from Ireland During the Famine of 1847*, 34.
57 Daly, "The Great Famine and Irish Society," 6.
58 Donnelly, *The Great Irish Potato Famine*, 59.
59 *Limerick Reporter*, 19 January 1847.
60 Archives of the Archdiocese of Dublin, (hereafter AAD) Daniel Murray Papers, vol. 35, folders 2–6 and 10–13 famine correspondence; folder 12, remittances from abroad, 1845–1850.
61 St Patrick's College Maynooth, Russell Library Special Collections, Laurence Renehan Papers. Note some sample letters from Father T. Kirby, Longford, 13 November 1851; Father M. Slattery, Thurles, 13 June 1847; Father C. Egan, Killarney, 22 April 1846.
62 *Limerick Reporter*, 19 January 1847.
63 Kerr, *A Nation of Beggars?*, 296–8; Kennedy, *Unhappy the Land*, 115.
64 Delaney, *The Great Irish Famine*, 136–8 and 181–2.
65 Daly, "The Great Famine and Irish Society," 17.
66 Kennedy, *Unhappy the Land*, 115–16.
67 Hickey, *Famine in West Cork*, 231–64; Whelan, "The Stigma of Souperism," 135–54.
68 Gray, *The Irish Famine*, 86.
69 Hickey, 262.
70 *The Berean*, 6 and 13 May 1847.

71 Cited in Moran, "Suffer the Children," 41.
72 Gray, *Famine Land and Politics*, 99 and 102–4; Gray, "Ideology and the Famine," 91–3.
73 MacAtasney, *This Dreadful Visitation*.
74 McGowan, *Death or Canada*, 91–2.
75 Larkin, "The Devotional Revolution In Ireland," 625–52.
76 The Repeal Association, headed by Daniel O'Connell applied pressure on the British government to repeal the Act of Union of 1801, which dissolved the Irish Parliament in Dublin and created the United Kingdom, with a single parliament at Westminster for England, Wales, Scotland, and Ireland. In 1829, The Catholic Relief Act marked the high point for O'Connell's Catholic Association, when Parliament finally permitted Catholics to be elected and sit in the House of Commons. The Catholic Association provided the foundation for the Repeal Association. Macauley, *The Catholic Church and the Campaign for Emancipation*.
77 Geoghegan, *Liberator*, 162–5; Kinealy, *Death-Dealing*, 28–9.
78 Daly, "The Great Famine and Irish Society," 4.
79 Geoghegan, *Liberator*, 220–1 and 228–9.
80 Wilson, *Thomas D'Arcy McGee*, 1:120.
81 Ibid.
82 MacArthur, "Medical History," in *The Great Famine*, 265–70 and 302–6.
83 AAD, Murray Papers, vol. 33, file 6, letter 13, "List of Deaths," 21 October 1847.
84 MacArthur, "Medical History," 314–5.
85 Board of Works, *Famine Ireland*, appendix F, "A Schedule showing the Names of persons injured, Nature of the Injury, Date of Occurrence, where Committed, the Officer by whom reported, with consequent Local Results," 60–1 and 66.
86 Board of Works, *Famine Ireland*, "Extract from Report of Lieutenant Miller, Inspecting Officer, County Tipperary, N.R., for the week ending 9 January 1847," 103.
87 Daly, *The Famine*, 88.
88 Kierse, *The Famine Years in the Parish of Killaloe*, 29.
89 Daly, *The Famine*, 29.
90 *Limerick Reporter*, 19 January 1847.
91 Ibid., 12 February 1847.
92 Ibid., 5 February 1847.
93 *Limerick Chronicle*, 29 May 1847
94 *Limerick Reporter*, 8 January 1847.
95 Kinealy, King, and Moran, *Children and the Great Hunger in Ireland*, xii; and Kinealy "Attenuated Apparitions of Humanity: The Innocent Casualties of the Great Hunger," 3.
96 Ibid, xiii.
97 Cited in Hamrock, *The Famine in Mayo*, 19.

98 Hickey, *Famine in West Cork*, 168.
99 Moran, "Suffer the Children," 29.
100 Kinealy, "Attenuated Apparitions," 21.
101 Gallaher, "Grim Scars of the Great Hunger," 61. Also Moran, "Suffer," 30.
102 Gallaher, "Grim Scars," 64.
103 Reid, *Farewell My Children*. For a Canadian variation see Conclusion and Moran, "'Permanent deadweight'": female pauper emigration from Mountbellew Workhouse to Canada," 109–21. More recently see Connolly, *On Every Tide*, 64.
104 *St Catharine's Journal*, 3 June 1847.
105 Akenson, *The Irish in Ontario*, 32.
106 *Boston Pilot*, 20 November 1847 cited in Woodham-Smith, *The Great Hunger*, 210.
107 *Limerick Reporter*, 4 May 1847.
108 Nova Scotia governor Sir John Harvey, in April 1847, warned the Colonial Office that the province could not sustain immigration that season. The office complied and redirected emigrants to other colonies. Public Record Office, Kew, England, Colonial Office Papers, 217, vol. 196, fols. 166r–168r, Sir John Harvey to Earl Grey, 1 April 1847. See also Susan Longley Morse, "Immigration to Nova Scotia, 1839–1851" (unpublished MA thesis, Dalhousie University, 1946), 88; *The Novascotian*, 24 May 1847.
109 De Vere testimony, Select Committee, 1847–1848; CO 384/79535 and Arthur Doughty, ed., *The Elgin-Grey Papers, 1846–1852* (Ottawa: J.G. Patenaude, King's Printer, 1937), "Stephen De Vere to Earl Grey, 30 November 1847, London, Canada West," 1341–42.
110 Whyte, *The Ocean Plague*, 46. See also McGowan, "Famine Facts, and Fabrications."
111 McGowan, *Death or Canada*, 28.
112 From a facsimile of a poster in the rebuilt *Jeanie Johnston*, where it is moored as a tourist attraction at Customs House Quay, Dublin, Ireland.
113 If the list of orphans compiled by the Catholic Ladies of Charity in Quebec is any indication, out of the 248 orphans whose origins could be identified: Ulster had forty-seven (19 per cent), Connaught had ninety-six (34.6 per cent), Munster had fifty-eight (23.4 per cent), and Leinster had fifty-seven (23 per cent). Taken from O'Gallagher, *Grosse Ile: Gateway to Canada*, appendix.
114 Duffy, *Atlas of Irish History*, 94–5.
115 Mannion, "Old World Antecedents, New World Adaptations," 30–95.
116 O'Grady, *Exiles and Islanders*, 141–73.
117 Spray, "The Reception of the Irish in New Brunswick," 9–26 and Toner, "The Irish of New Brunswick at Mid-Century," 106–32.
118 LAC, Colonial Office Papers, 384/80, "Guide for Emigrants to British North America," March 1847, 197.

119 Harvey, "The Canadian Response to the Irish Famine Migration of 1847," 27–30.
120 LAC, Colonial Office, 384/82, Colonial Land and Emigration Commission, *Eighth General Report*, (June 1848):15–17.
121 British Parliamentary Papers, volume 17, sessions 1847–48, report of A.C. Buchanan, 31 March 1848, 471–7.
122 Grace, "Irish Immigration and Settlement in a Catholic City, 1842–61," 240.
123 *The Kings County Chronicle*, 29 September 1847.

CHAPTER TWO

1 *Globe*, 27 September 1848; *St Catharine's Journal*, 8 June 1848; Joy Parr, "The Welcome and the Wake," 102.
2 Of particular note are: Bruce Elliott's pioneering work *Irish Migrants in the Canadas*, in which he tracked 775 Protestant Irish families from Tipperary to their resettlement in central Canada before the famine; Jim Rees *Surplus People* that traces the assisted migrants from Lord Fitzwilliam's estates in Wicklow between 1847 and 1856, over which time some 6,000 tenants migrated to Quebec and later to the colony of New Brunswick; Tyler Anbinder's, "From Famine to Five Points," 351–87, is a meticulous study of Lord Lansdowne's assisted migrants from Kerry to the Five Points neighborhood in New York; Robert Scally's *The End of Hidden Ireland* is a detailed examination of the migrants of the Ballykilcline estate, adjacent to Denis Mahon's lands at Strokestown. Similarly, Mary Lee Dunn's *Ballykilcline Rising* continues the story of this townland, tracking several families to Rutland, Vermont.
3 The one exception might be Kevin Lee and Tom Jenkins, *Shoeboxes* in which families themselves, as descendants of assisted migrants from Lord Fitzwilliam's estate in County Wicklow, work with local historian Kevin Lee. The Coollattin research is less systematic in approach, as individual descendants, anxious to reconnect with their Irish roots, reach out to Mr Lee, who is clearly the expert of the estate papers.
4 Irish term for the "Great Hunger," which to many nationalists is preferable to "Great Famine" because the latter term suggests there was no food in the land.
5 Duffy, *The Killing of Major Denis Mahon*.
6 Coleman, *Riotous Roscommon*. Orser, "An Archaeology of Famine-Era Eviction," 52.
7 Vesey, *The Murder of Major Mahon*, 13; a similar link between Mahon's actions in the migration scheme and his murder is offered in Kelly, *The Graves are Walking*, 284–5.
8 Duffy, *The Killing*, x–xi.
9 Scally, *The End of Hidden Ireland*; Dunn, *Ballykilcline Rising*.
10 The Molly Maguires was a term used for secret societies meting out vigilante

justice in rural areas to both landowners and tenants who violated local customs, such as assuming property from which a neighbour had been evicted.
11 Huggins, *Social Conflict in Pre-Famine Ireland*, 156–61.
12 Delaney, *The Great Irish Famine*, 195–6; Campbell, *The Great Irish Famine*, 47–8.
13 Reilly, *Strokestown and the Great Irish Famine*, 57. Reilly reports that "he has traditionally been portrayed as the villain in the Strokestown famine narrative." In March 2018, at a reception in Toronto, Irish TD McNaughton, the minister of communications, remarked on Mahon's draconian actions that forced his tenants to migrate. Local dramatizations in Strokestown, in 2019, in conjunction with the inaugural National Famine Way commemorative walk along the Royal Canal to Dublin, highlighted the victimization of the tenants by Mahon and his agent John Ross Mahon. The panels in the pre-renovated (2022) National Famine Museum, housed on the estate, were neutral about his actions. Local opinion was captured in Woodham-Smith, *The Great Hunger*. Woodham-Smith's reflections on local attitudes cannot be taken lightly since she spent considerable time on the Strokestown Estate doing research in preparation for the book. It was likely she picked up local opinion in the course of her sojourn there.
14 One should distinguish between landlords who were landowners and their middlemen who were land holders on long term leases and who sublet to tenants (cottiers and labourers). Proudfoot, "Landlords," 297.
15 Hood, "The Strokestown Park House Archive," 11. Although the family papers at Strokestown Park House Archives indicate that Charles II granted the lands of Ballynamully to Nicholas Mahon 26 March 1676. Strokestown Park Archive [hereafter SPA], STR/1B/2, "Names of Pantentee."
16 Hood, "The Landlord Influence in the Development of an Irish Estate Town," 119–21.
17 Hood, "The Famine in the Strokestown Park House Archive," 110–12. SPA, Box STR/1A/127, Census of 21 March 1847. This local census counted 68 townlands with 2,237 families constituting 11,958 persons.
18 Vesey, *The Murder*, 13.
19 Kelly, "The Great Famine in County Roscommon," 389. Kelly estimates that the average amount of land held by tenants and sub-tenants was between one and five acres, between a half and one third of average holdings in Kerry (five to fifteen acres).
20 Reilly, *Strokestown*, 49–64.
21 Huggins, *Social Conflict*, 13–16 and 113–14.
22 Duffy, *The Killing*, 66–7. Martin Browne, brother of Bishop George P Browne of Elphin (the Catholic diocese that contained Strokestown) rented 400 acres of Mahon land.
23 Kelly, "The Great Famine in County Roscommon," 389.

24. Coleman, *Riotous Roscommon*, 19.
25. SPA, STR 88, Book #8, Indian Meal Given Gratuitously, 6 August 1846. On that day 195 individuals received free meal. STR/1A/122 contains the names of those given free maize meal on Monday, 22 June 1846.
26. National Library of Ireland [hereafter NLI], Mahon Estate Papers, MS 10,102 (3), Major Denis Mahon to John Ross Mahon, 26 February 1847.
27. Vesey, *The Murder of Major Mahon*, 13–14.
28. Reilly, *Strokestown*, 26–7. SPA, Box STR/1A/37, Charitable Loan Fund, 31 December 1838 to 31 December 1839 and 5 November 1836 to December 1841.
29. NLI, Mahon Estate Papers, MS 10,102 (1), Major Denis Mahon to John Ross Mahon, 28 March 1847.
30. NLI, MS 10, 102 (1), Major Denis Mahon to John Ross Mahon, 7 March 1847; Major Mahon to John Ross Mahon, 30 March 1847; John Ross Mahon to Denis Mahon, April 1847. In the latter letter the agent indicates that he can get a rate per person to Quebec from Liverpool for between £3 10s and £4 10s, a substantial saving from having to support the tenants and the Poor Law at home. NLI, MS 10, 138, Denis Mahon Emigration File, no date, indicates that the passage of the first 405½ statute passengers came in at £1,400 1s 6d or roughly £3 13s per person.
31. NLI, MS 10,102 (1), Major Denis Mahon to John Ross Mahon, 2 April 1847 and NLI, MS 10, 102 (2), Major Denis Mahon to John Ross Mahon, 13 April 1847. The Major even claimed he might get a rate of £2 10s per person at Sligo.
32. NLI, MS 10, 102 (2), Major Denis Mahon to John Ross Mahon, 12 May and 25 May 1847; also MS 10,102 (1), Major Denis Mahon to Mr Samuel Gale, 8 April 1847.
33. Three families chose not to leave: William Dalton of Mullevetron remained because his wife was ill. James Egan and James Duffy of the more troubled Cregga House Townland elected to stay as did Widow Stuart of Tully. Patrick Leonard of Kilgraffy was going to stay but then elected to go, only to die on the *Virginius*. The names are on the draft and duplicate copies of the lists of tenants from the thirty-two townlands at SPA, STR/74, 1847.
34. NLI, MS 10,102 (2), Denis Mahon to John Ross Mahon, 14 April 1847.
35. SPA, Series STR/1A/150a, Agreements with 31 Tenants, Witnessed by Michael Dalton, 14 May 1847. Brennan and others sign with an "x." Also, Document 7, Duplicate Kilmackenny Townland Appraisal (8 April 1847). It should be noted that most of the other prospective migrants in Brennan's townland held over twice as many acres as he.
36. SPA, STR/1A/148 and STR/74, Copy of Lists of Tenants for an Assisted Emigration Scheme.
37. The list was compiled in 2014 by Dr Ciaran Reilly based on SPA, STR/1A/148, and STR/74, Lists of Tenants for Assisted Emigration Scheme.
38. NLI, MS 10, 138, Denis Mahon's Emigration, confirms that the assisted tenants

were sent to Liverpool from Dublin via "steam packet," at a cost to Mahon of 5 shillings each. The first group of 467 people cost him £116 15s.
39   Reilly, *Strokestown*, 70.
40   *The Pilot*, 28 May 1847. The article claims 300 to 400 families from "Colonel" Mahon's estate left Dublin on the 27th for Liverpool. He had supplied them with provisions.
41   *The Berean*, 24 June 1847 (vol. 4, no. 13). This item was credited as having been reprinted from the *Dublin Paper*, 24 May 1847, but no such publication is listed in the catalogues of either the National Archives of Ireland or the National Library if Ireland. This paper was likely *Saunder's News-letter*, in Dublin, where the article appeared 24 May 1847. Small weekly newspapers in British North America depended on other papers for "filler" in their columns and they anxiously awaited the latest steamships to land at New York or Boston and then have the latest European news cabled to them. *The Berean* would be little different from other dailies of its time. Founded in 1844 as an unofficial weekly publication of the Church of England in Quebec, the paper was published each Thursday by Charles L.F. Haersel, an Anglican minister of German origin. The paper itself was produced on rue Ste-Anne in Quebec City, by Stanley Printer & Bookseller, for a subscription price of 12 shillings 6 pence, or $3.50 American per year. It had distributers in New York, Brooklyn, and Boston in addition to its Canadian circulation. Named after the Christian community visited by Silas and Paul in northern Greece, as recorded in the book of Acts (17: 10–15), *The Berean*'s four pages were filled with Protestant theological writing, anti-Catholic diatribes and critiques, and generous news on the conversions being made by Protestant ministers among the starving Catholics of Achill and Dingle in Ireland. *The Berean*, 7 January 1847 and 8 and 13 May 1847. The story reprinted by *The Berean* later appeared in the *London Evening Standard*, 26 July 1847, and the *St James Chronicle*, 27 July 1847. The author would like to than Dr Ray O'Connor of Cork University for his assistance in tracking down the source of the report.
42   Mahon paid a least £9 for the baggage, in addition to the passengers' tickets. NLI, MS 10, 138, Denis Mahon's Emigration, 1847. Travel vouchers for emigrants in Canada demonstrated that most migrants had baggage with them upon their arrival. Library and Archives Canada, [hereafter LAC] RG 19-D-5, Emigrant Services Fonds, (Canada West), vol. 2532.
43   Houston and Smyth, *Irish Emigration and Canadian Settlement: Patterns, Links, and Letters*, 3–9 and 43–74. The fact that Upper Canada had been the target of previous state-supported assisted migrations from Ireland and that the Canada Company was aggressively advertising its available lands made the province a logical target for the Strokestown emigrants. See Cameron, "Selecting Peter Robinson's Irish Emigrants," 29–46; and Cameron, "Peter Robinson's Settlers in Peterborough," 343–53. These assisted settlements took

place between 1823 and 1825 and proved to be too costly for the British government to continue the scheme.
44 NLI, MS 10,102 (4), Major Denis Mahon to John Ross Mahon, 18 and 28 April 1847 and MS 10,102 (3) Denis Mahon to John Ross Mahon, 20 and 27 May 1847.
45 *The Albion*, 10 May 1847, 5.
46 Duffy, *The Killing*, 110–11. The firm was located at 48 Waterloo Road, Liverpool. *The Nation*, 10 June 1848.
47 Reilly, "Strokestown and the Pakenham Mahon Estate," 367. Reilly is citing the *Roscommon Messenger*, 19 July 1851.
48 NLI, MS 10,102 (1), Unknown (presumably JRM) to Mr Samuel Gale, 7 April 1847. Children under fourteen years of age usually were counted and charged as half a statute adult. Gale was from the Dublin land surveying firm of Brassington and Gale, which had been retained by the estate.
49 NLI, MS 10,102 (2), DM to JRM, 24 May 1847.
50 NLI, MS 10,102 (3), DM to JRM, 27 May 1847.
51 NLI, MS 10,102 (2), DM to JRM, 5 June 1847.
52 NLI, MS 10, 102 (3), DM to JRM, 13 June 1847; www/http/the shipslist.com/1847/index.html.
53 NLI, MS 10, 138, Invoice from John & William Robinson, June 1847.
54 It is difficult to determine the total number of families leaving the estate based on newspapers alone. While the estate papers carefully document 271 families, *The Armagh Guardian*, 8 June 1847, reported that "three and four hundred families ... embarked at Liverpool, whence they proceed to America – Colonel [sic] Mahon supplied them with the means of emigrating, and defraying the expenses of their passage and maintenance during the voyage."
55 Kinealy, *Hunger and Hope*, 43–58.
56 Here the registers of the assisted immigrants of Mahon's thirty-two townlands filed in SPA, STR/1A/148 are cross-referenced with Charbonneau and Drolet-Dubé, *A Register of Deceased Persons at Grosse Ile in 1847*.
57 *Belfast Newsletter*, 8 June 1847. Joseph Davidson was only thirty-six years old. *Belfast Commercial Chronicle*, 1 April 1848.
58 Ships List: http//www.shipslist.com/1847/index.htm.
59 *Belfast Newsletter*, 7 and 21 May 1847.
60 Ibid., 12 January 1847 and *Belfast Commercial Chronicle*, 1 April 1848.
61 LAC, Colonial Office Papers, CO384/79. Letter to the Right Honourable Earl Grey from the Honourable Adam Ferrie, Member of the Legislative Council, Chairman of the Executive Lay Commission for Emigration, 1847, Montreal, 1 December 1847, 199.
62 O'Gallagher and Dompierre, *Eyewitness Grosse Isle*, 52.
63 McCabe, "Denis Mahon," 295.
64 Duffy, *The Killing*, 129–30. *The Belfast Newsletter*, 3 September 1847 reported that 158 passengers died at sea and 186 were ill upon landing at the quarantine

station. *The Belfast Commercial Chronicle*, 4 September 1847, reported 178 dead and 186 sick. The "Return of the Passenger Ships" provided by Emigration Agent A.C. Buchanan at Quebec records that the *Virginius* lost 158 at sea, 19 at quarantine, and 90 in the quarantine hospital for a total of 267 dead.

65 *The Armagh Guardian*, 7 September 1847. Reprinted from the *Quebec Morning Chronicle*.
66 O'Gallagher and Dompierre, *Eyewitness Grosse Isle*, 349 and 352.
67 Harvey, "The Canadian Responses to the Irish Famine Migration of 1847," 63.
68 They received 119,000 emigrants from UK ports in 1847. Akenson, *The Irish in Ontario*, 30.
69 *St Catharine's Journal*, 3 June 1847. Reprinted from *Montreal Courier*. Also, *Quebec Morning Chronicle*, 7 August 1847; *The Belfast Commercial Chronicle*, 4 September 1847.
70 Cited in, *The British Colonist*, 28 May 1847.
71 Harvey, "The Canadian Responses," 72–5.
72 *British Colonist*, 4 June 1847.
73 Ibid., 15 June and 13 July 1847.
74 Charbonneau and Drolet-Dubé, *A Register of Deceased Persons*, 66. O'Gallagher and Dompierre, *Eyewitness*, table B, 384 and 394.
75 Reilly, *Strokestown*, 91–8; Duffy, *The Killing*, 131–4. *Globe*, 14 August 1847; Campbell, *The Great Irish Famine*, 48–9.
76 O'Gallagher, *Grosse Ile*, 56–7 and appendices. The transcribed ledgers of the Charitable Catholic Ladies of Quebec are like a mini census indicating the given and family names of the child, age, father and mother's name, parish of origin, county of origin in Ireland, ship from which he/she disembarked, when the child departed the orphanage, and any remarks regarding health or death of the child while in the care of the ladies. The information usually includes the head of the family with whom the child had been placed.
77 *The Berean*, 18 November 1847.
78 Parr, "The Welcome and the Wake," 101.
79 Runnalls, *The Irish on the Welland Canal*, 14–20. Runnalls reports that most of the workers from Munster were Corkmen who had emigrated from the United States, just having completed the Erie Canal. The Connaught men had been in Canada and had completed their work on the St Lawrence Canal systems. See Harris, *The Catholic Church in the Niagara Peninsula, 1626–1895*, 259–61. The canal would have been known to some Irish during the famine because the canal builder, William Hamilton Merritt, called for a collection to assist the famine victims in Ireland. LAC, RG 43, Department of Railways and Canals, volume 2359, Welland Canal, Pay Ledger, 1850–1856.
80 *St Catharine's Journal*, 8 June 1848. Weekly issues of this paper also included lists of persons receiving letters at the post offices of St Catharine's and Thorold, Lincoln County, which contained many names of Roscommon origin.

CHAPTER THREE

1. O'Gallagher, "The Orphans of Grosse Ile," 82.
2. Mary Tighe's name does not appear on the death registers for Grosse Ile, which recorded both deaths at sea and in the quarantine station, so it is likely she perished after arriving at Quebec and was probably buried at the Marine Hospital Cemetery in Lower Town.
3. Ibid., 71.
4. O'Gallagher, "The Orphans of Grosse Ile," 90–1.
5. The Tighe story is related in full in O'Gallagher, "Children of the Famine," 55–6 and Callery, "The Tye/Tighe Story," 5.
6. *Census of Canada*, 1871, Province of Quebec, County of Lotbiniere, District 155, Subdistrict C, Francois Coulombe.
7. *Census of Canada*, 1891, Province of Quebec, County of Lotbiniere, District 165, Catherine Tighe.
8. The mobility of migrants to the Canadas is evidenced in Gagan, *Hopeful Travelers*; and Katz, *The People of Hamilton, Canada West*.
9. Moir, *The Church in the British Era*, 35–79; Lemieux, *Les Années difficiles (1760–1839)*; Wallot, "Religion and French-Canadian Mores," 51–91; Neatby, *Quebec*.
10. Kinealy, *Charity and the Great Hunger in Ireland*, 135–6.
11. Harvey, "The Canadian Response to the Irish Famine Emigration of 1847," 77–8; originally in Jordan, "The Tragedy of Grosse Ile," 54.
12. *Hamilton Gazette*, 10 June 1847.
13. *British Whig*, 8 June 1847.
14. *The Berean*, 27 May 1847.
15. O'Gallagher, *Grosse Ile*, appendices. It was also coincidental that orphans from Roscommon accounted for the highest number of orphans from any single county, among the 360 orphans who had a county recorded beside their name on the list. After those declared dead were removed from the data sets, the researchers proceeded methodically to search orphan names through a variety of sources: the Canadian Census, beginning in 1851–52 and continuing to 1921, the Census of the United States, beginning in 1850, the databases at Ancestry.ca, FamilySearch.com, and parish registers and records for British North America. There were eight categories that would measure a match: 1. surname; 2. given name; 3. Irish birth; 4. "adoptive family"; 5. approximate age; 6. timing based on age and birthplace of children (for later censuses); 7. location of place of settlement; and 8. religion. The latter category (8) was problematic when using the American census, since religion is not recorded. Four colour-coded categories were created: Green (6–8 matches), Blue (4–5 matches); Orange (less than 4); Yellow (did not find). The team met weekly to discuss their findings and every month a new colour-coded master list was created, based on the revisions and additions up to that point. The research

project lasted just more than three months and has provided a relatively clean data set of names and locations, upon which a historical narrative might be constructed and the prevailing ideas about "orphan adoption" tested.

16 Belley, "Un exemple de prise en charge."
17 *The Berean*, 5 August 1847.
18 Ibid., 22 and 29 July.
19 Ibid., 23 September 1847.
20 *British Colonist*, 4 June 1847.
21 *The Berean*, 12 August 1847.
22 Ibid., 15 July 1847.
23 Belley, "Un exemple de prise en charge," 68–71 and O'Gallagher and Dompierre, *Eyewitness Grosse Ile*, 400.
24 Belley, 19 and 47; *Canada Gazette*, 12 July 1847.
25 *Canada Gazette*, 6 May 1848.
26 Reilly, *Strokestown and the Great Irish Famine*, 71–3.
27 O'Gallagher and Dompierre, *Eyewitness*, 166. Archives of the Archdiocese of Quebec [AAQ], Mandements, Vol. 3 (1806–1850), Circular Letter, 29 May 1847, Archbishop Signay as published by Felix Cazeau, 509.
28 Ibid., 398.
29 Belley, 62; O'Gallagher and Dompierre, *Eyewitness*, 58, cite AAQ, Mandements, vol. 3, (1806–1850), Circular Letter, 29 May 1847, 506; also O'Gallagher, "The Orphans of Grosse Ile," 105.
30 O'Gallagher, "The Orphans of Grosse Ile," 104–5.
31 AAQ, 210 A, Registre des lettres, vol. 22, Felix Cazeau to Dominick Daly, 1847, 202–5. Cited in Belley, 93.
32 I would like to thank one of my research assistants, Britany Powell, for bringing the case of the Mahoney's to my attention for further study.
33 *Census of Canada*, 1851–1852, Canada East, District 14 of Rimouski, 131, identifies Elizabeth Mahoney, seventeen, as living with the Levesque family as a non-family member; Patrick Mahoney, age forty-seven, is also included as a resident in the same household. The *Register of Baptisms, Marriages and Deaths* for the parish of St Germain de Rimouski, 247, identifies the marriage of Catherine Mahoney to Joseph Pineau, 25 October 1858.
34 *Census of Canada*, 1852, Canada East, District 14, Rimouski, Hubert Levesque, 131.
35 This practice is discussed in Bradbury, *Working Families: Age, Gender, and Daily Survival in Industrializing Montreal*, 208.
36 Roche, *L'Adoption dans la Province de Québec*, 25.
37 Hughes, "Adoption in Canada," 105.
38 O'Gallagher, "Children of the Famine," 56.
39 Hughes, "Adoption in Canada," 104; Goubau and O'Neill, "L'Adoption, L'Eglise et l'Etat," 771.
40 De Brou, "The Rose, the Shamrock, and the Cabbage," 305–34.

41 Houston and Smyth, *Irish Emigration and Canadian Settlement*, 13–42.
42 O'Gallagher List and basilica records.
43 O'Gallagher List and 1852 census (Aylmer).
44 O'Gallagher List and *Census of Canada*, 1851, Canada East, Portneuf County, Ste-Catherine, Agricultural Census; https://central.bac-lac.gc.ca/.item/?app=Census1851&op=img&id=e002310937. *Census of Canada*, 1851, Canada East, Portneuf County, St Catherine Parish, Neilan, 374, https://central.bac-lac.gc.ca/.item/?app=Census1861&op=img&id=4108810_00131.
45 United Province of Canada, Canada East, Census of 1851–1852, District 2, Rimouski, Village de Fraserville, 33 [17], John Kelly, line 35.
46 O'Gallagher List and census of 1851, 1861.
47 AAQ, 1 CB Vicaires Généraux, vol. XII, Bishop Thomas Cook to Coadjutor Bishop Flavien Turgeon, 18 July 1847, 40. Cited in O'Gallagher and Dompierre, *Eyewitness*, 106.
48 O'Gallagher, "Children of the Famine," 50–6.
49 Strong-Boag, *Finding Families, Finding Ourselves*, 18.
50 Bradbury, "The Fragmented Family," 109–11.
51 Strong-Boag, *Finding Families*, 11–12; Perkhoff and Brickey, "Creating Precious Children and Glorified Mothers," 29–31; On discipline, see Cliché, *Abuse or Punishment?*
52 The 170 children located in the routinely generated records constitute about 28 per cent of the O'Gallagher List.
53 Larrivée, "Une Ville en Pline nature," 3–4.
54 Gosselin, "Les terretoires et ses premiers occupants," 21–2.
55 Ibid., 27.
56 The census of 1851–52 indicates that 3,653 were in the district, most of whom were rural dwellers. See also, Larocque, "Un Region de Peuplement (1790–1855)," 95–112.
57 Larocque, "Un Region," 114–17.
58 Ibid., 100. The parish was erected in the 1820s and named after St Germain d'Auxerre, the patron of Paris. Coincidentally, the father of the first seigneur was Germain Lepage. Langlois, *Dossier Sur La Paroisse de Saont-Germain de Rimouski*, 12 and 55–6.
59 O'Gallagher and Dompierre, *Eyewitness*, 253 and 262–4.
60 Lebel to Cazeau, 18 April 1848 as cited in Larocque, "Un Region," 116–17.
61 Ibid., 117. For more on Father Destroismaisons, see Langlois, "Dossier sue las Paroisse," 151.
62 "Monsieur l'abbé Thomas Quinn, 1841–1923. Souvenirs D'Enfance (Arrivée au Canada)," in *Metáire St-Joseph, Nicolet (Chronique). 1895–1935*, 1, 58–60.
63 Watts, "L'emigration britannique de 1847–1848," 21–3.
64 O'Gallagher and Dompierre, *Eyewitness*, 352.
65 The census indicates Roscommon 7; Mayo 4; Clare 4; Fermanagh, Tipperary, Tyrone, Galway, and Leitrim each with one, and three unknown.

66 Twenty-three were listed as non-family members and one was included in the family count. Family membership is indicated by sex in four columns on the second page of teach return – a page that has not been used carefully by historians in assessing the issue of orphans and legal adoption.
67 Neff, "The Education of Destitute Homeless Children," 3–46.
68 All case studies are derived from the data in the Census of 1851–1852, Canada East, District of Rimouski.
69 *Census of Canada*, 1851, Canada East, Rimouski, Ann Kane, 33, https://central.bac-lac.gc.ca/.item/?app=Census1851&op=img&id=e002313113.
70 *Census of Canada*, 1851, Canada East, District 5, Chambly, St-Jean, Mary Joice, 43, https://central.bac-lac.gc.ca/.item/?app=Census1851&op=img&id=e002300738.
71 The entire genealogy is recreated in ancestry.com with some minor errors in transcription by the family. https://www.ancestry.ca/family-tree/person/tree/53223284/person/13473817770/facts?ssrc=.
72 Mary Dempsey, Register of Baptisms, Marriages and Burials, St-Germain de Rimouski Parish, 23 July 1858, 236.
73 *The Berean*, 18 November 1847.
74 *Census of Canada*, 1851, Canada East, District 14, Rimouski, George Cocs [sic], 95, https://central.bac-lac.gc.ca/.item/?app=Census1851&op=img&id=e002313113.
75 Census of Canada, 1851, Canada East, District 14, Rimouski, Henry Olden, 69 https://central.bac-lac.gc.ca/.item/?app=Census1851&op=img&id=e002313086.
76 *The Berean*, 13 May 1847.
77 Delaney, *The Great Irish Famine*, 198–9; Donnelly, *The Great Irish Potato Famine*, 234–5. Robins, "The Emigration of Irish Workhouse Children," 32–4.
78 *The Berean*, 2 September 1847.
79 *The Church*, 28 May 1847.
80 Millman, "The Church's Ministry," 12; Harvey, "The Canadian Response to the Irish Famine Emigration of 1847," 77.
81 George Mountain to the Hon. T.C. Alwyn, MPP, 25 July 1847, cited in O'Gallagher and Dompierre, *Eyewitness*, 205.
82 Millman, "The Church's Ministry," 133.
83 *The Berean*, 22 July 1847.
84 Millman, "The Church's Ministry," 133; *The Berean*, 7 October 1847.
85 *The Berean*, 16 September 1847.
86 Ibid., 22 July 1847 and *The Church*, 16 July 1847.
87 Naylor, "WILLOUGHBY, MARK."
88 *The Berean*, 23 September 1847.
89 *Canada Gazette*, 6 May 1848.
90 Census of 1851–52, Canada East, Quebec City District, https://central.bac-lac.gc.ca/.item/?app=Census1851&op=img&id=e002334348. Alice was a witness to

her sister's marriage at the Anglican Church in Valcartier in 1854; Drouin List, https://www.ancestry.ca/discoveryui-content/view/13731764:1091?tid=&pid= &queryId=efbdc725d4b52ee91dcc1b8426834962&_phsrc=cPz209&_phstart= successSource.

91 Census of 1851–52, District 3, Sherbrooke, Compton Subdivision, Item 736566; https://central.bac-lac.gc.ca/.item/?app=Census1851&op=&img&id=e00 2318006.
92 *Canada Gazette*, 6 May 1848, 5337.
93 Harvey, "The Protestant Orphan Asylum," 2–3.
94 Neff, "The Education of Destitute Homeless Children," 4 and 6.
95 Ibid, 4–12; *Constitution and By-Laws of the Montreal Protestant Orphan Asylum* (Montreal: John Lovell, 1860).
96 The author was not admitted access to the files of the Montreal Protestant Orphans Asylum, now housed at Library and Archives Canada, but are restricted (MG 28 I 388). No inquiries to the proprietor of the collections, Summerhill Home of Montreal, were answered. The lists were gleaned from the *Canada Gazette*, the O'Gallagher List, and the Ship's List, https://www.theshipslist.com/1847/orphans.html.
97 Charbonneau and Drolet-Dubé, *Register of Deceased Persons*, 105; The *John and Robert* left Liverpool with 348 passengers on 9 June 1847 and arrived in Quebec on 6 August of that year. Of the thirty-four deaths, twenty were in quarantine, seven on board ship at Grosse Ile, and seven at sea. It had been fifty-three days at sea and spent five extra days in quarantine. O'Gallagher and Dompierre, *Eyewitness*, 351. The Pickering brothers also appear on the Ships List, on a transcription of the "Semi-Monthly Return of Government Orphans in charge of the Montreal Protestant Orphan Asylum from 31st Day of August to the 15th September 1847," which was transcribed from LAC, RG4, C1, vol.208: files 3500-3699, 1847. I would like to thank my research team member Jaime McLaughlin for bringing the Pickering Brothers to my attention.
98 *Census of Canada*, 1851–52, Canada West, York County, Markham Township, Adam Wideman, age fifty-four, Francis Pickering, age twenty-three, not a family member. https://central.bac-lac.gc.ca/.item/?app=Census1851&op =&img&id=e002374209.
99 Census of 1861, Canada West, York County, Markham Township, Andrew Pickering, labourer; https://central.bac-lac.gc.ca/.item/?app=Census1861&op =&img&id=4108435_00138.
100 Charbonneau and Drolet-Dubé, *Register of Deceased Persons*, 51 and 92. See also chapter 6 for more information on the Pickering brothers.
101 Charbonneau and Drolet-Dubé, *Register of Deceased Persons*, 95.
102 Ibid., 101.
103 He was buried 30 May 1847. O'Gallagher and Dompierre, *Eyewitness*, 78.
104 Ibid, 345.

NOTES TO PAGES 89–92

105   *The Berean*, 12 August 1847. In August the temperatures in the St Lawrence Valley sometimes exceeded 102 degrees fahrenheit.
106   *British Colonist*, 22 June 1847.
107   *St Catharine's Journal*, 24 June 1847.
108   *British Whig* (Kingston), 3 and 7 July 1847.
109   *British Colonist*, 22 June 1847. Leslie Anne Harvey, "The Canadian Response," 89.
110   Millman, "The Church's Ministry," 135. Newspapers kept an ongoing tally of the dead. At the end of July, it was reported that 2,046 people had died in Montreal: 596 residents, 316 immigrants in town, and 1,134 immigrants in the sheds. The dead in Montreal for the same period in 1846 had been only 325, only 7 of whom were immigrants. *Quebec Morning Chronicle*, 2 August 1847.
111   *The Berean*, 29 July 1847. LAC, Department of Finance, Emigration Service Fund, R200-161-)-E, 1843–1847 are the vouchers redeemed by carters for their expenses incurred by taking emigrants away from the major ports of entry.
112   Annals of the Sisters of Charity of Montreal (Grey Nuns), *Ancien Journal*, vol. 1 (1847) ed. by Jason King and trans. by Jean-Francois Bernard, 7 June 1847, 493.
113   Harvey, "The Canadian Response," 90, citing *Montreal Transcript*, 29 June 1847.
114   *The Berean*, 29 July 1847. The numbers in the sheds at Point St Charles gradually decreased as the sailing season tapered off. By 22 August 1847, there were 1,330 people in the sheds, of whom 27 died including 5 children. The following day 220 out of 1,304 patents were children. *The Mirror*, 27 August 1847.
115   *The Cross*, 31 July 1847, citing the Montreal *Pilot*.
116   Archives of the Religious Hospitallers of St Joseph (Kingston) [ARHSJK], typescript the RHSJ and the Famine, 12. The ten dead sisters were in addition to eight dead Catholic priests. Lettre pastoral, XXXVIII, "Epidemie de 1847," in *Fioretti Vescovile: Extraits de Mandements, Lettres Pastorales et Circulaires de Monseigneur Ignace Bourget* (Montreal: Imprimerie "Le Franc-Parleur," 1872), 22–3.
117   Lord Elgin to Parliament, British Parliamentary Papers, Vol. 17, 1847, 381; O'Gallagher and Dompierre, *Eyewitness*, 56.
118   *Ancien Journal*, 1 (1847): 9 June 1847, 500.
119   Lettre pastorale XXXVII, "Orphenilat," in *Fioretti Vescovile: Extraits de Mandements, Lettres Pastorales et Circulaires de Monseigneur Ignace Bourget* (Montreal: Imprimerie "Le Franc-Parleur," 1872), 22.
120   *Ancien Journal*, 1 (1847): 24 June 1847, 500.
121   APM, M6, "Les notes ont été prise par Sr. Wilson."
122   King, "Remembering Famine Orphans," 122. Lettre pastoral, XLIV, "Orphelins Irlandais – Asile St Jérome-Emilien," 9 mars 1848, in *Fioretti*, 28.
123   APM, M6, "Les notes ont été prise par Sr Wilson."
124   Pastoral Letter, XLIV, "Orphelins Irlandais," 9 Mars 1848, in *Fioretti*, 28. Translation by the author.

125 Archives of the Archdiocese of Montreal [AAM], 525.103, 848-2, Category of the Orphans at Point St Charles, 12 March 1848.
126 AAM, 901.103, Emigration, 1842–1849, M Sullivan to Bourget, 11 July 1848, 848-7 and Dominick Daly to Bourget, 21 October 1847, 847-5a. Daly remitted the sum of £755/17/1 for the Church's expenses at the shed thus far in the year.
127 Archives Bon-Pasteur [ABP], 501-004, 847, Transcript of Letter from Bourget to the Community, 30 November 1847. Archives Providence Montreal [APM], M6 Registre des orphelins du typhus Chroniques, Hospice St-Jerome-Emilien et Hôpital St-Patrice, 1847–1852.
128 ASBP, "Names of the Orphan Children Entrusted to the Care of the Ladies of the Good Pastor, Montreal, 18 August 1847" although the list appears on a LAC microfilm from the RG 4, C 1 vol. 204: files 3000-3099 of 1847, image number 016863. Census of 1851–52, Canada West, Hastings County, Belleville.
129 Driedger, *An Irish Heart*, 45.
130 King, "Remembering Famine Orphans," 124.
131 Lettre pastoral, XXXIX, "Prière, Voeu, et Consecration á la Ste-Vièrge, 13 August 1847, in *Fioretto*, 24.
132 *The Berean*, 9 September 1847.
133 Ibid., 18 November 1847. Vicar General Hyacinthe Hudon's death was announced in the *British Colonist*, 20 August 1847. ARHSJK, typescript, 11–12.
134 *Armagh Guardian*, 12 October 1847.
135 *British Whig*, 25 July 1847.
136 *British Colonist*, 27 July 1847.
137 AAM, Bourget Papers, 525.103, 848-2, SGM 89, "Category of Orphans at Point St Charles," 12 March 1848.
138 Ibid.
139 Providence Archives, Montreal, M6, Registre des Orphelins du Typhus Chroniques Hospice St-Jerome Emilien et Hopital Saint-Patrice, 1847–1852, Liste des Filles.
140 McGowan, *Michael Power: The Struggle to Build the Catholic Church on the Canadian Frontier*, 44–5.
141 Census of 1851–52, Lower Canada, Boucherville, J.P. Proulx, http://www.bac-lac.gc.ca/eng/census/1851/Pages/item.aspx?itemid=1166519. My thanks to research student Emma McKeen for uncovering Dr Proulx's identity and largesse.
142 Gavan, *Teachers of a Nation: The Jesuits in English Canada, 1842–2013*, 23, 39, and 47; Monet, *Dictionary of Jesuit Biography: Ministry to English Canada*, 333.
143 Voisine, "Calixte Marquis," Dictionary of Canadian Biography, XIII (1901–1910), University of Toronto/Université Laval; http://www.biographi.ca/en/bio/marquis_calixte_13E.html.
144 My thanks to research student Sofia Romaschenko for uncovering the story of the Cuthberts. Census of 1851–52, Canada East, Nicolet, http://www.bac-ac.gc.ca/eng/census/21851/Pages/item.aspx?itemid=340835, http://data2.collec

NOTES TO PAGES 96–101

tionscanada.gc.ca/e/e093/e002309367.jpg, http://www.bac-ac.gc.ca/eng/census/1851/Pages/item.aspx?itemid=340779.
145 *The Canada Gazette*, no. 345, Montreal, Saturday, 6 May 1848.
146 Census of Canada West, 1851–52, Glengarry County, Lochiel Township, Harold Kennedy.
147 Pastoral Letter, XLIV, "Orphelins Irlandais," 9 Mars 1848, in *Fioretti*, 29. Translated by the author.

CHAPTER FOUR

1 Strokestown Park Archives [SPA], Townland of Culliagh, List of Strokestown Passengers Prepared by Dr Ciaran Reilly.
All of the dead from the Cox's Townland were passengers on board the *Virginius*. SPA, Strokestown Passengers List, cross referenced with Charbonneau and Drolet-Dubé, *A Register of Deceased Persons at Sea and on Grosse Ile in 1847*.
Hamilton Gazette, 27 September 1847.
There were two Widows Cox from the Mahon estate, both from the Culliagh townland in the civil parish of Bumlin. Neither widow is recognized in the Strokestown record by her given name. One is identified as the widow of John Cox, who travelled to Quebec with four persons in her party. Little else survives to indicate whatever happened to this Widow Cox and her children. What is clear is that in the death register for Grosse Ile, a Patrick Cox, with no age given, is recorded to have died after his voyage on the *Naomi* (Charbonneau and Drolet-Dubé, 71). If this was the child of the Widow Cox who placed her advertisement in September 1847, her journey ended in the tragedy of perhaps never knowing that the son for whom she yearned had died shortly after she left him. There is a second Widow Cox, also from Bumlin, who left Strokestown with a party of eight in tow. Susan Cox, a "knit worker" appears on the census of 1851–52, living in "a hovel" in Hamilton, Canada West, and with her are listed three children, including a son Patrick, aged fifteen. Much of the census profile of the second Widow Cox matches information on the original Strokestown list and the advertisement in the *Hamilton Gazette*. There is no definitive answer to this mystery, but the best evidence available points to a happy ending to the tale of at least one of Major Mahon's "assisted" families. Susan Cox, *Census of Canada, 1851–1852*, Canada West, Hamilton, St George's Ward, Queen Street.
5 Millman, "The Church's Ministry," 126–36; *The Church*, 28 May and 18 June 1847; *The Berean*, 3 June 1847.
6 *The Canada Gazette*, Number 345, Montreal, 6 May 1848. See also Harvey, "The Protestant Orphan Asylum."
7 King, "Remembering Famine Orphans," 118; the role of religious orders in Montreal is covered by O'Gallagher, "The Orphans of Grosse Ile," 97–101.

8 *British Colonist*, 11 May 1847.
9 Library and Archives Canada [LAC], RG 10, Vol. 162, pp. 94332-55 and vol.163, pp. 94944-55.
10 Archdiocese of Dublin Archives, [AAD], Dr Daniel Murray Papers, 34-12-115, Rev P. Connell, Richmond, CW to Murray, 21 July 1847, offers a donation of £18; 34-12-78, WG Hines, Treasurer, Relief Committee of Kingston, to Murray, 18 March 1847, offers a donation of £200; and 34-12-81, E Curran of Bytown to Murray, 18 March 1847, offers £52-2s-6d for Irish famine relief.
11 The most popular currency used in Upper Canada at the time was the Halifax pound (£) which was valued at about 10 per cent less than the pound sterling. The Halifax pound was usually valued at four Canadian or USA dollars. Decimal currency was being phased into the province by the 1850s. Lee, *The Canada Company and the Huron Tract*, 12–13.
12 *Bytown Packet* (reported in *Ottawa Citizen*), 8 May 1847. For more information on the area consult McCuaig, *People of St Patrick's*.
13 LAC, RG 5 C1, Provincial Secretary, Correspondence Files, 1844–1867, Reel 11, vol. 204-211. Daly would issue warrants for up to £300 to cover a variety of local costs for both Boards of Health and Boards of Police who handled the influx of Irish migrants.
14 Archives of the Roman Catholic Archdiocese of Toronto [ARCAT] Michael Power Papers, AA10.10, Copy of letter from Michael Power to the Propaganda Fide, Rome, 12 April 1847. Also Archives of the Sacred Congregation of the Propaganda Fide [APF], Scritture riferte nei congress. America Settentionale. Canada ecc. Dal 1841–1848, vol 5, Bishop Power to PF, 12 April 1847; PF to Power, 12 June 1847.
15 Paul-Émile (Louise Guay), "BRUYÈRE, ÉLISABETH."
16 Paul-Emile, "Mère Élisabeth Bruyère: fille de l' glise et femme d'oeuvres," 55–6.
17 Lamirande, *Élisabeth Bruyère*, 167.
18 McBane, *Bytown 1847*, 55–84.
19 Paul-Emile, "Mère Élisabeth Bruyère," 51–2.
20 City of Ottawa Archives, Sisters of Charity of Bytown (Grey Nuns), Hospital Ledger, Bytown, 1847. My thanks to colleague Michael McBane for sending me a digitized version of the ledger. See also McBane, *Bytown*, 320.
21 *Census of Canada*, 1851, Canada West, Renfrew District, Township of Bagot, https://central.bac-lac.gc.ca/.item/?app=Census1851&op=img&id=e002368965.
22 LAC, RG 5 C1, vol. 204, Provincial Secretary, Correspondence Files, 1844–1867, Reel 11, Image #17,264, Returns of Board of Health, Cornwall to Dominick Daly, 6/7 July, 1847; RG 5 C1 vol. 207, Reel 11, Image #1078, Returns from Board of Police, Prescott to Daly, 14 June 1847. The provincial secretary's correspondence indicates that, in 1847, the following towns had established boards of health: Cornwall, West Williamsburgh, Matilda (Dundas Co.), Brockville,

Picton, Bytown, Kingston, Belleville, Toronto, West Toronto, Simcoe (police), Barrie, Hamilton, Niagara, Brantford, Dunville, London, Chatham, Guelph, and Sandwich (Windsor).

23 *British Whig*, 11 August 1848.
24 Errington, *Greater Kingston*, 32–4.
25 *The Berean*, 1 July 1847.
26 Malcomson, "The Poor in Kingston," 281–4.
27 *Berean*, 1 July 1847.
28 Towns, "Relief and Order," 123. The number appears a little high given the recorded deaths, the expeditious way migrants were moved through the port, and the fact that just more than 38,000 made the next stop in Toronto.
29 Archdiocese of Kingston, St Mary's Cathedral, Register of Baptisms, Marriages, and Burials, 1843–1849. Accessed on Familysearch.org, 29 March 2018. The emigrants were almost all Irish, with 328 (33.2 per cent) being identified by county of origin.
30 O'Gallagher and Dompierre, *Eyewitness*, 52.
31 *British Whig*, 22 June 1847.
32 McGowan, *Death or Canada*, 40–1. Also see *British Colonist*, 20 August 1847 and *St Catharine's Journal*, 26 August 1847. Kingston was well connected by steamship to Hamilton, Lewiston (NY), and Toronto. *British Colonist*, 9 July and 20 August 1847, and *British Whig*, 11 August 1847.
33 Archives of Ontario [hereafter AO], RG 11-3, Anthony Hawke Letterbooks, Hawke to J.E. Campbell, Civil Secretary, 16 October 1847.
34 McMahon, "Les Religieuse Hospitalières," 47.
35 Errington, *Greater Kingston*, 59; Flynn, *Built on a Rock*, 5–8.
36 Corcoran and Smith, "Bishop Macdonell and the Friends of Ireland," 7–23.
37 *Lord Durham's Report (1839)*, 98.
38 McMahon, "Les Religieuse Hospitalières," 41–2.
39 Ibid., 46.
40 Ibid.; Osborne and Swainson, *Kingston*, 128–9.
41 Religious Hospitallers of St Joseph (Kingston), Archives [hereafter RHSJA], Typescript History/Memoire, 19.
42 RHSJA, Annals of the Hotel Dieu, Kingston, typescript, volume 1, 26 December 1847.
43 RHSJA, Annals of the Hotel Dieu, Kingston, typescript, volume 1, December 1847.
44 Ibid.
45 Ibid.
46 Ibid.
47 Ibid
48 RHSJA, Annals, 26 December 1847.
49 RHSJA, Annals, January 1847.

50 Queen's University Archives [hereafter QUA], House of Industry, Inmate Registers, 2262-Box 7, Ledger 1, December 1847.
51 McGowan, "Rethinking the Irish Famine Orphans," 108.
52 Bradbury, *Working Families*, 208.
53 Register of St Mary's Cathedral, Kingston, 12 September 1856.
54 *Census of Canada*, 1851–1852, Canada West, Northumberland County, River Trent, Patrick Flannigan.
55 *Census of 1861*, Canada West, City of Kingston, Mary Ryan.
56 LAC, RG 19 D5, Department of Finance, vol. 2533, Civil Secretary, Major T Campbell to Anthony B Hawke, 7 May 1847. The government had remitted funds to hospitals in Bytown, Kingston, Toronto, and Hamilton, so that Phelan was quite correct in his allegations that precedents had already been set. Prior to Phelan's letter, the government had also subsidized the hospital in Toronto to the sum of £75. *British Colonist*, 9 July 1847.
57 LAC, RG 5 C1 Canada West, Provincial Secretary Correspondence, Vol. 206, File 17400, Letter from Bishop Patrick Phelan (Bishop of Carrhae) to Provincial Secretary Dominick Daly, 19 July 1847 and Daly to Phelan, 19 July 1847.
58 Ibid, Daly to "Mr Panet," 20 July 1847.
59 *British Whig*, 31 July 1847 and 18 December 1847.
60 McMahon, "Les Religieuse Hospitalières," 56; *British Whig*, 18 December 1847; and QUA, House of Industry, Inmate Registers, 2262-Box 7, Ledger 1, December 1847–July 1848.
61 QUA, House of Industry, Inmate Registers, 2262-Box 7, Ledger 1, Michael Grady (10), 28 April–28 July 1848; James Dowling (7), 4 May–19 July 1848; Jane Feeny (7), 1 December 1847–16 July 1848; Patrick Maloney (14), 21–26 June 1848.
62 Ibid, Bridget Maloney, 1 December 1847 to 6 May 1848.
63 *British Whig*, 21 August 1847.
64 Ibid., 11 August 1847.
65 Ibid., 25 August 1847.
66 Ibid., 18 August 1847.
67 RHSJA, Annals, 26 December 1847 to 22 January 1848.
68 RHSJA, Annals, 22 January 1848.
69 Samples of these interior destinations mentioned in *British Colonist*, 9 and 20 August 1847 and *St Catharine's Journal*, 26 August 1847.
70 *British Whig*, 1 September 1847.
71 Minutes of the board of health, Toronto, 26 August 1847 as printed in the *British Colonist*.
72 LAC, RG 5 C1, vol. 210, Provincial Secretary's Office, Board of Health (Constable J.B. Townsend, clerk) to Dominick Daly, 30 August 1847, Reel C-10802, Image 838.
76 *British Colonist*, 3 September 1847.
74 AO, Anthony B Hawke Papers, Convalescent Hospital Ledger, lines 315 and 752.

75 Smyth, *Toronto, the Belfast of Canada*; Moir, "Toronto's Protestants," 1313–27; a revision of this theme appears in McGowan, *The Waning of the Green*.
76 *The Mirror* (Toronto), 18 February 1848.
77 *British Whig*, 6 November 1847.
78 McGowan, *Death or Canada*, 52–5.
79 LAC, RG 19-D-5, volumes 2531–2535, Emigration Service Fund, 1847–1853, Travel Vouchers and Vouchers for Payment, 1843–1855; Lee, *The Canada Company*, 172–6; Huron County Museum and Archives, Assessment Roll, District of Huron, 1848. These assessment rolls for townships now in Huron, Perth, and Wellington Counties reveal the presence of hundreds of Irish settlers, both pre-famine and famine era. As see Tucker, "Successful Pioneers: Irish Catholic Settlers in Hibbert [Township]." See also *Globe*, 12 February 1848. The report from the Toronto clerk indicates that 26,700 migrants of the 38,560 who landed in Toronto, were sent on to Niagara and Hamilton.
80 McGowan, *Death or Canada*, 91.
81 *Report of the Managing Committee of the Widows' and Orphans' Asylum* (Toronto: Bowsell and Thompson, 1848), 18.
82 *The Mirror*, 20 August 1847.
83 Ibid., 2 July 1847.
84 McGowan, *Michael Power*, 199–226.
85 *St Catharine's Journal*, 14 October 1847; *Quebec Chronicle*, 4 October 1847; *The Berean*, 7 October 1847; *The Mirror*, 8 October 1847.
86 Norman, "Making a Path by Walking," 92–106.
87 *The Berean*, 8 July 1847 [Grasett appointed]; *The Church*, 16 July 1847; *British Colonist*, 20 July 1847 and 31 August 1847 [Susan Bailey].
88 Neff, "Pauper Apprenticeship," 149.
89 *Report of the Managing Committee*, 6–7.
90 Ibid, 12, 15.
91 *Report of the Managing Committee*, appendix.
92 ARCAT, Special Collections, Holograph Collection, HO, Series 20.67, Father T. Kirwan, List of Farmers from Adjala Township Who Request Orphan Children, 18 April 1848.
93 *Report of the Managing Committee*, appendix.
94 *Census of Canada*, 1851–1852, Canada West, York County, Vaughan Township, Michael O'Connor.
95 All cases are listed in the *Report of the Managing Committee*, appendix. *Census of Canada*, 1851–1852, Canada West, Ontario County, Whitby Township, Richard Butler.
96 Ibid, Maria Mooney, Orphan #59.
97 *Censuses of Canada*, 1665–1871, vol 4. *Census of Canada*, 1870–1871 (Ottawa: I.B. Taylor, 1876): 165–6; Table 11. In 1848, the home district around Toronto had a population of 84,312 with Catholics accounting for 7,949 people, or 9.4 per cent.

98 Smyth and Houston, "Community and Institutional Supports," 5–22.
99 ARCAT, Special Collections, Holograph Collection, HO 20.67, Publication of Banns from St Paul's, 1849 and List of Farmers from Adjala Who Request Orphan Children, 18 April 1848 (Father Thaddeaus Kirwan and Mr Robert Keenan).
100 *Report of the Managing Committee*, appendix, orphan #36; *Census of Canada*, 1851–1852, Canada West, Blenheim.
101 Hughes, "Adoption in Canada," 105.
102 *Census of Canada*, 1851–1852, Canada West, Peel County, Chinguacousy Township, Jane Hamilton. *Report of the Managing Committee*, appendix, orphan #197.
103 LAC, RG 5, C 1, Provincial Secretary's Office, vol 210, Image 689, Guelph Board of Health to Dominick Daly, 24 August 1847.
104 *British Whig*, 6 November 1847.
105 See chapter 2.
106 Neff, "The Education of Destitute Homeless Children," 3–46.

CHAPTER FIVE

1 Steele, "Henry John Temple," 9.
2 Norton, "On Landlord-Assisted Emigration," 27.
3 Cited in Anbinder, "Lord Palmerston," 461.
4 *British Whig*, 17 November 1847.
5 Despatch from Lt Gov. W.M.G. Colebrooke to Earl Grey, 6 July 1847, No. 60, enclosure 10, United Kingdom Parliamentary Papers (hereafter UKPP), Emigration to the British Provinces in North America and to the Australian Colonies, Part I, House of Commons, 20 December 1847.
6 Osborne, "The Right Reverend William Dollard, D.D.," 23. Toner, "The Foundations of the Catholic Church in English-speaking New Brunswick," 66.
7 I am heavily indebted to the work of Peter D. Murphy, *Poor Ignorant Children*, and Koral LaVorgna, "Not Standing Idly By," 139–57. Both Murphy and LaVorgna have published on the work at the Orphan Asylum, and Murphy's list of orphans and linkage to the 1851 census have been invaluable. All line items were rechecked by my assistant Louis Reed-Wood, who made further cross-references to both the 1851 and 1861 censuses of New Brunswick.
8 *New Brunswick Reporter & Fredericton Advertiser*, 12 February 1847.
9 Archives of the Diocese of Saint John [ADSJ], Dollard Papers, Correspondence #666, Earl Gray to Lieutenant-Governor Sir William Colbrooke, 17 May 1847. Copy.
10 Murphy, *Poor Ignorant Children*, 13.
11 Ibid, 14.
12 *New Brunswick Reporter and Fredericton Advertiser*, 27 August 1847.

13 Spray, "'The Difficulties Came Upon Us Like a Thunderbolt,'" 124; Wright, "Partridge Island," 136. Wright cites that about 16,000 landed in New Brunswick in 1847. The Colonial Office officially registered 16,589 emigrants to New Brunswick from United Kingdom ports in 1847. Library and Archives Canada [hereafter LAC], Colonial Office Papers, CO 384/78-83, "Report of the Colonial Land and Emigration Commissioners, 1848."
14 See, "The Orange Order," 71–89.
15 See, *Riots in New Brunswick*, 115–32.
16 *The New Brunswick Reporter and Fredericton Advertiser*, 28 November and 5 December 1845.
17 Rees, *Surplus People*, 82–116.
18 See, *Riots in New Brunswick*, 61–5 and 90–6.
19 UKPP, Part 1, Despatch from Lt Gov. Colebrooke to Earl Grey, 30 July 1847, 73. An excellent analysis of denominational relations in Saint John can be found in Acheson, "The Irish Community in Saint John," 27–54.
20 Osborne, "The Right Reverend," 32.
21 Assumption Chapel was built in 1847 in Carleton, now in the western section of Saint John; http://www.ourladyoftheassumptionnb.com/history; see also Chilton, "Des morts sur la Miramichi: reactions de la population a arrive de immigrants maladies au Nouveau Brunswick au milieu de XIXe siècle," 89.
22 Rees, *Surplus People*, 89.
23 McGowan, *Pax Vobis*, 16–18; See, *Riots*, 35.
24 Houston and Smyth, *Irish Emigration and Canadian Settlement*, 203–4.
25 Murphy, *Poor Ignorant Children*, 11.
26 *New Brunswick Courier*, 7 July 1847. Chilton, "Des morts," 83.
27 *New Brunswick Courier*, 21 August 1847.
28 Ibid., 28 August 1847. A general assessment of the condition at the quarantine station can be found in ADSJ, Partridge Island Fonds, Robert Bayard, MDH, "Report of the Commission Appointed by the Lieutenant Governor to Inquire into the State of Immigrants Upon Partridge Island," September 6, 1847.
29 UKPP, Part 1, Enclosure 2, no. 37, letter from Stewart & Kincaid to Viscount Palmerston, 3 December 1847.
30 Punch, *North America's Maritime Funnel*, 87.
31 Murphy, *Poor Ignorant Children*, 50–1 and 76. The *Lady Sale* carried 150 assisted migrants from the Gore-Booth estate and 200 from Palmerston's, although there is no list indicating which estate the Foleys had been assisted from. No name is given for Mrs Foley.
32 Whelan, "The Nineteenth-Century Almshouse System," 9–11.
33 Paupers were segregated by race.
34 Whelan, "The Nineteenth-Century Almshouse System," 11–13.
35 Ibid., 16. The numbers of inmates and deaths were recorded between March 1847 and March 1848.

36 Murphy, *Poor Ignorant Children*, 17.
37 Ibid., 5–7.
38 Nova Scotia also had one.
39 Rees, *Surplus People*, 22. Rees comments that Fitzwilliam was "generally regarded as a 'good' landlord." In 1847, Fitzwilliam assisted tenants headed to Quebec and St Andrew's New Brunswick. See also Lee, *Coollattin*, 155–71. On Lord Lansdowne, see Anbinder, "From Famine to Five Points," 351–87.
40 Gray, *The Irish Famine*, 101; McDonagh, "Irish Emigration," 338. Gore-Booth spent about £15,000 to assist 1,340 of his "surplus" tenants off the estate.
41 Swords, *In Their Own Words*, 132 [Garrett to Sir Randolph Routh, Chairman of the Relief Commission, 7 February 1847], and 146–8 [Captain O'Brien to Colonel Harry Jones, former Chair of the Relief Commission, 2 March 1847].
42 Punch, *North America's Maritime Funnel*, 74. Punch reports that twenty-six passengers (5.3 per cent) of the 493 passengers died at sea.
43 Archives of New Brunswick (ANB), Mattias Ferguson, Head Manager, Committee of Ship Aeolus to Robert Gore Booth, 5 June 1847. Archives.gnb.ca/Documents/IrishPortal/Letters/SC/04/Committee-1847.06.05. Accessed 29 November 2021.
44 This was a reference to the revision of the Irish Poor Law in June 1847, which placed the burden of poverty on Ireland strictly on the property holders of Ireland and would require anyone seeking poor relief to hold a quarter acre or less.
45 *Saint John Courier*, cited in *The New Brunswick Reporter and Fredericton Advertiser*, 3 September 1847.
46 *New Brunswick Reporter*, 3 September 1847.
47 UKPP, Part 1, Enclosure 2, "Extract Resolutions Passed by the Common Council of the City of Saint John, 3 September 1847.
48 The *Transit* arrived at Quebec on 3 June 1847 with 149 assisted passengers from the Sligo estates. Of the 158 passengers only six died at sea. The *Springhill* arrived at Quebec, 10 June 1847 with 220 assisted passengers, and 7 who paid individually. Only nine of the 227 passengers died on route. The *Numa* arrived at Quebec on 27 July with 244 assisted passengers. Only 37 of the 257 passengers died either at sea or in quarantine. The *Marchioness of Breadalbane* landed at Quebec on 12 August, the same day as the notorious *Virginius*, but with only 27 dead among its 187 passengers. The *Richard Watson* was the last ship to arrive at Quebec during the sailing season of 1847. It held 164 assisted passengers from Palmerston's estates of whom only 4 died on the voyage. O'Gallagher and Dompierre, *Eyewitness Grosse-Ile*, 342–3, 349, 352, 356. Anbinder, "Lord Palmerston and the Irish Famine Emigration," 457–60. For an inventory of Palmerston's ships carrying assisted migrants see UKPP, Part 1, Enclosure 2, no. 37, Stewart & Kincaid to Palmerston, 3 December 1847.
49 The *Carricks* sank in the Gulf of St Lawrence, 10 May 1847, with a loss of 75 per cent of its passengers and crew.

NOTES TO PAGES 131–6

50 Anbinder, "Lord Palmerston," 458.
51 *St Catharine's Journal*, 14 September 1847; *New Brunswick Courier*, 25 August 1847.
52 *New Brunswick Courier*, 6 November 1847.
53 Anbinder, "Lord Palmerston," 461–2.
54 UKPP, Part 1, Enclosure 1, no.31, Moses Perley to John Saunders, Provincial Secretary, 2 November 1847.
55 UKPP, Part 1, Enclosure 1, no. 67, Stewart & Kincaid to Palmerston, 16 December 1847.
56 Ibid and Enclosure 2, no. 37, Stewart & Kincaid to Palmerston, 3 December 1847.
57 McDonagh, "Irish Emigration," 339–40; Gray, *The Irish Famine*, 101; Donnelly, *The Great Irish Potato Famine*, 115.
58 Norton, "Lord Palmerston and the Irish Famine Emigration," 155–65.
59 Cited in Gray, *Famine, Land, and Politics*, 192.
60 *New Brunswick Courier*, 13 November 1847.
61 LAC, Colonial Office Papers, 384/81, Adam Ferrie to Governor General Elgin, 1 December 1847, 365–72.
62 Derived from the Emigrant Orphan Asylum Admittance Ledger in Murphy, *Poor Ignorant Children*, 32–75. The number of 302 comes from the following calculation. There are 330 entries for orphans in the ledger. Deduct the ten children who are local and one arrives at a subtotal of 320. Deduct from this the 18 children who are repeated because they return to the asylum and one arrives at the grand total of 302 orphans.
63 Cited in Anbinder, "Lord Palmerston," 460.
64 Peter Murphy estimates that Irish orphans from all counties were dominated by Catholic children at a rate of 91 per cent. Protestant children were mostly natives of New Brunswick, Cork, Donegal, or Derry, 32, 44, 50, 51, 62, 66, 72. Thomas and Betsy McNab were the only two orphaned children recorded from the Gore-Booth Estate. They had survived the voyage on the *Yeoman*. Murphy, *Poor Ignorant Children*, 66.
65 All calculations are derived from the "Ledger" provided in Peter Murphy's *Poor Ignorant Children*.
66 Rooke and Schnell, "Childhood and Charity," 160–2.
67 Prentice, *The School Promoters*, 66–87.
68 LaVorgna, "Not Standing Idly By," 140.
69 Ibid., 143 and 145–7.
70 Murphy, *Poor Ignorant Children*, "Ledger," 52 and 54.
71 Murphy, *Poor Ignorant Children*, 5.
72 LaVorgna, "Not Standing Idly By," 144.
73 Murphy, *Poor Ignorant Children*, "Ledger," 50–1.
74 Murphy, *Poor Ignorant Children*, 5.
75 Murphy, *Poor Ignorant Children*, "Ledger," 42–3.

76 Ibid., 52–3.
77 Ibid.
78 Ibid., 68–9.
79 Ibid., 42–3.
80 Ibid., 34–5.
81 Moran, "Suffer the Children," 27–50.
82 Lee, *Coollattin*, chapter 9.
83 Murphy, *Poor Ignorant Children*, "Ledger," 42–3.
84 Ibid., 50–3.
85 Strong-Boag, *Funding Families, Funding Ourselves*, 25.
86 Murphy, *Poor Ignorant Children*, "Ledger," 70–1.
87 Murphy, *Poor Ignorant Children*, 7.
88 On Portland, across the St John River from Saint John. See, *Riots in New Brunswick*, 27.
89 LaVorgna, 143.
90 Murphy, *Poor Ignorant Children*, "Ledger," 42–3.
91 Census of 1851, New Brunswick https://www.bac-lac.gc.ca/eng/census/1851/Pages/item.aspx?itemid=320388. Accessed 22 July 2020.
92 The case of Flannagan is in Murphy, *Poor Ignorant Children*, "Ledger," 52–3 and https://central.bac-lac.gc.ca/.item/?app=Census1851&op=pdf&id=e00 2294414. Accessed 22 July 2020.
93 Parker, "Henry Chubb (1787–1855)."
94 Obituary at https://archives.gnb.ca/Search/NewspaperVitalStats/Details.aspx?guid=6f80cb77-3751-464a-b9fa-75e5e658237c&culture=en-CA. Accessed 31 December 2021. Murphy, *Poor Ignorant Children*, 17.
95 Murphy, *Poor Ignorant Children*, 22.
96 Ibid., 26.
97 Ibid., 7–10.
98 Ibid., 26.
99 See, *Riots in New Brunswick*, 54–64.
100 Toner, "The Irish of New Brunswick," 111.
101 Ibid., 107.
102 Murphy, *Poor Ignorant Children*, "Ledger," 52–3.
103 Whelan, "Hatheway, Calvin Luther," *Dictionary of Canadian Biography*, vol. 9 (University of Toronto/Universite laval, 2003). Accessed 20 December 2021.
104 https://central.bac-lac.gc.ca/.item/?app=Census1851&op=pdf&id=e0022 94400. Accessed 22 July 2020.
105 Census of 1861, New Brunswick Census of 1861, New Brunswick, https://www.bac-lac.gc.ca/eng/census/1861/Pages/item.aspx?itemid=231534. Accessed 4 April 2021.
106 Murphy, *Poor Ignorant Children*, "Ledger," 56–9. The records of the emigrant hospital and emigrant orphan asylum differ on the ages of the children. I have elected to use the asylum ages.

107 Saint John almshouse records, https://archives.gnb.ca/Irish/Databases/Almshouse/NameResults.aspx?culture=en-CA&letter=H&data=un53sMSVeFFkJXt9fvZuXvKlzFuXtj3sFufTNdgi5hY=. Accessed 4 January 2022.
108 Census of 1861, New Brunswick https://central.bac-lac.gc.ca/.item/?app=Census1861&op=img&id=4108518_00115. Accessed 4 January 2022.
109 Census of 1861, New Brunswick https://www.bac-lac.gc.ca/eng/census/1851/Pages/item.aspx?itemid=679899. Accessed 22 July 2020; also William McLean, census of 1861, Barton, King's County https://central.bac-lac.gc.ca/.item/?app=Census1861&op=img&id=4108531_00047. Accessed 4 January 2022.
110 Murphy, *Poor Ignorant Children*, 26. He refers to the asylum as a "vehicle of religious and cultural assimilation." This may have been true in a general sense but there are cases like that of Hurley that run contrary to this assumption.
111 https://www.bac-lac.gc.ca/eng/census/1861/Pages/item.aspx?itemid=173154. Accessed 4 April 2021.
112 McGowan, *A History of the Diocese of Saint John*, 71.
113 https://www.bac-lac.gc.ca/eng/census/1851/Pages/item.aspx?itemid=679942. Accessed 22 July 2020.
114 Murphy, *Poor Ignorant Children*, "Ledger," 62–3.
115 Thomas Kelley, https://www.bac-lac.gc.ca/eng/census/1851/Pages/item.aspx?itemid=719728. Accessed 22 July 2020.
116 Ibid. Accessed 4 April 2021.
117 Murphy, *Poor Ignorant Children*, "Ledger," 76–7.
118 The census returns for Saint John, New Brunswick are missing for 1861.
119 John Moran, https://www.bac-lac.gc.ca/eng/census/1861/Pages/item.aspx?itemid=222591. Accessed 4 April 2021.
120 Murphy, *Poor Ignorant Children*, "Ledger," 72–3.
121 Timothy Purcell, spelled Percel, https://www.bac-lac.gc.ca/eng/census/1851/Pages/item.aspx?itemid=1126306. Accessed 22 July 2020.
122 ANB, Archives.gnb.ca/Documents/IrishPortal/Letters/SC/14/Hennegan-1848.02.15.pdf. Accessed 29 November 2021.
123 *New Brunswick Courier*, 11 December 1847.
124 Ibid., 4 December 1847.
125 Ibid., 18 December 1847.
126 Wilson, "The Most Reverend Thomas L. Connolly," 55–108. The best biography of Connolly is Tromblay's doctoral dissertation "Thomas Louis Connolly (1815–1876)."
127 McGahan, "The Sisters of Charity," 99–133.
128 Murphy, *Poor Ignorant Children*, "Ledger," 66–7.

NOTES TO PAGES 146–50

CHAPTER SIX

1 *Census of Canada*, Canada East, 1851, Portneuf County, Ste-Catherine, Agricultural Census; https://central.bac-lac.gc.ca/.item/?app=Census1851&op=img&id=e002310937. Cornelius held seventy-five acres, of which 1.5 were reserved for wheat. Thirty of his acres were cleared.
2 *Census of Canada*, Canada East, 1851, Portneuf County, Ste-Catherine, Cornelius McCarty; https://central.bac-lac.gc.ca/.item/?app=Census1851&op=img&id=e002310897. Other locals included Fogartys, Meaghers, Landrigans, and Donovans. The enumerator was careful to give their Irish county of birth, instead of just listing Ireland.
3 *Census of Canada*, Canada East, Portneuf County, Ste-Catherine, Dennis and Mary McCabe McCarty; https://central.bac-lac.gc.ca/.item/?app=Census1851&op=img&id=e002310893. Dennis McCarty also hailed from Cork but was thirty-one. His wife Mary was born in Quebec and was only twenty-two. It is possible that Dennis and Cornelius travelled together and the elder married earlier. Or Dennis followed Cornelius as part of a McCarty migration chain to Quebec before the famine. The farm was ninety acres but less of it than that of Cornelius had been cleared and only one acre was under wheat cultivation. In any event, James Neilan was working for Dennis in 1851–52 because the McCarty children, at four and two years of age, were too young. James is not listed as a family member.
4 *Census of Canada*, Canada East, 1861.
5 *Census of Canada*, Canada East, 1851, Portneuf County, Ste-Catherine, Patrick and Mary Kelly Irish; https://central.bac-lac.gc.ca/.item/?app=Census1851&op=img&id=e002310917.
6 Larry Zolf, *Zolf* (Toronto: Exile Editions, 1999), 103. My thanks to my student Brittany Powell who helped bring the story of Edward Nealon and his family to life.
7 O'Gallagher, *Grosse Ile*, appendix 1, 118.
8 Anbinder, *City of Dreams: The 400-Year Epic History of Immigrant New York*, 149–71.
9 O'Gallagher, *Grosse Ile*, appendix 1, 119.
10 *US Census*, 1850, Matthew Carroll, Pittsburgh, Ward 6, Alleghany County.
11 *US Census*, 1870, Matthew Carell, Hazel Green, Grant County, Wisconsin.
12 Murphy, *Poor Ignorant Children*, 64–5.
13 https://www.ancestry.com/family-tree/person/tree/113431713/person/390113795192/facts.
14 *Census of Canada*, 1861, Canada West, Glengarry County, Locheil Township.
15 https://www.ancestry.com/family-tree/person/tree/113431713/person/390113796181/facts.
16 My appreciation to my student-researcher Bridget Hager, who searched for Bart Furlong and discovered his many travels. The Alpine House can be

17. Katz, *The People of Hamilton*, 94–111.
18. Mary Blair Conlan to Benjamin Conlan, 3 June 1847. Courtesy of descendent Brenda Sissons.
19. She died in Saltfleet of myocarditis, 16 December 1928. Hiram died in 1897. Conversation with Brenda Sissons, great-granddaughter, 29 January 2018.
20. O'Gallagher, *Grosse Ile*, appendix 1, 135.
21. *Elmira Star-Gazette*, 27 June 1939.
22. *Census of the United States of America*, 1850, New York State, Chemung County, Elmira, John Sheridan, family, 667. Ann's age is off by two years, but it is still within the realm of possibility that she was a niece or cousin of the priest.
23. "Irish Relatives and Friends," *Irish American*, 11 February 1871.
24. Runnalls, *The Irish on the Welland Canal*, 14–20.
25. *Census of Canada*, 1851, Canada West, Welland County, Bertie, John Fritz, farmer, "Manonist." John O'Connor is listed as nine years old, a non-family member, and a Quaker.
26. "Irish Relatives and Friends," *Irish American*, 11 February 1871.
27. *Census of Canada*, 1851–1852, Canada East, Nicolet, Becancour, 115; *Census of Canada*, 1861, Canada East, Nicolet, Becancour, "Helene Harrighton," 13.
28. Roby, *Les Franco-Americains de la Nouvelle Angleterre*.
29. Helene Lamontagne, https://www.ancestry.ca/discoveryui-content/view/6722 1113:60525.
30. https://search.ancestry.ca/cgi-bin/sse.dll?indiv=1&dbid=1061&h=2807143 &tid=&pid=&usePUB=true&_phsrc=NxZ46&_phstart=successSource.
31. *Census of Canada*, 1851, Canada East, Quebec City, "Alice Edmonds," 119.
32. Drouin List, 1621–1968, Alice Edmonds, Quebec, Holy Trinity Anglican Cathedral, 1854. https://www.ancestry.ca/discoveryui-content/view/14045410 :1091?tid=&pid=&queryId=1cb8f025c281a2add24f78f0e468538a&_phsrc=cPz21 4&_phstart=successSource. Reference to her death can be found at https://applications.banq.qc.ca/apex/f?p=118:11:0::NO::P11_CLE:6454.
33. My appreciation to Michaela Vukas, one of my researchers, for tracking down the story of Catherine Kennedy.
34. O'Gallagher, *Eyewitnesss Grosse Ile*, table 8, 355.
35. Charbonneau and Drolet-Dube, *A Register of Deceased Persons*, 37 and 82.
36. *Census of Canada*, 1851, Canada East, District 13, L'Islet, Clovis Caron; *Drouin Collection of Vital and Church Records, 1681–1968*, Marriage Record, L'Islet-sur-Mer, 1853, Catherine Kennedy and Louis Caron. For a more complete compilation of her records see: https://www.ancestry.ca/search/?name= Catherine_Kennedy&event=_l+islet-quebec-canada_1654516&count=50 &event_x=_1-0&name_x=1_1.

37 https://www.ancestry.ca/family-tree/person/tree/151727196/person/3020571 31655/facts?_phsrc=cPz187&_phstart=successSource.
38 O'Gallagher, *Grosse Ile*, appendix 1, 140–1.
39 My appreciation to Britany Powell, one of my researchers, who discovered the initial leads to the O'Mahoney family.
40 Family search, *Register of St Germaine de Paris Parish*, Rimouski, 15 February 1858 and 25 October 1858, 220 (image 493) and 247 (image 522).
41 Testimony of Yolande Miller (my translation), Ancestry.com.
42 Drouin collection, *Register of St Patrick's Church*, Quebec, 14 May 1871.
43 *Census of Canada*, 1871, District 155, Lotbinière, Subdistrict C, Daniel Tye.
44 *Census of Canada*, 1891, Quebec, District 165, Lotbinière, St-Croix., Catherine Tye.
45 Parish Register, Ste-Croix, Lotbinière, Quebec, 1898. https://www.ancestry.ca/discoveryui-content/view/7798160:1091?tid=&pid=&queryId=9bab293c1990b9febf92bfc0b6e8d058&_phsrc=cPz210&_phstart=successSource.
46 *Census of Canada*, 1921, Quebec, District 179, Lotbiniere, Subdistrict 16, Daniel Tye.
47 Callery, "Making History Visible," 156–9.
48 *Census of Canada*, 1871, Quebec, Nicolet, Ste-Gregoire, Année Kilmartin.
49 *Register of the Parish of St-Germain de Rimouski*, 236, 23 July 1858; *Census of Canada*, 1851, Canada East, District 24, Rimouski, Mary Damphery [sic], 65. https://central.bac-lac.gc.ca/.item/?app=Census1851&op=img&id=e00 2313082.
50 *Census of Canada*, 1851–1852, Canada East, Montreal, Bridget Brown.
51 *Census of Canada*, 1851–1852, Canada East, Terrebonne, Fanny Armour.
52 *Census of Canada*, 1871, Ontario, Essex County, Windsor, Fanny Armour.
53 *Census of Canada*, 1881, Quebec, Montreal, Mary Bridget Carter.
54 The *Avon* arrived from Cork on 26 July 1847, taking fifty-four days to cross the Atlantic and spending thirteen days in quarantine; of the 552 passengers, 246 (44.6 per cent) either died at sea or in quarantine. O'Gallagher and Dompierre, *Eyewitness*, 349.
55 Charbonneau and Drolet, *A Register of Deceased Persons*, 52.; O'Gallagher, *Gateway*, 133–4.
56 O'Gallagher, "Children of the Famine," 50.
57 Smyth, *Changing Habits*, 7–18.
58 For helpful references to French Canadian Ultramontanism consult: Voisine et Hamelin, *Les Ultramontains Canadiens Français*; Sylvain et Voisine, *Réveil et consolidation, tome 2, 1840–1898*, 265–94.
59 O'Gallagher, *Grosse Ile*, 143.
60 Ibid.
61 Ibid., 122.
62 King, "Finding a Voice," 123–4.

63 Maguire, *The Irish in America*, 143. Archives of the University of St Michael's College, Accounts Register, Robert Walsh.
64 King, "Finding a Voice," 127–36.
65 Charbonneau and Drolet, *A Register of Deceased Persons*, 52. Elzéar Bellemare's eulogy of Thomas Quinn mentions a third sibling dying at Grosse Ile but this cannot be verified by the Grosse Ile death register. Archives de Province de Nicolet [APN], Chroniques de la Metairie St-Joseph, vol. 1 (1895–1935), "Monsieur l'abbe Thomas Quinn," 54–5, second section of the volume.
66 APN, Chroniques de la Metairie St-Joseph, vol. 1 (1895–1935), "Monsieur l'abbe Thomas Quinn," 58–60, first section of the volume. My thanks to Dr Jason King for copies of the memoir.
67 Ibid.
68 O'Gallagher, *Grosse Ile*, 133.
69 Richmond County Historical Society Archives (Melbourne, Quebec), Code 03-G-F26.62, typescript biography of Patrick Quinn.
70 APN, Chroniques de la Metairie St-Joseph, vol. 1 (1895–1935), "Monsieur l'abbe Thomas Quinn," 54, second section of the volume.
71 For more background see Choquette, *Language and Religion*; Fiorino, "The Nomination of Bishop Fallon," 33–46; Zucchi, *The View from Rome*; McGowan, *The Waning of the Green*.
72 APN, Chroniques de la Metairie St-Joseph, vol. 1 (1895–1935), "Monsieur l'abbe Thomas Quinn," 58, second section of the volume.
73 *Sherbrooke Daily Record*, 12 March 1915.
74 Ibid., and Richmond County Historical Society Archives (Melbourne, Quebec), Code 03-G-F26.62, typescript biography of Patrick Quinn.
75 Ibid.
76 *Sherbrooke Daily Record*, 12 March 1915.
77 O'Gallagher, *Eyewitness*, 351.
78 *Census of Canada*, 1881, Ontario, Simcoe County North, Sunnidale, District 139, "William Pickering," 97.
79 *Census of Canada*, 1901, Ontario, Simcoe County North, Sunnidale, District 114, Sub-District 4, "John Pickering Sr," np. The census of 1901 confirms for the first time the date of emigration and John's year of arrival as 1847.
80 Akenson, *The Irish in Ontario*, 3–47.
81 Lee, *The Canada Company*, 5–12.
82 Ibid, 96-8 and 132.
83 *St Catharine's Journal*, 26 August 1847 and *The Mirror*, 28 July 1847. Lee, *The Canada Company*, 172–5.
84 *British Colonist*, 14 and 28 May 1847
85 *The Mirror*, 2 August 1847.
86 O'Gallagher, *Eyewitness*, 353.
87 O'Gallagher, *Grosse Ile*, 136.

88 *Census of Canada*, 1851, Canada West, Middlesex County, Adelaide Township, "Thomas Woodlock," "Edward Woodlock," 39; Both were labourers. The rest of the family resided with farmer Patrick Woodlock, age twenty-nine. Ibid, 43.
89 *Census of Canada*, 1851, Canada West, Middlesex County, Adelaide Township, Agricultural Census, 87.
90 McCallum, *Unequal Beginnings*.
91 *Census of Canada*, 1891, Ontario, Middlesex County, Adelaide Township, District 93, "John Woodlock," 9; Census of Canada, 1911, Ontario, Middlesex North, District 93, Adelaide, Sub-District 1, "John Woodlock," 7. The census also confirms that John arrive on Canada in 1847.
92 Bleasdale, *Rough Work*, 60–3.
93 Hutchison and Power, *Goaded to Madness*, 11–22. The lists of Connaught names is evident in the payrolls of the canal, Library and Archives Canada, RG 43, Department of Railways and Canals, vol. 2358, Paylists, 1843–1851.
94 *St Catharine's Journal*, 28 October 1847. This issue advertised job openings on the Michigan and Illinois Canal. Workers were enticed by $1 per day wages and the promise that "boarding houses are provided." Such advertisement underscores the sojourning nature of labourers engaged in large public works and also helps to explain why emigrants, who are constantly on the move, are so difficult to track.
95 Ibid., 137.
96 *Census of Canada*, 1851, Canada East, Rimouski, Line 36, file #1105922.

CONCLUSION

1 Parr, *Labouring Children*; McEvoy, "'These Treasures of the Church,'" 50–70.
2 Robins, "The Emigration of Irish Workhouse Children," 29–45.
3 McIntyre, "Remembering and Commemorating."
4 Moran, "Suffer the Little Children," 48. See also Collingwood, "Irish Workhouse Children in Australia," 46–61. Collingwood's essay offers some negative views of local Australians on the behavior of the Irish workhouse girls. A comprehensive study of assisted migration to Australia can be found in Reid, *Farewell My Children*.
5 *The Mirror*, 15 October 1852.
6 *Tyrone Constitution*, 29 November 1850.
7 The fleeing of placements also was a cause of concern in Australia, where many orphans in the Earl Grey scheme fled their placements. Collingwood, "Irish Workhouse Children in Australia," 52.

Bibliography

CIVIL AND PUBLIC ARCHIVES AND LIBRARY COLLECTIONS

Archives of New Brunswick [ANB]
Archives.gnb.ca/Documents/IrishPortal/Letters/SC/04/.

Archives of Ontario [AO]
RG 11-3 Anthony B. Hawke Papers, Letterbooks.
RG 11-3 Anthony B Hawke Papers, Convalescent Hospital Ledger.

City of Limerick Library [CLL]
Board of Works, *Famine Ireland,* Appendix F, "A Schedule showing the Names of persons injured, Nature of the Injury, Date of Occurrence, where Committed, the Officer by whom reported, with consequent Local Results," 60–1 and 66.
Board of Works, *Famine Ireland,* "Extract from Report of Lieutenant Miller, Inspecting Officer, County Tipperary, N.R., for the week ending 9 January 1847," 103.

City of Ottawa Archives [COA]
Sisters of Charity of Bytown (Grey Nuns), Hospital Ledger, Bytown, 1847.

City of Toronto Archives [CTA]
Minutes of the Board of Health, Toronto, 1847.

Huron County Museum and Archives [HMCA]
Assessment Roll, District of Huron, 1848.

Library and Archives Canada [LAC]
Census of Canada, 1851–52, 1861, 1871, 1881, 1891, 1901.
MG 30 D314, Robert Sellar Fonds, Volume 10, "*Gleaner* Tales—Summer of Sorrow," File 16.
RG 4, C 1 vol. 204: files 3000-3099 of 1847.
RG 5 C1, Provincial Secretary, Correspondence Files, 1844–1867, Reel 11, vol. 204–11.
RG 10, Indian Affairs and Northern Development, vol. 162–3.

RG 19-D-5, Emigrant Services Fonds, (Canada West), vol. 2532.
RG 43, Department of Railways and Canals, volume 2359.
R200-161-E, 1843–1847, Department of Finance, Emigration Service Fund.
Colonial Office Papers, CO 384/78-83, "Report of the Colonial Land and Emigration Commissioners, 1848."
Colonial Office Papers, CO384/79.
Colonial Office Papers, 384/80, "Guide for Emigrants to British North America," March 1847.
Colonial Office, Papers 384/82, Colonial Land and Emigration Commission, *Eighth General Report*, (June 1848).

National Library of Ireland [NLI]

MS 10,102 (1-4) Pakenham-Mahon Estate Papers, Major Denis Mahon Correspondence
MS 10, 138, Denis Mahon Emigration File

Public Record Office, Kew, England, UK [PROUK]

Colonial Office Papers, 217, vol 196, Fols. 166r-168r.

Queen's University Archives, Kingston, Ontario [QUA]

House of Industry, Inmate Registers, 2262-Box 7.

Richmond County Historical Society Archives (Melbourne, Quebec) [RCHCA]

Code 03-G-F26.62, typescript biography of Patrick Quinn.

St Patrick's College Maynooth, Russell Library Special Collections, [SPCM]

Laurence Renehan Papers.

Strokestown Park Archive [SPA]

STR/1B/2
STR/1A
STR 88, Book #8
STR 74

Trinity College Dublin [TCD]

Stephen De Vere Famine Diary. MS 5061. Vol. 1 April 29 – December 1, 1847

ECCLESIASTICAL ARCHIVES

Archives of the Archdiocese of Dublin [AAD]
Daniel Murray Papers, vol. 35, folders 2–6, and 10–13 famine correspondence; folder 12, remittances from abroad, 1845–1850.

Archives of the Archdiocese of Kingston [AAK]
St Mary's Cathedral, Register of Baptisms, Marriages, and Burials, 1843–1849.

Archives of the Archdiocese of Montreal [AAM]
Fonds Bishop Ignace Bourget, Correspondence 1847
901.103, Emigration, 1842–1849 Fonds

Archives of the Archdiocese of Quebec [AAQ]
Mandements, vol. 3 (1806–1850)
Fonds Archbishop Joseph Signay
210 A, Registre des lettres, vol. 22
1 CB Vicaires Généraux, vol. XII

Archives Bon-Pasteur [ABP]
501-004, 847, Transcript of Letter from Bourget to the Community, 30 November 1847.
"Names of the Orphan Children Entrusted to the Care of the Ladies of the Good Pastor, Montreal, 18 August 1847."

Archives of The Diocese of Saint John, New Brunswick [ADSJ]
Partridge Island Files
William Dollard Papers

Archives Providence Montreal [APM]
M6 Registre des orphelins du typhus Chroniques, Hospice St-Jerome-Emilien et Hôpital St-Patrice, 1847–1852.

Archives de Providence de Nicolet [APN]
Chroniques de la Metairie St-Joseph, Vol 1 (1895–1935)

Archives of the Religious Hospitallers of St Joseph (Kingston) [ARHSJK]
Typescript the RHSJ and the Famine.
Annals of the Hotel Dieu, Kingston, typescript, volume 1.

Archives of the Roman Catholic Archdiocese of Toronto [ARCAT]
Michael Power Papers.
Special Collections, Holograph Collection, HO, Series.

Archives of the Sacred Congregation of the Propaganda Fide [APF]
Scritture riferte nei congress. America Settentionale. Canada ecc. Dal 1841–1848, vol 5.

CONTEMPORARY SOURCES

Annals of the Sisters of Charity of Montreal (Grey Nuns), *Ancien Journal*, vol. 1 (1847). Edited by Jason King and translated by Jean-Francois Bernard, 7 June 1847.
British Parliamentary Papers, volume 17, sessions 1847–48. Report of A.C. Buchanan, 31 March 1848, 471–7.
Charbonneau, André, and Doris Drolet-Dubé, eds. *A Register of Deceased Persons at Sea and on Grosse Ile in 1847*. Ottawa: Canadian Heritage, Parks Canada, 1997.
Constitution and By-Laws of the Montreal Protestant Orphan Asylum. Montreal: John Lovell, 1860.
Craig, Gerald M., ed. *Lord Durham's Report (1839)*. Carleton Library Series. Toronto: McClelland and Stewart, 1963.
"De Vere Testimony, Select Committee, 1847–1848, CO 384/79535." In *The Elgin-Grey Papers, 1846–1852*, edited by Arthur Doughty. Ottawa: J.G. Patenaude, King's Printer, 1937.
Fioretti Vescovile: Extraits de Mandements, Lettres Pastorales et Circulaires de Monseigneur Ignace Bourget. Montreal: Imprimerie "Le Franc-Parleur," 1872.
Harris, Dean William Richard. *The Catholic Church in the Niagara Peninsula, 1626–1895*. Toronto: William Briggs, 1895.
"Monsieur l'abbé Thomas Quinn, 1841–1923. Souvenirs D'Enfance (Arrivée au Canada)." In *Metáire St-Joseph, Nicolet (Chronique), 1895–1935*, vol. 1, edited by Gerald M. Craig, 58–60.
Mitchel, John. *The Last Conquest of Ireland (perhaps)*. London: R & T Washbourne, 1861.
Register of Baptisms, Marriages and Deaths for the parish of St Germain de Rimouski.
Report of the Managing Committee of the Widows' and Orphans' Asylum. Toronto: Bowsell and Thompson, 1848.
Somerville, Alexander. *Letters from Ireland During the Famine of 1847*. Dublin: Irish Academic Press, reprinted 1994.
United Kingdom Parliamentary Papers (UKPP), Emigration to the British Provinces in North America and to the Australian Colonies, Part I, House of Commons, 1847.
Whyte, Robert. *The Ocean Plague: A Voyage to Quebec in an Irish Emigrant Vessel*. Boston: Coolidge and Wiley, 1848.

BIBLIOGRAPHY

NEWSPAPERS AND PERIODICALS

Canada

Ancien Journal (Montreal)
The Berean (Quebec City, Quebec)
The British Colonist (Toronto)
British Whig (Kingston)
Bytown Packet (Ottawa)
The Canada Gazette (Montreal)
The Catholic Record (London, Ontario)
The Church (Toronto)
The Cross (Halifax)
Globe (Toronto, Ontario)
Hamilton Gazette
The Mirror (Toronto)
Montreal Transcript
New Brunswick Courier (Saint John)
New Brunswick Reporter & Fredericton Advertiser (Fredericton, NB)
The Novascotian (Halifax)
The Pilot (Montreal)
Quebec Morning Chronicle
St Catharine's Journal (St Catharine's, Ontario)
Sherbrooke Daily Record

Ireland and United Kingdom

The Albion (Liverpool)
The Armagh Guardian
Belfast Commercial Chronicle
Belfast Newsletter
The Kings County Chronicle
Limerick Reporter
Limerick Chronicle
London Evening Standard
The Nation (Dublin)
Saunders News-Letter (Dublin)
Tyrone Constitution

United States of America

Boston Pilot
Elmira Star-Gazette
Irish American (New York)

MONOGRAPHS, BOOKS, ARTICLES, AND BOOK CHAPTERS

Acheson, T.W. "The Irish Community in Saint John." In *New Ireland Remembered: Historical Essays on the Irish in New Brunswick*, edited by Peter Toner, 27–54. Fredericton: New Ireland Press, 1988.

Akenson, Donald Harmon. *The Irish in Ontario: A Study in Rural History*. Montreal and Kingston: McGill-Queen's University Press, 1984.

Anbinder, Tyler. *City of Dreams: The 400-Year Epic History of Immigrant New York*. New York: Houghton Mifflin Harcourt, 2016.

– "From Famine to Five Points: Lord Lansdowne's Irish Tenants Encounter North America's Most Notorious Slum." *American Historical Review* 107, no.2 (April 2002): 351–87.

– "Lord Palmerston and the Irish Famine Emigration." *The History Journal* 44, no. 2 (June 2001): 441–69.

Bleasdale, Ruth. *Rough Work: Labourers on the Public Works of British North America and Canada, 1841–1882*. Toronto: University of Toronto Press, 2018.

Bradbury, Bettina. "The Fragmented Family: Family Strategies in the Face of Death, Illness, and Poverty in Montreal, 1860–1885." In *Childhood and Family in Canadian History*, edited by Joy Parr, 109–28. Toronto: McClelland and Stewart, 1982.

– *Working Families: Age, Gender, and Daily Survival in Industrializing Montreal*. Toronto: University of Toronto Press, 1993.

Brundage, David. *Irish Nationalists in America: The Politics of Exile, 1798–1998*. New York: Oxford University Press, 2016.

Callery, Caroilin. "Making History Visible: Strokestown and the Famine Story." In *Hunger and Hope: The Irish Famine Migration from Strokestown, Roscommon in 1844*, edited by Christine Kinealy, Jason King, and Mark G. McGowan, 153–64. Cork: Cork University Press, 2023.

– "The Tye/Tighe Story." In *Strokestown Gathering Celebration, Commemoration Booklet*. Strokestown: Strokestown Community Development Association, 2013.

Cameron, Wendy. "Peter Robinson's Settlers in Peterborough." In *The Untold Story: The Irish in Canada*, edited by Robert O'Driscoll and Lorna Reynolds, vol.1, 343–53. Toronto: Celtic Arts of Canada, 1988.

– "Selecting Peter Robinson's Irish Emigrants." *Social History-Histoire sociale* 9, no. 17 (1976): 29–46.

Campbell, Malcolm. *Ireland's New Worlds: Immigrants, Politics, and Society in the United States and Australia, 1815–1922*. Madison: University of Wisconsin Press, 2008.

Campbell, Stephen J. *The Great Irish Famine: Words and Images from the Famine Museum, Strokestown Park, County Roscommon*. Strokestown: The Famine Museum, 1994.

Chilton, Lisa. "Des morts sur la Miramichi: reactions de la population a arrive de immigrants maladies au Nouveau Brunswick au milieu de XIXe siècle." *Histoire Sociale/Social History* 52 (May 2019): 71–91.

Choquette, Robert. *Language and Religion: A History of French-English Conflict in Ontario*. Ottawa: University of Ottawa Press, 1975.

Cliché, Marie-Aimé. "*Abuse or Punishment? Violence Toward Childhood in Quebec Families, 1850-1969*. Translated by W. Donald Wilson. Waterloo: Waterloo University Press, 2014.

Collingwood, Judy. "Irish Workhouse Children in Australia." In *The Irish Emigrant Experience in Australia*, edited by John O'Brien and Pauric Travers, 46–61. Dublin: Poolbeg Press, 1991.

Coleman, Anne. *Riotous Roscommon: Social Unrest in the 1840s*. Maynooth Studies in Local History, no. 27. Dublin: Irish Academic Press, 1999.

Connolly, Sean. *On Every Tide: The Making and Remaking of the Irish World*. New York: Basic Books, 2022.

Coogan, Tim Pat. *The Famine Plot: England's Role in Ireland's Greatest Tragedy*. New York: Palgrave MacMillan, 2012.

Corcoran, Brandon, and Laura J Smith. "Bishop Macdonell and the Friends of Ireland: Mixing Politics and Religion in Upper Canada." Canadian Catholic Historical Association, *Historical Studies* 79 (2013): 7–23.

Crawford, E. Margaret. "Food and Famine." In *The Great Irish Famine*, edited by Cathal Póithiér, 60–73. Dublin: Mercier Press, 1995.

Daly, Mary. *The Famine in Ireland*. Dundalgan: Dublin Historical Society, 1986.

– "The Great Famine in Irish Society." In *Ireland: The Haunted Ark*, edited by Cecil J. Houston and Joseph Leydon, 3–20. Toronto: Celtic Arts of Canada, 1996.

De Brou, David. "The Rose, the Shamrock, and the Cabbage: The Battle for Irish Voters in Upper-Town Quebec, 1827–1836." *Histoire sociale/Social History* 24, no. 48 (November 1991): 305–34.

Delaney, Enda. *The Great Irish Famine: A History in Fours Lives*. Dublin: Gill and Macmillan, 2012.

Devine, Thomas. *The Great Highland Famine: Hunger, Emigration, and the Scottish Highlands*. Edinburgh: A. Donald, 1988.

Donnelly, James S. *The Great Irish Potato Famine*. Gloucestershire: Sutton Publishing, 2001.

– "Irish Property Must Pay for Irish Poverty." In *Fearful Realities: New Perspectives on the Famine*, edited by Chris Morash and Richard Hayes, 60–76. Dublin: Irish Academic Press, 1996.

Driedger, Sharon Doyle. *An Irish Heart: How a Small Immigrant Community Shaped Canada*. Toronto: Harper-Collins, A Phyllis Bruce Book, 2010.

Duffy, Peter. *The Killing of Major Denis Mahon: A Mystery of Old Ireland*. New York: Harper, 2007.

Duffy, Sean, et. al., eds., *Atlas of Irish History*. Dublin: Gill and MacMillan, 2000.

Dunn, Mary Lee. *Ballykilcline Rising: From Famine Ireland to Immigrant America*. Amherst: University of Massachusetts Press, 2006.

Edwards, R. Dudley, and T. Desmond Williams, eds. *The Great Famine: Studies in Irish History 1845–1852*. Dublin: Browne and Nolan, 1956.

Elliott, Bruce. *Irish Migrants in the Canadas: A New Approach*. Montreal and Kingston: McGill-Queen's University Press, 1988.

Errington, Jane. *Greater Kingston: Historic Past, Progressive Future*. Burlington: Windsor Publications, 1988.

Fiorino, Pasquale. "The Nomination of Bishop Fallon as Bishop of London." CCHA *Historical Studies* 62 (1996): 33–46.

Flynn, Louis J. *Built on a Rock: The Story of the Roman Catholic Church in Kingston, 1826–1976*. Kingston: Roman Catholic Archdiocese of Kingston, 1976.

Gagan, David. "Enumerator's Instructions for the Census of Canada 1852 and 1861." *Social History/Histoire sociale* 7, no. 14 (November 1974): 355–65.

– *Hopeful Travelers: Families, Land, and Social Change in Mid-Victorian Peel County, Canada West*. Toronto: University of Toronto Press, 1981.

Gavan, Joseph B, SJ. *Teachers of a Nation: The Jesuits in English Canada, 1842–2013*. Toronto: Novalis, 2014.

Geoghegan, Patrick M. *Liberator: The Life and Death of Daniel O'Connell 1830–1847*. Dublin: Gill and Macmillan, 2010.

Gosselin, Sylvain. "Les terretoires et ses premiers occupants." In *Rimouski Depuis Ses Origines*, edited by Jeannot Bourdages et al. Rimouski: Société d'histoire du Bas Saint-Laurent, 2006.

Goubau, Dominic, and Claire O'Neill. "L'Adoption, L'Eglise et l'Etat : les origines tumultueuses d'une institution légale." *Les Cahiers de Droit* 38, no. 4 (December 1997): 769–804.

Grace, Robert. "Irish Immigration and Settlement in a Catholic City, 1842–61." *Canadian Historical Review* 84 (June 2003): 217–52.

Gray, Peter. *Famine, Land and Politics: British Government and Irish Society, 1843–1850*. Dublin: Irish Academic Press, 1999.

– "Ideology and the Famine." In *The Great Irish Famine*, edited by Cathal Póithiér, 86–103. Dublin: Mercier Press, 1995.

– *The Irish Famine*. London: Harry N Abrams, 1995.

– "Memory and the Great Irish Famine." In *The Memory of Catastrophe*, edited by Peter Gray and Kendrick Oliver, 46–64. Manchester: Manchester University Press, 2004.

Hamrock, Ivor, ed. *The Famine in Mayo: A Portrait from Contemporary Sources, 1845–1850*. Castlebar: Mayo County Council, 1998, third printing, 2010.

Hickey, Patrick. *Famine in West Cork: The Mizen Peninsula Land and People 1800–1852*. Dublin: Mercier, 2002.

Hill, Robert, "From Famine to Fraud: The Truth About Ireland's Best Selling Famine Diary." *Matrix* no. 38 (1992): 5–12.

Hood, Susan, "The Famine in the Strokestown Park House Archive." *The Irish Review*, no. 17/18 (Winter 1995): 109–17.

- "The Landlord Influence in the Development of an Irish Estate Town: Strokestown, County Roscommon." *Irish Geography* 28, no. 2 (1995): 118–30.
- "The Strokestown Park House Archive." *History Ireland* 3, no. 4 (winter 1995): 11–15
Houston, Cecil J., and William J. Smyth. *Irish Emigration and Canadian Settlement: Patterns, Links, and Letters*. Toronto: University of Toronto Press, 1990.
Huggins, Michael. *Social Conflict in Pre-Famine Ireland: The Case of County Roscommon*. Dublin: Four Courts, 2007.
Hughes, Margaret E. "Adoption in Canada." In *Studies in Canadian Family Law*, vol.1, edited by D. Mendes da Costa, QC, 108–13. Toronto: Butterworth, 1972.
Hutchison, Paul, and Michael Power. *Goaded to Madness: The Battle of Slabtown*. St Catharine's: Slabtown Press, 1999.
Jackson, Jim. "Famine Diary: The Making of a Best Seller." *The Irish Review* 11 (Winter1991/1992): 1–8.
James, Dermot. *John Hamilton of Donegal, 1800–1884: This Recklessly Generous Landlord*. Dublin: Woodfield Press, 1998.
Katz, Michael. *The People of Hamilton, Canada West: Family and Class in a Mid-Nineteenth-Century City*. Cambridge: Harvard University Press, 1975.
Kelly, John. *The Graves are Walking: A History of the Great Irish Famine*. New York: Henry Holt and Co., 2012.
Kelly, Mary. "The Great Famine in County Roscommon." In *Roscommon: History and Society*, edited by Richie Farrell, Kieran O'Conor, and Matthew Potter, 385–410. Dublin: Geography Publications, 2018.
Kennedy, Liam. *Unhappy the Land: The Most Oppressed People Ever, the Irish?* Kildare: Merrion Press, 2016.
Kerr, Donal A. *A Nation of Beggars? Priests, People, and Politics in Famine Ireland, 1846–1852*. Oxford: Clarendon Press, 1994.
Kierse, Sean. *The Famine Years in the Parish of Killaloe, 1845–1851*. Killaloe: Boru Books, 1984.
Kinealy, Christine, Jason King, and Mark G. McGowan, eds. *Hunger and Hope: The Irish Famine Migration from Strokestown, Roscommon in 1847*. Cork: Cork University Press and The Great Hunger Institute, Quinnipiac University, CT, 2023.
Kinealy, Christine, Jason King, and Gerard Moran. *Charity and the Great Hunger in Ireland: The Kindness of Strangers*. London: Bloomsbury, 2013.
- eds. *Children and the Great Hunger in Ireland*. Hamden, CT: Quinnipiac University Press, 2018.
- *A Death-Dealing Famine: The Great Hunger in Ireland*. London & Chicago: Pluto Press, 1997.
- "'This Great Agony of the Empire': The Great Famine in Ulster." In *Irish Hunger and Migration: Myth, Memory and Memorialization*, edited by Patrick Fitzgerald, Christine Kinealy, and Gerard Moran, 43–55. Hamden, CT: Quinnipiac University Press, 2015.

– *This Great Calamity: The Irish Famine, 1845–1852*. Dublin: Gill and Macmillan, 1994.

King, Jason. "Finding a Voice: Irish Famine Orphan Robert Walsh's Search for His Younger Sister." In *Children and the Great Hunger in Ireland*, edited by Christine Kinealy, Jason King, and Gerard Moran, 123–38. Hamden, CT: Quinnipiac University Press, 2018.

– "Remember Your Souls and Your Liberty." In *Hunger and Hope: The Irish Famine Migration from Strokestown, Roscommon in 1847*, edited by Christine Kinealy, Jason King, and Mark G. McGowan, 109–28. Cork: Cork University Press and The Great Hunger Institute, Quinnipiac University, 2023.

– "Remembering Famine Orphans: The Transmission of Famine Memory Between Ireland and Quebec." In *Holodomor and Gorta Mor: Histories, Memories, and Representations of Famine in Ukraine and Ireland*, edited by Christian Noack, Lindsay Janssen, and Vincent Comerford, 115–40. London: Anthem Press, 2012.

Lamirande, Emilien. *Élisabeth Bruyère: Fondatrice des Soeurs de la Charité d'Ottawa*. Montreal: Bellaramine, 1998.

Larkin, Emmet. "The Devotional Revolution in Ireland, 1850–1875." *American Historical Review* 77 (1972): 625–52.

Larocque, Paul. "Un Region de Peuplement (1790–1855)." In *Rimouski Depuis Ses Origines*, edited by Jeannot Bourdages et. al. Rimouski: Société d'histoire du Bas Saint-Laurent, 2006.

Larrivée, Jean. "Une Ville en Pline nature." In *Rimouski Depuis Ses Origines*, edited by Jeannot Bourdages, et al. Rimouski: Société d'histoire du Bas Saint-Laurent, 2006.

LaVorgna, Koral. "Not Standing Idly By: Educating Famine Orphans at the Emigrant Orphan Asylum in Saint John, New Brunswick, 1847 to 1849." In *Children and the Great Hunger in Ireland*, edited by Christine Kinealy, Jason King, and Gerard Moran, 139–57. Hamden, CT: Quinnipiac University Press, 2018.

Lee, Kevin. *Coollattin: The History of Ireland's Mysterious Estate & Its Pivotal Role in the Birth of Canada*. Carnew: Coollattin–Canada Connection, 2022.

Lee, Kevin, and Tom Jenkins. *Shoeboxes: From Irish Roots to Canadian Branches*. Dublin: Coollattin–Canada Connection, 2022.

Lee, Robert C. *The Canada Company and the Huron Tract, 1826–1853: Personalities, Profits, and Politics*. Toronto: Natural Heritage Books, 2004.

Lemieux, Lucien. *Les Années difficiles (1760–1839)*. Montreal: Boréal, Histoire du Catholicisme Québécois [series], 1989.

Lepage, Germain, and Gabriel Langlois. *Dossier Sur La Paroisse de Saont-Germain de Rimouski (histoire religieuse) 1701–1987*. Rimouski: Centre Pastorale, 1988.

MacAtasney, Gerard. *This Dreadful Visitation. The Famine in Lurgan and Portadown*. Belfast: Beyond the Pale, 1997.

Macauley, Ambrose. *The Catholic Church and the Campaign for Emancipation in England and Ireland*. Dublin: Four Courts Press, 2016.

Mackay, Donald. *Flight from Famine: The Coming of the Irish to Canada*. Toronto: McClelland and Stewart, 1990.

Maguire, John Francis. *The Irish in America*. New York: D&J Sadlier, 1880.

Malcomson, Patricia. "The Poor in Kingston, 1815–1850." In *To Preserve and Defend: Essays on Kingston in the Nineteenth Century*, edited by Gerald Tulchinsky, 281–97. Montreal and Kingston: McGill-Queen's University Press, 1976.

Mangan, James J. *The Voyage of the Naparima*. Ste-Foy, QC: Carriag Books, 1982.

Mannion, John. "Old World Antecedents, New World Adaptations: Inistioge (Co. Kilkenny) Immigrants in Newfoundland." In *The Irish in Atlantic Canada, 1780–1900*, edited by Thomas Power, 30–95. Fredericton: New Ireland Press, 1991.

Mark-Fitzgerald, Emily. *Commemorating the Irish Famine: Memory and the Monument*. Liverpool: Liverpool University Press, 2013.

Maurutto, Paula. *Governing Charities: Church and State in Toronto's Catholic Archdiocese, 1850–1950*. Montreal and Kingston: McGill-Queen's University Press, 2003.

McBane, Michael. *Bytown 1847: Élisabeth Bruyère & the Irish Famine Refugees*. Ottawa: Michael McBane, 2022.

McCabe, Desmond. "Denis Mahon." In *The Dictionary of Irish Biography*, 295–6. Cambridge: Cambridge University Press and Royal Irish Academy, 2009.

McCallum, John. *Unequal Beginnings: Agricultural and Economic Development in Quebec and Ontario until 1870*. Toronto: University of Toronto Press, 1980.

McCuaig, Carol Bennett. *People of St Patrick's: Mount St Patrick Parish, 1843–1993*. Renfrew: Juniper Books, 1993.

McDonagh, Oliver. "Irish Emigration to the United States of America and the British Colonies During the Famine." In *The Great Famine: Studies in Irish History, 1845–52*, edited by R. Dudley Edwards and T. Desmond Williams, 319–88. Dublin: Browne and Nolan Ltd., 1956; reprint Dublin: Lilliput Press, 1994.

McEvoy, Frederick J. "'These Treasures of the Church': Catholic Child Emigration to Canada." *Canadian Catholic Historical Association, Historical Studies* 65 (1999): 50–70

McGahan, Elizabeth. "The Sisters of Charity of the Immaculate Conception: A Canadian Case Study." *Canadian Catholic Historical Association, Historical Studies* 61 (1995): 99–133.

McGowan, Mark G. "Contemporary Links between Canadian and Irish Famine Commemoration." In *Global Legacies of the Great Irish Famine: Transnational and Interdisciplinary Perspectives*, edited by Marguerite Corporaal et al., 267–84. Bern: Peter Lang, 2014.

– *Creating Canadian Historical Memory: The Case of the Irish Famine Migration of 1847*. Ottawa: Canadian Historical Association, 2006.

– *Death or Canada: The Irish Famine Migration to Toronto, 1847*. Toronto: Novalis, 2009.

– "Famine, Facts, and Fabrication: An Examination of Diaries from the Irish Famine Migration to Canada." *Canadian Journal of Irish Studies* 35, no. 2 (Fall 2007): 48–55.

- Michael Power: *The Struggle to Build the Catholic Church on the Canadian Frontier.* Montreal and Kingston: McGill-Queen's University Press, 2005.
- "Rethinking the Irish Famine Orphans in Quebec, 1847–1848." In *Children and the Great Hunger in Ireland*, edited by Christine Kinealy, Jason King, and Gerard Moran, 95–122. Hamden, CT: Quinnipiac University Press, 2018.
- "A Tale of Two Famines: Famine Memory in Nova Scotia, Canada." In *Irish Hunger and Migration: Myth, Memory and Memorialization*, edited by Patrick Fitzgerald, Christine Kinealy, and Gerard Moran, 57–68. Hamden, CT: Quinnipiac University Press, 2015.
- The *Waning of the Green: Catholics, the Irish, and Identity in Toronto, 1887–1922.* Montreal and Kingston: McGill-Queen's University Press, 1999.

McGowan, Michael. *Pax Vobis: A History of the Diocese of Saint John its Bishops and Parishes.* Strasbourg: Editions du Signe, 2004.

McIntyre, Perry. "Remembering and Commemorating the Great Famine and Emigration to Australia." *Breac: A Digital Journal of Irish Studies* (University of Notre Dame: 28 January 2018).

McMahon, Cian. *The Coffin Ship: Life and Death at Sea During the Great Irish Famine.* New York: New York University Press, 2021.

McMahon, Nancy. "Les Religieuse Hospitalières de St Joseph and the Typhus Epidemic, Kingston, 1847–1848," *Canadian Catholic Historical Association, Historical Studies* 58 (1991): 41–55.

Miller, Kerby. *Emigrants and Exiles: Ireland and the Irish Exodus to North America.* New York: Oxford University Press, 1985.

Millman, Thomas R. "The Church's Ministry to Sufferers of Typhus Fever, in 1847." *Canadian Journal of Theology* 8, no. 2 (1962): 126–36.

Moir, John S. *The Church in the British Era: From the British Conquest to Confederation.* Toronto: McGraw-Hill Ryerson, 1972.
- "Toronto's Protestants and Their perceptions of Their Roman Catholic Neighbours." In *Catholics at the Gathering Place: Historical Essays on the Archdiocese of Toronto, 1841–1991*, edited by Mark G. McGowan and Brian P. Clarke, 313–27. Toronto: Canadian Catholic Historical Association, 1993.

Mokyr, Joel. *Why Ireland Starved: A Quantitative and Analytical History of the Irish Economy 1800–1850.* London: George Allen and Unwin, 1983.

Monet, Jacques, ed., *Dictionary of Jesuit Biography: Ministry to English Canada.* Toronto: Canadian Institute of Jesuit Studies, 1991.

Moran, Gerard. "'Permanent Deadweight': Female Pauper Emigration from Mountbellew Workhouse to Canada." In *Women and the Great Hunger*, edited by Christine Kinealy, Jason King, and Ciaran Reilly, 109–21. Hamden, CT: Quinnipiac University Press, 2016.
- *Sending Out Ireland's Poor: Assisted Emigration to North America in the Nineteenth Century.* Dublin: Four Courts, 2004.
- "Suffer the Children: Life in the Workhouse During the Famine." In *Children and the Great Hunger in Ireland*, edited by Christine Kinealy, Jason King, and Gerard

Moran, 27–50. Hamden, CT: Quinnipiac University Press/Cork: Cork University Press, 2018.
Morgan, Robert. *Early Cape Breton: From Founding to Famine, 1784–1851*. Sydney, NS: Breton Books, 2000.
Murphy, Peter D. *Poor Ignorant Children: Irish Famine Orphans in Saint John New Brunswick*. Halifax: D'Arcy McGee Chair in Irish Studies, St Mary's University, 1999.
Naylor, Mary. "WILLOUGHBY, MARK." In *Dictionary of Canadian Biography*, vol. 7, University of Toronto/Université Laval, 2003–http://www.biographi.ca/en/bio/willoughby_mark_7E.html.
Neatby, Hilda. *Quebec: The Revolutionary Age, 1760–1791*. Toronto: McClelland and Stewart, 1977.
Neff, Charlotte, "The Education of Destitute Homeless Children in Nineteenth-Century Ontario." *Journal of Family History* 29 no.1 (January 2004): 3–46.
– "Pauper Apprenticeship in Early Nineteenth Century Ontario." *Journal of Family History* 21 (April 1996): 144–71.
Norman, Marion. "Making a Path by Walking: Loretto Pioneers Facing Challenges of Catholic Education on the North American Frontier." *Canadian Catholic Historical Association, Historical Studies* 65 (1999): 92–106.
Norton, Desmond. "Lord Palmerston and the Irish Famine Emigration: A Rejoinder." *The History Journal* 46 no.1 (March 2003):155–65.
– "On Landlord-Assisted Emigration from Some Irish Estates in the 1840s." *The Agricultural History Review* 53, no. 1, (2005): 1254–74.
O'Driscoll, Robert, and Lorna Reynolds, eds. *The Untold Story: The Irish in Canada*, 2 vols. Toronto: Celtic Arts of Canada, 1988.
O'Gallagher, Marianna. "Children of the Famine." *The Beaver* (February–March 2008): 50–6.
– *Grosse Ile: Gateway to Canada, 1832–1937*. Ste Foy: Carraig Books, 1984.
– "The Orphans of Grosse Ile and the Adoption of Irish Famine Orphans, 1847–48." In *The Meaning of the Famine*, edited by Patrick O'Sullivan. London: Leicester University Press, 1997.
O'Gallagher, Marianna, and Rose Masson Dompierre. *Eyewitness Grosse Ile, 1847*. Ste-Foy: Carraig Books, 1995.
Ó Gráda, Cormac. *Black '47 and Beyond: The Great Irish Famine*. Princeton: Princeton University Press, 2000.
– *The Great Irish Famine*. New York Macmillan, 1989.
O'Grady, Brendan. *Exiles and Islanders: The Irish Settlers of Prince Edward Island*. Montreal and Kingston: McGill-Queen's University Press, 2004.
O'Murchadha, Ciaran. *The Great Famine: Ireland's Agony, 1845–1852*. London: Continuum, 2011.
Osborne, W.J., "The Right Reverend William Dollard, D.D." *Canadian Catholic Historical Association, Report* 9 (1941–42): 23–8.

Orser Jr, Charles E. "An Archaeology of Famine-Era Eviction." *New Hibernia Review* 9, no. 1 (Spring, 2005): 45–58.

Parr, Joy. *Labouring Children: British Immigrant Apprentices to Canada, 1869–1924*. Montreal and Kingston: McGill-Queen's University Press, 1980.

– "The Welcome and the Wake: Attitudes in Canada West toward the Irish Famine Migration." *Ontario History* 66 (1974): 101–13.

Parker, George L., "Henry Chubb (1787–1855)." *Dictionary of Canadian Biography*, vol. 8. Toronto: University of Toronto/Laval University, 2003.

Paul-Émile (Louise Guay), Souer. "BRUYÈRE, ÉLISABETH." In *Dictionary of Canadian Biography*, vol. 10. Toronto: University of Toronto/Laval University, 2003. http://www.biographi.ca/en/bio/bruyere_elisabeth_10E.html.

– "Mère Élisabeth Bruyère: fille de l' glise et femme d'oeuvres." *La Société Canadienne d'histoire de l' glise Catholique, Rapport*, 29 (1961).

Peikoff, Tannis, and Stephen Brickey "Creating Precious Children and Glorified Mothers: A Theoretical Assessment of the Transformation of Childhood." In *Dimensions of Childhood: Essays on the History of Children and Youth in Canada*, edited by Russell Smandych, Gordon Dodds, and Alvin Esau, 29–42. Winnipeg: Legal Research Institute, University of Manitoba, 1991.

Prentice, Alison. *The School Promoters: Education and Social Class in Mid-Nineteenth Century Upper Canada*. Toronto: McClelland & Stewart, 1977.

Proudfoot, Lindsay. "Landlords." In *The Oxford Companion to Irish History*, edited by S.J. Connolly, 297. Oxford: Oxford University Press, 1998.

Prunty, Jacinta, "Battle Plans and Battle Grounds: Protestant Mission Activity in the Dublin Slums, 1840-1880." In *Protestant Millennialism, Evangelicalism, and Irish Society, 1790-2005*, edited by Crawford Gribben and Andrew Holmes, 119–43. New York: Palgrave McMillan, 2006.

Punch, Terence M. *North America's Maritime Funnel: The Ships that Brought the Irish 1749–1852*. Baltimore: Genealogical Publishing Company, 2012.

Quigley, Michael, "Grosse Ile: Canada's Irish Famine Memorial." *Labour/Le Travail* 39 (Spring 1997): 195–214.

Rees, Jim. *Surplus People: From Wicklow to Canada*. Cork: The Collins Press, 2000.

Reid, Richard. *Farewell My Children: Irish Assisted Immigration to Australia, 1848–1870*. Spit Junction, NSW: Anchor Books Australia, 2011.

Reilly, Ciaran. *John Plunket Joly and the Great Famine in King's County*. Maynooth Studies in Local History, No. 103. Dublin: Four Courts Press, 2012.

– *Strokestown and the Great Irish Famine*. Dublin: Four Courts Press, 2014.

– "Strokestown and the Pakenham Mahon Estate." In *Roscommon: History and Society*, edited by Richie Farrell, Kieran O'Conor, and Matthew Potter, 367–84. Dublin: Geography Publications, 2018.

Robins, Joseph. "The Emigration of Irish Workhouse Children to Australia in the Nineteenth Century." In *The Irish Emigrant Experience in Australia*, edited by John O'Brien and Pauric Travers, 29–45. Dublin: Poolbeg Press, 1991.

Roby, Yves. *Les Franco-Americains de la Nouvelle Angleterre, 1776–1930*. Quebec: Septentrion, 1990.

Roche, Hervé. *L'Adoption dans la Province de Québec*. Montreal: Wilson et Lafleur Ltée, 1951.

Rooke, Patricia, and R.L. Schnell, "Childhood and Charity in Nineteenth-Century British North America." *Social History / Histoire sociale* 15, no. 20 (May/mai 1982): 157–79.

Runnalls, J. Lawrence. *The Irish on the Welland Canal*. St Catharine's: St Catharine's Public Library, 1973.

See, Scott. "The Orange Order and Social Violence in Mid-Nineteenth Century Saint John." In *New Ireland Remembered: Historical Essays on the Irish in New Brunswick*, edited by Peter Toner, 71–89. Fredericton: New Ireland Press, 1988.

– *Riots in New Brunswick: Orange Nativism and Social Violence in the 1840s*. Toronto: University of Toronto Press, 1993.

Sen, Armatya. *Development as Freedom*. New York: Anchor Books, 1999.

Scally, Robert. *The End of Hidden Ireland: Rebellion, Famine and Emigration*. New York: Oxford University Press, 1995.

Smyth, William J. *Toronto, the Belfast of Canada: The Orange Order and the Shaping of Municipal Culture*. Toronto: University of Toronto Press, 2015.

Smyth, William, and Cecil Houston, "Community and Institutional Supports: Life on the Agricultural Frontier of Mono and Adjala." In *Catholics at the Gathering Place*, edited by Mark George McGowan and Brian P. Clarke, 5–22. Toronto: Canadian Catholic Historical Association, 1993.

Spray, William A. "'The Difficulties Came Upon Us Like a Thunderbolt': Immigrants and Fever in New Brunswick." In *The Irish in Atlantic Canada, 1780–1900*, edited by Thomas P. Power, 107–26. Fredericton: New Ireland Press, 1991.

– "The Reception of the Irish in New Brunswick." In *New Ireland Remembered: Historical Essays on the Irish in New Brunswick*, edited by P.M. Toner, 9–26. Fredericton: New Ireland Press, 1988.

Steele, David. "Henry John Temple, 3rd Viscount Palmerston (1784–1865)." *Oxford Dictionary of National Biography*, 9 May 2009.

Stout, Matthew. "The Geography and Implications of Post-Famine Population Decline in Baltyboys, County Wicklow." In *Fearful Realities: New Perspectives on the Famine*, edited by Chris Morash and Richard Hayes. Dublin: Irish Academic Press, 1996.

Strong-Boag, Veronica. *Finding Families, Finding Ourselves: English Canadian Accounts of Adoption from the Nineteenth Century Through to the 1990s*. Toronto: Oxford University Press, 2006.

Sutherland, Neil. *Children in English Canadian Society: Framing the Twentieth Century Consensus*. Toronto: University of Toronto Press, 1976.

Swords, Liam. *In Their Own Words: The Famine in North Connaught, 1845–1849*. Dublin: The Columba Press, 1999.

Sylvain, Philippe, and Nive Voisine. *Réveil et consolidation, Histoire du Catholicisme Québécois, vol. 2 1840–1898*. Montreal: Boréal Express, 1991.
Toner, Peter. "The Foundations of the Catholic Church in English-speaking New Brunswick." In *New Ireland Remembered: Historical Essays on the Irish in New Brunswick*, edited by P.M. Toner, 63–70. Fredericton: New Ireland Press, 1988.
– "The Irish of New Brunswick at Mid-Century: The 1851 Census." In *New Ireland Remembered Historical Essays on the Irish in New Brunswick*, edited by P.M. Toner, 106–32. Fredericton: New Ireland Press, 1988.
Vesey, Padraig. *The Murder of Major Mahon, Strokestown, County Roscommon, 1847*. Dublin: Four Courts, Maynooth Studies in Local History, no. 80, 2008.
Voisine, Nive. "Calixte Marquis." *Dictionary of Canadian Biography, XIII (1901-1910)*. University of Toronto/Université Laval. http://www.biographi.ca/en/bio/marquis_calixte_13E.html.
Voisine, Nive, and Jean Hamelin, eds. *Les Ultramontains Canadiens Français*. Montreal: Boréal Express, 1985.
Wallot, Jean-Pierre. "Religion and French-Canadian Mores in the Early Nineteenth Century." *Canadian Historical Review* 52 (March 1971): 51–91.
Watts, Jacques. "L'emigration britannique de 1847–1848." *L'Estuaire* 21 (June 1998), 21–3.
Whelan, Irene. "The Stigma of Souperism." In *The Great Irish Famine*, edited by Cathal Póirtéir, 135–54. Dublin: Mercier Press, 1995.
Whelan, J.M. "HATHEWAY, CALVIN LUTHER." In *Dictionary of Canadian Biography*, vol. 9. Toronto: University of Toronto/Universite laval, 2003.
Wilson, David A. *Thomas D'Arcy McGee: Passion, Reason, and Politics, 1825–1857*. Montreal and Kingston: McGill-Queen's University Press, 2008.
– *Thomas D'Arcy McGee: Volume 2 – The Extreme Moderate, 1857–1868*. Montreal and Kingston: McGill-Queen's University Press, 2011.
Wilson, F.J. "The Most Reverend Thomas L. Connolly, Archbishop of Halifax." *Canadian Catholic Historical Association, Report* 11 (1943–44): 55–108.
Woodham Smith, Cecil. *The Great Hunger, 1845–1849*. New York: Old Town Books, 1962.
Wright, H.E. "Partridge Island: Re-discovering the Irish Connection." In *The Irish in Atlantic Canada, 1780-1900*, edited by Thomas P. Power, 127–49. Fredericton: New Ireland Press, 1991.
Zucchi, John. *The View from Rome: Archbishop Stagni's 1915 Reports on the Ontario Bilingual Schools Question*. Montreal and Kingston: McGill Queen's University Press, 2002.

UNPUBLISHED THESES AND DISSERTATIONS

Belley, Marie-Claude. "Un exemple de prise en charge de l'enfance dependente au milieu du XIXe siècle : Les orphelins Irlandais á Québec en 1847–1848." MA mémoire, Laval University, 2003.

Harvey, Janice. "The Protestant Orphan Asylum and the Montreal Ladies Benevolent Society: A Case Study in Protestant Child Charity in Montreal, 1822–1900." PhD diss., McGill University, 2001.

Harvey, Lesley Anne. "The Canadian Response to the Irish Famine Migration of 1847." MA thesis, University of British Columbia, 1973.

King, Jason. "Famine Diaries: Narratives About Emigration from Ireland to Lower Canada and Quebec, 1832–1853." MA thesis, Simon Fraser University, 1996.

Morse, Susan Longley. "Immigration to Nova Scotia, 1839–1851." MA thesis, Dalhousie University, 1946.

O'Reilly, Rebecca. "In a Situation of Great Distress: The Emigrant Agency, Poverty, and the Irish in Nineteenth Century Upper Canada." MA thesis, Guelph University, 2006.

Ryan, Michael D'Arcy. "Commissioners, Guardians, and Paupers: Life and Death in the Limerick Poor Law Union, 1838–1850. PhD diss., Concordia University, 2005.

Towns, Colleen M. "Relief and Order: The Public Response to the 1847 Famine Migration to Upper Canada." MA thesis, Queen's University, 1990.

Tromblay, Faye K. "Thomas Louis Connolly (1815–1876)." PhD diss., Louvain, 1983.

Tucker, Derek Nile. "Successful Pioneers: Irish Catholic Settlers in Hibbert [Township]." MA thesis, McMaster University, 2002.

FILMS AND WEBSITES

Ancestry.ca.

Historica Canada, *Heritage Minutes*, DVD, Heritage Minute #16 "Orphans," CRB Foundation, 1991–2012.

Irish Poor Law Unions to New South Wales: https://irishfaminememorial.org/orphans/.

Our Lady of the Assumption, Saint John, NB: http://www.ourladyoftheassumptionnb.com/history.

The Ship's List: https://www.theshipslist.com/1847/orphans.shtml.

Index

Adoption, 6, 66, 73, 121, 175; in New Brunswick, 72–3, 137; notaries, 14; as a political tool, 164
Aeolus, 70, 125, 131, 132, 133, 135, 136, 137, 138, 141
Anglican Church (Church of England), 7, 66, 68, 85, 87, 90, 94, 101, 151, 154; clergy, 86
Australian emigration, 11, 172; orphans, 35

Barnardo children, 5, 171–2
Belley, Marie-Claude, 12
Bingham, George (Lord Lucan), 24
Bourget, Ignace (bishop of Montreal), 7, 8, 67, 91–2, 93, 98, 128, 164
Brennan, Mary, 114–15
Brennan, Thomas, 43, 47, 50, 59, 62, 123, 152–3, 168
Bruyère, Élisabeth, 12, 103–4, 123. *See also* Grey Nuns (Sisters of Charity of Ottawa)
Buchanan, A.C., 68, 172

Cahill, Philip, 105
Catholic Church: in Bytown, 5, 100, 103, 123; in Ireland, 27–8; in Kingston, 100, 106–7, 109, 114, 123; in Montreal, 5, 90, 93; in Nicolet, 162–3; in Quebec City, 5, 64–5, 66–7, 92, 94, 148; in Saint John, 5, 101, 128, 143–4, 173; Saint John religious census, 139; in Toronto, 5, 100, 115–16, 120, 123. *See also* orphans: placement, of; Protestants: sectarian strife
Cazeau, Charles-Felix (Rev.), 70, 72, 81, 84, 144
census problems, 13–14
Charitable Society of Catholic Ladies (Quebec), 11, 63, 66, 68, 69, 75, 88, 148, 156, 161, 168

Church of Ireland (Anglican), 29; and proselytizing, 7
City Almshouse (Saint John), 130
coffin Ship, 5, 16, 36–7, 45, 55, 129; and Cian McMahon, 11
Collins, James Patrick, MD, 129
conacre farmers, 47–8
Conlan, Margaret, 22, 86–7, 151, 152, 165
Connolly, Thomas Louis (bishop of Saint John), 145
Coogan, Tim Pat, 18
Coulombe family (François and Marie), 64, 73, 158
Corn Laws, 31. *See also* Peel, Sir Robert
Coyne family, 137–8
Cox family (George and Mary), 62, 84, 98
Cox, Patrick, 99–100, 197n1
Cullen, Paul (archbishop of Armagh), 28, 30

Daly, Dominick, 103, 111, 114
Dempsey, Mary, 83–4, 159
de Valera, Éamon, 17
De Vere, Stephen, 25, 37
Dollard, William (bishop of New Brunswick), 126, 128, 143, 144; death of, 145
droit civile (Canada East), 5, 72
Dunn, Mary Lee, 11

Edmonds, Alice, 87, 154, 165
Elgin, Lord (James Bruce), 9
Eliza Liddell, 131–2
Emigrant Orphans Asylum (Saint John), 13, 125, 130, 133, 134; and education, 135
emigration, 35–6; assisted, 41–2; children and, 50; fares, 41; paupers and, 131; ports of arrival, 38

Erin's Queen, 54, 55–6, 57, 58; and casualties, 59

Faucher, Edouard (Rev.), 63, 64
Fitzwilliam, Earl (Charles Wentworth), 26, 130, 136
Foley, Bartholomew, 140
Foley family, 129–30, 135
Furlong, Bartholomew, 149–50, 169

Gore-Booth, Robert, 129, 130–1, 133, 136, 173
Grasset, George, MD, 116
Gregory clause, 24
Grey, Earl (Henry George, Colonial Secretary), 9, 7, 126; and emigration schemes, 11, 148, 172–3; Mountbellew workhouse, 172
Grey Nuns (Sisters of Charity of Montreal), 6, 69, 90, 91, 92–4, 96, 149, 160, 172; Elisabeth Forbes McMullen (superior), 12, 94, 95, 103
Grey Nuns (Sisters of Charity of Ottawa), 6, 12, 103, 104–5. *See* Bruyère, Élisabeth
Grosse Ile, 45, 57–8, 81, 83, 85, 89, 99, 102, 106, 126, 152, 153, 160, 162; Celtic Cross at, 8; Dr George Mellis Douglas, 58, 59, 67; Mahon emigrant casualties at, 60

Hamilton, John, 26
Harding, J.G., MD, 129
Harding, William S., MD, 129, 133–4
Hawke, Anthony B., 172–3
Heritage Minutes (Historica), 3, 4, 5, 8, 66, 70, 77, 81, 146, 170, 174
Holden children (Bridget and Henry), 84
Hospital Island. *See* St Andrew's, New Brunswick
Hurley family, 140–1
Huron Tract, 148, 166

Indigenous donations to famine relief, 102
Indigenous residential schools, xv
Irish Heritage Trust, 14

John Munn, 54, 57; casualties on, 59
Johnson, Molly, 3, 5, 17, 19, 66, 70, 155, 164, 169, 170–1, 174–5
Joice sisters (Honora and Mary), 83
Joly, John Plunket, 25

Keegan, Gerald, 16, 32, 37; diary, 17
Kelly, Thomas, 141–2, 143
Kennedy, Catherine, 155–6
Kennedy, Liam, 18–19
Kingston, 105–6; General Hospital, 106, 107, 109, 111, 114; House of Industry, 111–12. *See* Religious Hospitallers of St Joseph; Kirkpatrick, Thomas
Kirkpatrick, Thomas (Mayor of Kingston), 106–7
Kirwan, Thaddeus (Rev.), 117, 118, 120, 121, 144

Lady Sale, 70, 129, 131, 133, 135
laissez-faire economics, 19, 21, 22, 26–7, 28, 175; and providence, 28
landlords, 19, 20, 23–6; and evictions, 24; and plantation, 46. *See* Bingham, George; Dè Vere, Stephen; Fitzwilliam, Earl; Gore-Booth, Robert; Hamilton, John; Mahon, Major Denis; Palmerston, Lord; Smith, Elizabeth
LeBel, Antoine (Rev.), 81, 87
Lee, Kevin, 10
Liverpool, 49, 50, 52, 54, 63; and fares, 35; and spillage, 55
Loyal Orange Order, 127

Macdonell, Alexander (1st bishop of Kingston), 107
Maguire, John Francis, 8, 162
Mahoney family, 70, 72, 74, 82–3, 156–7; Elizabeth Mahoney, 157, 165
Mahon, John Ross, 45, 48, 54, 55; emigration scheme, 49–53, 60; and J&W Robinson, 53–4
Mahon, Major Denis, 10, 25, 28, 41, 42, 43, 44–5, 46, 70, 82, 99, 130, 136, 148, 151, 152, 153, 159, 160, 162, 168; death of, 45–6, 58, 61, 168; emigration scheme, 49–54, 60–1, 103; family, 46–7; in Liverpool, 53–4, 55; relief, 48–9
Mahon, Maurice (3rd Baron Hartland), 47
maize, 21, 48–9. *See* Corn Laws
Marine Hospital (Quebec), 64, 68–9, 74, 85
Marquis, Calixte (Rev.), 95, 96, 153
McGee, Thomas D'Arcy, 8, 31, 164
McHale, John (archbishop of Tuam), 28, 102
McMahon, Cian, 11

INDEX

McManus brothers (Patrick and John), 74, 154–5
McMullen, Elisabeth Forbes. *See* Grey Nuns (Sisters of Charity of Montreal)
McNulty, John (Rev.), 102
Middle Island (New Brunswick), 127, 128
middlemen farmers, 27, 47
Mills, J.E. (mayor of Montreal), 93
Mitchel, John, 17, 18, 23, 31
Molly Maguires, 45, 47
Montreal Protestant Orphan's Home, 12, 87, 101, 151, 165
Mooney, Ellen, 125, 145
Mooney, Mary, 118
Moran, Gerard, 11
Mountain, George J. (Anglican bishop of Quebec), 12, 85, 86, 88, 96, 101, 151, 154
Murphy, Peter, 12
Murray, Daniel (archbishop of Dublin), 28, 32, 102

Naomi, 54, 55, 57, 58, 61, 70, 82, 84, 148, 151, 159, 162; casualties on, 59
National Famine Museum (Ireland), 14, 159; founder James Callery, 159
National Famine Way, 14
Nealon, Edward, 73–4, 146–7, 154; granddaughter Senator Josie Quart, 147

O'Connell, Daniel, 30–1; repeal, 30; death of, 31
O'Connor, John, 43, 123, 152–3
O'Dowd, Patrick (Rev.), 8
O'Gallagher, Marianna, 11, 159; O'Gallagher List, 11, 69, 73, 76, 81
O'Neill, Patrick, 3, 170
O'Reilly sisters (Helena, Bridget, and Mary), 160–1
orphans, 34–5, 68, 130; and agency, 150, 152, 174; as apprentices, 6, 77; as child labour, 77, 82, 84, 138; contracts and, 117–20; definition of, 14, 109–10, 135, 143; myths, 4, 66; placement of, 14, 69, 70–83, 86–7, 94–7, 101–5, 109–10, 117, 120–2, 138–9, 142–3, 175; productivity of, 6, 120; Protestant, 85–9; of Roscommon, 10, 61–2, 69–70, 71; of Sligo, 133–4; teen orphans, 88, 137; of Tipperary, 69, 71; travelling alone, 136, 140; as vectors of infection, 93–4, 100. *See* Charitable Society of Catholic Ladies; Emigrant Orphans Asylum

Palmerston, Lord (Henry John Temple), 125, 129, 130, 131–3, 134, 137, 145, 173
Partlow, John H. (mayor of Saint John), 133
Partridge Island, 126, 127, 128–9, 130, 132, 153
Peel, Sir Robert, 21 23, 48
Perley, Moses Henry, 126, 128, 129, 132—3, 136, 137
Phelan, Patrick (coadjutor bishop of Kingston), 107, 110–11, 113, 128
phytophthora infestans (potato blight), 20
Pickering brothers (William, Andrew, and John), 88, 89, 165–6
Point St Charles, 90–1, 93–4, 96, 98, 106
Poor Law, 23, 24, 32, 136; and children 34–5; in Saint John, 130, 133, 173, 175; unions, 22, 48, 172–3; and workhouses, 34
Power, Michael (bishop of Toronto), 7, 103, 116, 121, 123
Presbyterian Church, 127
Princess Royal affair, 112–13
Protestants, 30, 66; anti-Catholic, 100, 143; and assimilation, 126, 139; Catholic fear of proselytism, 84, 90–1, 100, 107–8, 141–2; cooperation with Catholics, 101, 106–7, 108–9, 113, 115, 123–4, 144, 173; fear of Catholics, 85, 87, 92, 101; orphans, 85, 87–9; sectarian strife, 126–7, 139
providentialism, 29–30

Quinn brothers (Patrick and Thomas), 62, 81, 162–4; and French language rights, 163–4
Quinn, Edmund (Rev.), 128, 144

Rees, Jim, 10
Reid, C.B. (Rev.), 87
Religious Hospitallers of St Joseph, 6, 12, 92, 107, 109, 111, 112, 114; and Amable Bourbonnière (Superior), 108; and Hotel Dieu, Kingston, 107–8, 109, 110, 111, 112, 114
Rimouski, 74, 77–83, 96, 118, 156–7, 159, 168
Roscommon (county), 10; and orphans, 46, 69–70, 112, 123, 148, 152, 160, 163, 168
Royal Canal (Ireland), 50, 52
Russell, Lord John, 21, 23, 25, 31

Ryan, Kathleen, 3, 170

Scally, Robert, 10
Scott family, 89
Sellar, Robert, 17
Sheridan family, 61–2, 151–2, 169, 174
Signay, Joseph (archbishop of Quebec), 8, 66–7, 68, 70, 81, 128, 170; and deployment of priests, 70
Sisters of Providence, 6, 91–2, 93, 95, 160; Emilie Tavernier Gamelin, 91, 92. *See also* St Jerome Emilien Orphanage
Sisters of the Good Shepherd, 6, 12, 92, 93, 95, 160
Sligo, Lady Hester Catherine, 25
Smith, Elizabeth, 25
soup kitchen, 22, 28, 32; in Limerick, 32; souperism, 29, 84–5, 100
St Andrew's, New Brunswick, 127; and Little Hardwood Island (Hospital Island), 128
St Jerome Emilien Orphanage, 12, 19, 94, 95, 96, 98, 153, 160
Strokestown, 14, 99, 168; Ballynamully, 46; estate children, 50, 53, 54; the "1490," 43, 44. *See* Mahon, Major Denis
Sweeney, John (Rev.), 128

Tellier, Remi-Jospeh, S.J., 95–6
Tighe Family (Daniel and Catherine), 62, 63–4, 66, 70, 73, 98, 157–9, 169, 174
Toronto, 5, 115, 120; Belfast of North America, 115; Widows' and Orphans' Asylum, 5, 115–17, 118–20, 121. *See also* Protestants
Trevelyan, Charles Edward, 18, 21, 22, 23, 26, 29, 31
typhus (*rickettsia prowazecki* or ship's fever), 32, 44, 56–7, 64, 67, 89–90, 93, 116; in Kingston, 106; *Le Typhus* (Theophile Hamel), 93

violence, 32–3, 43–5. *See* Molly Maguires
Virginius, 54, 55, 57, 58, 60, 62, 70, 82, 84, 99, 159; casualties on, 59; outrage, 61

Walsh, Robert (Rev.), 161–2
Welland Canal, 63, 152, 168
Whatley, Richard (Anglican archbishop of Dublin), 29
Willoughby, Mark (Rev.), 86
Woodham-Smith, Cecil, 18
Woodlock family, 167–8, 174

Yeoman, 131, 136, 142
Young Ireland, 23, 30–1